"Many in the West are unfamiliar with any view of judgment not resulting in some sort of eternal conscious torment for the unbeliever. However, the alternative views of Christian Universalism and Conditional Immortality have also been held by faithful believers throughout church history. Steve Gregg's treatment of this topic opened my eyes to the theological landscape some thirteen years ago, and I'm so grateful."

—*Braxton Hunter,* president, Trinity College
of the Bible & Theological Seminary

"I am grateful that Steve Gregg has entered the arena of discussion on hell. First, Steve is a devoted student of the Bible. Second, Steve openly and fairly presents each position's strengths and weaknesses. Third, Steve's work respects and shows grace to those he quotes regardless of their beliefs. *Why Hell?* will give you a clear and unbiased perspective on one of Christianity's most sensitive subjects."

—*Chuck Smith Jr,* pastor and Bible teacher, author
of *There Is a Season* and a biography of his father's
ministry, *Chuck Smith: A Memoir of Grace*

"Contemporary evangelical debates about hell can easily feel like a vast and shifting maze of arguments and counterarguments. If you feel that way, fear not! Steve Gregg is sure-footed, evenhanded, and clear-sighted. He is the best guide to help you navigate your way through the confusion!"

—*Robin A. Parry [aka Gregory MacDonald],*
author of *The Evangelical Universalist*

"*Why Hell?* is the premier work covering every angle and argument for the three Christian views of hell. Steve Gregg presents an unbiased case for each view while giving its strengths and weaknesses. I pray this book leads to more openminded discussion on the Christian views of hell in the church, resulting in further unity in the body of Christ."

—*Dr. Matt Mouzakis,* professor of biblical
studies and theology at Covenant Theological
Seminary, Greenville, North Carolina

"... a phenomenal job in bringing the reader back to what Scripture says about hell. We have been using Gregg's work in our core curriculum line for years at Covenant Theological Seminary."

—*Will Ryan,* PhD, president, Covenant Theological
Seminary, Greenville, North Carolina

"Steve Gregg has given us a fulfilling commonsense, comprehensive, and fair treatment on the uncomfortable yet thoroughly biblical doctrine of hell. I came to the manuscript as a committed traditionalist, but ended up thoroughly fed with my cage rattled. While my stance has not changed, I found myself significantly, in the words of Elvis Presley, 'All shook up!'"

—*Danny Lehmann,* international dean,
College of Christian Ministries University
of the Nations, Youth With a Mission

"However disagreeable a topic, hell remains an important, yet debated subject for the Christian. Steve Gregg's clear, informative, and helpful overview of the arguments provides all of us an important service."

—*Robert K. Johnston,* professor of theology
and culture, Fuller Theological Seminary

"The doctrine of hell is not as straightforward as many once believed. Steve Gregg's guide to the three main theological positions is both comprehensive and accessible. Evangelicals need to talk about hell, and Gregg has given an admirable model for doing so."

—*Justin Brierley,* former presenter of the
Unbelievable? radio show and podcast

"Steve Gregg has produced a well-written, scholarly, and judicious survey of three different Christian views concerning the ultimate fate of the wicked. He uniquely summarizes the various arguments for and against each position, using the relevant literature, and offers an unbiased perspective; he even admits uncertainty about which view is most faithful to Scripture. This book should be an ideal starting point for any Christian wishing to explore these matters."

—*Thomas Talbott,* author of
The Inescapable Love of God

WHY HELL?

WHY HELL?

THREE CHRISTIAN VIEWS CRITICALLY EXAMINED

STEVE GREGG

ZONDERVAN
REFLECTIVE

ZONDERVAN REFLECTIVE

Why Hell?
Copyright © 2013, 2024 by Steve Gregg

Originally published as *All You Want to Know about Hell: Three Christian Views of God's Final Solution to the Problem of Sin.*

Published in Grand Rapids, Michigan, by Zondervan. Zondervan is a registered trademark of The Zondervan Corporation, L.L.C., a wholly owned subsidiary of HarperCollins Christian Publishing, Inc.

Requests for information should be addressed to customercare@harpercollins.com.

Zondervan titles may be purchased in bulk for educational, business, fundraising, or sales promotional use. For information, please email SpecialMarkets@Zondervan.com.

ISBN 978-0-310-15831-8 (audio)

Library of Congress Cataloging-in-Publication Data

Names: Gregg, Steve, 1953- author. | Gregg, Steve, 1953- All you want to know about hell.
Title: Why hell?: three Christian views critically examined / Steve Gregg.
Description: Nashville, Tennessee: Thomas Nelson, [2024] | Originally published as All You Want to Know about Hell: Three Christian Views of God's Final Solution to the Problem of Sin, 2013. | Includes bibliographical references.
Identifiers: LCCN 2023044346 (print) | LCCN 2023044347 (ebook) | ISBN 9780310158295 (paperback) | ISBN 9780310158301 (ebook)
Subjects: LCSH: Hell--Christianity. | BISAC: RELIGION / Biblical Reference / Handbooks | RELIGION / Demonology & Satanism
Classification: LCC BT836.3 .G74 2024 (print) | LCC BT836.3 (ebook)
LC record available at https://lccn.loc.gov/2023044346
LC ebook record available at https://lccn.loc.gov/2023044347

This book is dedicated to my wife, Dayna,
at whose urging it came to be written.

CONTENTS

PART 4:
The Good News Is Better Than You Thought

PREFACE TO THE
FIRST EDITION

W*hat kind of God do Christians worship?*

That is the question most crucial to the church and her message, and is, essentially, the matter explored in this book. The question of hell is necessarily central to this inquiry, since a person's character is revealed as much (if not more) by how he treats his enemies as it is in his conduct toward his friends. Jesus was clear in teaching how His disciples should treat their enemies. He said that we should love them, bless them, and do good to them, so that we could be as merciful as God is (Luke 6:27–28, 35–36).

Here is a thought experiment: If the Bible said nothing specific about hell's nature and purpose, then, based upon your knowledge of God's character, which of the alternatives available to Him—eternal torment, annihilation, or reconciliation—would you expect for Him to choose for His enemies?

Based upon *your* character, which would you *wish* for Him to choose?

You may think that the Bible gives a clear and consistent picture of hell. If so, you will have occasion to be surprised in considering the biblical evidence in the following pages. I have no intention of telling you which of the alternative views is correct (since I am still waiting for someone who really knows to tell me which is correct!), but I can tell you with certainty that the correct view, if discovered, would tell you more about the nature and character of God than would most other theological inquiries.

In dealing ultimately with His enemies, who hate and curse Him, does God behave otherwise than He has instructed us to do toward ours? Does He have options? Is He forced by factors outside Himself (like human free will) to follow a course of action contrary to His preferences, or has the ultimate means of punishing sinners been deliberately designed to accomplish some inevitable sovereign purpose? If God is purposeful, what purpose does He have in mind? Why is there a hell—and what is actually accomplished there?

Since we are not competent to do so, God has pledged to resolve the perennial problem of sin in the universe—to rectify the results of the fall. Those who, above all things, seek the kingdom of God, and His righteousness, desire earnestly to see God's final, righteous solution implemented.

The manner in which He plans to do so is what is debated in these pages, and is more than worth the effort to discover.

PREFACE TO THE
SECOND EDITION

This book was originally published a decade ago by Thomas Nelson under the rather unwieldy title *All You Want to Know about Hell: Three Christian Views of God's Final Solution to the Problem of Sin*. This title was given by the publisher, which intended it to become part of a series of books that would bear similar titles— "All You Want to Know about. . . ."

Actually, I never preferred the original title—due, partly, to its length, and also because to me it sounded too much like a book of the "for Dummies" genre. My book was not written with the intention of discussing everything anyone might wish to know about hell. More specifically, I wrote the book to explore the possible reasons for God's creating hell—and what such a discovery might tell us about God's own character. Three different evangelical theories are explored in this book.

Why Hell? Three Christian Views Critically Examined was my original choice for the title, and I am pleased that Zondervan, in publishing this second edition, has chosen to honor my original preference. Very little has been changed from the first edition. A few additional quotations and entries to the bibliography, as well as the improvement of a few sentences and footnotes, are the extent of the changes I have made. Zondervan has also made, in my opinion, aesthetic improvements over the earlier page designs. I pray that this new edition will bless many.

PART 1

PRELIMINARY CONSIDERATIONS

INTRODUCTION

I can conceive of no more powerful and irrefutable argument in favor of atheism than the eternal torments of hell.
—*Russian theologian Nicholas Berdyaev*[1]

Misery which is eternal and therefore infinite would constitute the largest part of the problem of evil.
—*British philosopher of religion John Hick*[2]

The existence of both evil and suffering in the world is thought by many to be the most cogent testimony against the existence of the Christian's God. The prolific atheist writers of our day resort to this argument, almost exclusively, in the absence of other proofs for the universal negative that they wish to affirm.

The conundrum is well known, and the challenge well worn: If God is good and loving, as Christians say He is, then He certainly would not wish for innocent people, including babies and small children, to suffer horribly, as many millions do every day. If He is all-powerful, it would be in His power to prevent all such sufferings. The fact that He allows unjust suffering to continue means either that He is not good or that He is not all-powerful—or, possibly, that He does not exist!

---

1. Quoted by Robert Short, *Short Meditations on the Bible and Peanuts* (Louisville: Westminster John Knox Press, 1990), 127.
2. John Hick, *Evil and the God of Love* (London: Macmillan, 1966), 378.

A significant part of the Christian response must be that sufferings, like surgery, may tend toward a positive end, which (for all we know) may prove to be more than worth the pain endured by the sufferer. This observation banks on the fact that earthly sufferings are always temporal. They come to an end after a finite duration, and often result in a lasting improvement of happiness and quality of life—if not in this life, then, possibly, in the next.

No one would say that this fully answers every case of human suffering, and we acknowledge that much human suffering produces no perceptible positive outcome. Nonetheless, the fact that sufferings are temporal[3] and are often justly punitive,[4] corrective,[5] sanctifying,[6] and ennobling[7] stands as one of the important aspects of a biblical worldview that somewhat ameliorates the otherwise unanswerable problem of pain.

On the other hand, the problem of the miseries associated with the standard view of hell—conceived, as it is, as a place of endless torment and misery—does not easily yield to such a pastoral solution. On the traditional view, the misery in hell is not temporal and has no positive end in view. It is sheer misery, which appears to accomplish no purpose other than divine vengeance. Most Christians will allow that God has the right to execute whatever degree of vengeance upon His enemies He may judge to be fitting. However, a sovereign being who finds it necessary to punish endlessly, without accomplishing thereby any ultimate improvement in the universe or the individual, seems to welcome the criticism that, were He a God of both love (at least as loving as most humans), and of infinite wisdom, He ought to have been able to come up with something better than this.

What possible good purpose could justify hell in God's mind? Perhaps God does not owe us an explanation—just as He did not

---

3. 2 Corinthians 4:17; Hebrews 12:11.
4. Psalm 119:75; Revelation 16:5–6.
5. Psalm 119:67, 71; Hebrews 12:11.
6. Hebrews 12:10.
7. Acts 5:41; Romans 8:18; 2 Corinthians 4:17; Job 23:10.

owe Job an explanation of the seeming injustice of his afflictions, which were the occasion of such theological perplexity in his friends and himself. On the other hand, perhaps God *has* told us what He is seeking to accomplish in consigning sinners to the lake of fire. If so, the answer is not easily agreed upon among Christians. For centuries, three alternative reasons for hell have been scripturally defended by various Christian theologians.

Some say that damnation is merely God's giving incorrigible rebels what they deserve, and is, thus, a final settling of scores, such as any just judge would be obliged to do. The righteous penalty for rebellion against the Creator is eternal misery, and God will not (perhaps *can* not) mitigate the sentence by one degree.

Others argue that this traditional position has been read wrongly out of ambiguous passages of Scripture, and that there is abundant scriptural evidence to support one of two alternative possibilities.

One camp holds that God annihilates the lost, putting them out of their misery. Thus He rids the universe of sin once and for all (as the traditional hell would never actually do). It is analogous to our taking the worthless rubbish to the dump to have it burned up, so as to have it no longer around fouling the air and occupying otherwise useful space.

Others see hell as the place where the dross of sin is purged from the rebellious creation, resulting, ultimately, in repentance and restoration. Sinners, for whom the trials of this life were insufficient to inspire reform, will find the process continued after this life, only more intensely. Ultimately, it is believed by those in this camp, none will remain unconverted.

It should be borne in mind that none of these views necessarily denies any major affirmation of the gospel, as traditionally conceived or as proclaimed in the New Testament or in the early church. The reader who is hearing of these options for the first time may be as surprised as I was to learn that each view can marshal an exegetical case from Scripture, and that all three were acceptable theological options for the first four centuries of the church.

MY OWN JOURNEY TO THE
CENTER OF THE EARTH

For the first fifteen or more years of my own ministry, I heard no cogent challenges to the traditional view of hell that were not easily disposed of with pat answers. I encountered no one—at least none who seemed to be committed to biblical authority, as I was—who seemed to feel the need even to question whether or not the traditional view had a compelling scriptural case in its favor.

Then, in the mid-1980s, I became aware that two evangelical leaders whom I had always admired—John R. W. Stott and Clark Pinnock—had embraced "conditional immortality" (also known as "conditionalism" and "annihilationism"), a view that I had formerly associated only with Jehovah's Witnesses and Seventh-Day Adventists. This is the view that, rather than experiencing eternal torment in hell, the lost will eventually pass from existence entirely, and suffer no more. I was shocked to learn that these two champions of evangelicalism had rejected the traditional vision of hell in favor of what I considered to be a "fringe" doctrine.

A similar jolt came when I read the book *The Fire That Consumes* —a thorough defense of the conditionalist position, written by Edward William Fudge. Fudge was not otherwise known to me as a theologian, and this might have given me greater comfort in questioning his evangelical credentials, if not for the fact that the foreword to the book was written by Professor F. F. Bruce—arguably the world's most respected evangelical scholar of the time. Nothing could have surprised me more than to find Professor Bruce recommending a book on annihilationism and suggesting that evangelicals give serious consideration to this thesis.

I was being forced to conclude that a departure from the traditional view of hell could no longer be regarded as a departure from a commitment to biblical authority. Nor could I comfortably assume that the company of those who challenge the traditional view is comprised, exclusively, of those who do not know as much as I do about biblical exegesis. Stott, Pinnock, and Bruce (and, possibly, Fudge) were not inferior to any other evangelical theologians I knew of, in terms of either exegetical skill or commitment to evangelical theology.

During the same period, I began hearing of yet another alternative to the tradition of eternal torment, often referred to as "universal reconciliation." Some call it "universalism," but it should not be referred to by this term without some modifier, such as *Christian* universalism or *evangelical* universalism. This is because it differs from other forms of universalism, such as may be found among non-evangelicals. Some forms of universalism suggest that all people will be saved, with or without faith in Christ, merely through their good intentions or through following faith systems other than Christianity.

By contrast, evangelical forms of "universalism" (a.k.a. "universal reconciliation" or "restorationism") hold to every essential doctrine of evangelical Christianity, affirming that Christ alone is the Savior of the world, and that none will ever be reconciled to God apart from their faith in Jesus. The principal difference in the soteriology of the evangelical universalist from that of other evangelicals is that the latter usually affirm that the death of an individual is the end of opportunities to repent and to believe in Christ. Advocates of universal reconciliation reject this assumption. They believe that God can, and will, accept the sincere repentance and faith of the individual, whether before or after death. Given enough time and inducements, all men who die as unbelievers will eventually repent at some interval after death. Most evangelicals rule out postmortem conversion as a possibility, almost as an impulse, though many scholars acknowledge that the Scriptures are silent on the matter.[8]

---

8. The appeal to Hebrews 9:27—"It is appointed unto men once to die, but after this the judgment" (KJV)—is answered by pointing out that, while judgment is experienced after death, postmortem repentance might yet occur at some time after the judgment.

I had known that Origen, the third-century head of the Alexandrian catechetical school, had promoted some form of universal restorationist doctrine, but I also knew that he commonly followed an allegorical approach to Scripture (which evangelicals today generally do not) and that he had ultimately been branded as a heretic by the Catholic Church. These things made it easy enough to disregard any form of universalism as an evangelical option.[9]

I eventually learned that universal reconciliation was alive and well in the modern church, and had been held among some Christian writers, whose works I had appreciated without knowing that they held this view. The preacher and novelist George MacDonald—one of C. S. Lewis's most admired writers—was among them. Hannah Whitall Smith, author of the classic *The Christian's Secret of a Happy Life*, was another. Over a period of years, I heard rumors about other Christian writers, whom I had respected, also being Christian universalists, including William Law, William Barclay, Jacques Ellul, and others.

Initially, I was disturbed to learn that writers who had positively impacted me in other ways had drifted into what seemed to me a heterodox position about hell, but I could not deny that they seemed, otherwise, to be true Christians, from whose works I had derived great spiritual benefit. I responded to this knowledge simply by relegating their universalism to the margins of my thinking, and was willing to give them a pass, since they were, as I considered, true Christians, exhibiting the Spirit of Christ—though not exactly mainstream, evangelical theologians.

In researching for this book, I have found evangelical universalists to be a prolific sector of the modern church, so there may be more recent books espousing this view among evangelicals than there are championing traditionalism or conditionalism.

---

9. For some reason, the fact that Hus and Luther had also been branded as heretics by the Catholic Church did not seem to have the same negative impact upon my opinions of them.

Introduction

CONSIDERING THE ALTERNATIVES

Edward Beecher (1803–1895), the Congregational theologian and former president of Illinois College, was, I think, correct in making the following observation: "Though the subject [of hell] has been often discussed, yet it is thought by some learned and pious divines that the full energy of investigation in the Church has never yet been put forth on this subject, and that a more profound discussion is needed and is at hand."[10]

In the quarter of a century since I first learned of these alternative views of hell, I have read widely from the advocates of all three views, in order to acquaint myself with the biblical bases of each viewpoint. From this reading, and as a result of spending decades contemplating these options, I have come to believe that none of these positions can justly be called "heretical." All are held by evangelicals who accept the absolute authority of Scripture.

The three camps are not internally monolithic. In each, differences of opinion upon details will be found, but the main distinctives that define the three camps are my main concern in writing—as well as the scriptural and logical basis claimed for each view by its proponents.

All three views seek to explain God's ultimate purpose in judging the lost, and to identify from Scripture what ultimate solution to the problem of sin is the best that divine wisdom and benevolence can accomplish. The reader is likely to be surprised by the unexpected strength of each case. I cannot promise that, after hearing all sides, it will immediately be possible to choose one of the alternatives as the clear winner. That is something that I, having studied the alternatives for years, have not yet been able to do.

If, with all the biblical data before us, we still find ourselves unable to place complete confidence in one particular view over

---

10. Edward Beecher, *History of Opinions on the Scriptural Doctrine of Retribution* (New York: D. Appleton and Company, 1878), 2, online version found at http://www.tentmaker.org/books/DoctrineOfRetribution.html.

the others, we may nonetheless take comfort in knowing that the most disconcerting answer to the question is not the only reasonable option on the table.

A summary of the main arguments for each view is presented below.[11] What one cannot gain from this summary alone is the full weight of the various arguments, the exegesis of the relevant passages of Scripture with their application to each argument, or the critique that each view presents in the cross-examination of the rival views. All of the above will be presented in the body of this work.

However, an overview of the three views, and their respective scriptural defenses, follows:

1. Eternal Torment (a.k.a. "Traditionalism")

Primary Texts: Matt. 25:41, 46; Mark 9:43–48; 2 Thess. 1:9; Rev. 14:10–11; 19:20; 20:10, 15

Notable advocates: Tertullian, Augustine, Thomas Aquinas, and the majority of evangelical theologians throughout most (though not all) of church history

Affirmations and Arguments

    a. As a consequence of being made in the image of God (Gen. 1:26–27), people, unlike animals, are immortal beings, and must necessarily spend eternity consciously in one state or another (alternatively: immortality is not innate, but will be conferred by God after the resurrection).

    b. Though the wages of sin is "death," this does not preclude continuing conscious existence beyond the grave, as is seen in the story of Lazarus and the rich man (Luke 16:19ff.). The terms "dead" and "death" do not necessarily refer to a cessation of existence, nor of consciousness, in Scripture (Eph. 2:1; Col. 2:13; 1 Tim. 5:6).

---

11. The charts in the Appendix will serve a similar purpose.

c. Only those who believe in Christ may dwell in God's presence for all eternity (John 3:16). All others must remain forever absent from God, apart from all light, joy, and consolation (2 Thess. 1:9).

d. After the final judgment, the souls, as well as the bodies, of the lost will be cast into Gehenna (Matt. 10:28; Mark 9:43, 45, 47), which is also called "the lake of fire" (Rev. 20:10, 14–15).

e. In Gehenna, the unbeliever will suffer torment, possibly of both body and soul, suggested by terms like "furnace of fire . . . weeping and gnashing of teeth" (Matt. 13:42, 50 NASB) and "cast out into outer darkness" (Matt. 8:12; 22:13; 25:30).

f. That this torment never ends for the lost in hell is suggested by terms "eternal" and "forever" in phrases like "eternal fire" (Matt. 25:41 NASB), "eternal punishment" (Matt. 25:46 NASB), "eternal destruction" (2 Thess. 1:9 NASB), and "tormented . . . forever" (Rev. 20:10). All this is contrasted with the "eternal life" enjoyed by the redeemed (John 3:16 NASB).

g. Justice demands eternal punishment. Only a punishment that is eternal is suited to the crime of sinning against the eternal God. Sinning against God is a crime against infinite Majesty, and warrants punishment of infinite duration.

h. There will be no eternal grieving on the part of believers for those who are lost. God will wipe away all tears from their eyes (Rev. 21:4). This may involve the erasing of memories about former relationships (Isa. 43:18), or it may involve a change in perspective on the part of believers, once they see the matter from God's point of view (Isa. 55:8–9; Job 42:5–6).

2. Conditional Immortality (a.k.a. "Conditionalism," "Annihilationism," "Extinctionism," "Terminalism")

Notable advocates: John R. W. Stott, Clark Pinnock, Greg Boyd, Roger Forster, John Wenham, Michael Green, Edward William Fudge, Glenn Peoples, Ben Witherington III, F. F. Bruce (open but undecided)

Affirmations and Arguments

    a. Only God is immortal by nature (1 Tim. 6:16).

    b. Man, not innately possessing immortality, must seek to obtain it (Rom. 2:7).

    c. God gives eternal life (immortality) to men, on the condition of their believing in Christ (John 3:16; 10:28; Rom. 6:23; 1 John 5:11–12).

    d. In Scripture, the lost are never declared to be immortal. Their fate is described using terms such as "destroy," "consume," "perish," and "death" (Matt. 10:28; John 3:16; Rom. 2:12; 1 Thess. 5:3; 2 Thess. 1:9; 2:8).

    e. Certain Scriptures assert that conscious existence does not continue beyond the grave (Pss. 6:5; 146:4; Eccl. 9:5).

    f. After death, the wicked will be punished proportionately to their guilt (Luke 12:47–48), and not all suffer equally (Matt. 11:22, 24), which means that the suffering is not infinite or eternal.

    g. The *punishment* (though not the *punishing*) of the wicked is eternal, permanent, and irrevocable (Matt. 25:46).

    h. God's eternal loss of those who will not repent is the terrible cost that He Himself endures out of His determination to honor the creature's freedom of choice (Isa. 5:3–7; 66:3–4; Ezek. 33:11; Matt. 23:37; Luke 19:41–44). Nonetheless, it brings a just and final solution to the problem of sin in the universe, and does not require God (or us) to eternally endure the grief of knowing that millions of souls who were loved in this life are being tormented endlessly in the next.

    i. The lost will be resurrected, along with the righteous, in order to face the judgment (John 5:28–29; Acts 24:15). Upon being condemned, they will be cast into the lake of fire (hell) where they will either be immediately consumed, and cease to exist, or suffer punishment proportionate to their guilt (Luke 12:47–48), after which they will be allowed to pass into natural nonexistence (the same condition they were in before they were born). In the end, it will be as if they never existed.

j. Though this view does not have as happy an ending as does Christian universalism, it nonetheless ends with a tolerable and just resolution to the problem of sin in the world, and it takes seriously the Scriptures about the eternal forfeiture of eternal life by those who die in rebellion against Christ.

3. Universal Reconciliation (a.k.a. "Christian Universalism," "Restorationism")

Notable advocates: Clement of Alexandria (150–215), Origen (185–254), Gregory of Nyssa (332–398), Gregory of Nazianzus (329–390), William Law, George MacDonald, Hannah Whitall Smith, F. W. Farrar, William Barclay, Jacques Ellul, Thomas Talbott, Rob Bell (apparently, but not certainly)

Affirmations and Arguments

a. God desires for all people to be saved (Ezek. 18:23, 32; John 3:16; 1 Tim. 2:4; 2 Peter 3:9).

b. Christ died to redeem the whole world (John 1:29; 1 Tim. 2:6; 1 John 2:2).

c. If all for whom Christ died are not ultimately reconciled, then Christ will never receive all that He died to obtain, and He becomes the cosmic Loser for all eternity, while the devil wins his desired object—which hardly agrees with biblical statements about Christ's victory over sin, death, and Satan (Isa. 42:1–4; Col. 2:15; Heb. 2:14; 1 John 3:8).

d. The Bible often speaks in terms of universal salvation and restoration (Isa. 53:11; John 12:32; Rom. 5:18–19; Eph. 1:9–10; Col. 1:19–20; 1 Tim. 4:10).

e. After death, the wicked will be punished proportionately to their guilt, or until they are brought to repentance (Luke 12:47–48).

f. There is no obvious reason (in Scripture or in logic) why the God who desires that all would repent, and who will accept the genuine repentance of a lifelong sinner even in the moment before death, would arbitrarily declare death to be the cut-off point for any opportunity to repent and be forgiven.

g. Given enough pressure and time, all men will—if not before death, then afterward—turn to Christ and be saved (Phil. 2:10–11).

h. There is nothing in this teaching to offend the sentiments of Christians, since it affirms every cardinal doctrine of the evangelical faith—in fact, it is the view that would most satisfy those who share God's heartfelt desire for the salvation of the lost.

i. Throughout certain periods of early church history, some argue, this was a major view of the church.

DISCLAIMERS

Since the subject matter of the book is controversial, and I do not regard myself as a controversialist, I would offer the following disclaimers:

1. In the course of presenting a given argument, I generally have written sympathetically, as if it were my own argument, and as if I am personally defending the view of hell that seems favored by that particular point. In fact, my own opinions about hell remain unsettled, and I do not write to promote any one view. As in my book *Revelation: Four Views—A Parallel Commentary*, I do not have an interest in promoting one view over another, but in allowing the proponents of each view to speak, as much as possible, in their own voices. In any chapter defending a particular viewpoint, my

own comments are deliberately meant to sound favorable to that view, so that they can be integrated into the argument itself. Likewise when writing the chapters critical of each view, I may sound as if I am myself a critic, though I will be depending upon the criticisms presented by other authors to carry the argument.

2. The chapters defending traditionalism and restorationism are about equal in length, whereas that defending conditionalism is only about two-thirds their length. This does not reflect favoritism on this author's part (the chapters *critiquing* traditionalism and restorationism are, likewise, the longest chapters in this book). The length of the chapters was determined by the number of arguments advanced in the literature for each view. The arguments advanced for conditionalism are fewer in number than for the other views, but this fact does not reflect negatively on the relative strength of the view. It is the weight of the arguments—not their number—that will demonstrate which view is more scripturally valid. A view that has four strong arguments in its favor may be better-grounded than one defended by ten weak arguments.

3. I can anticipate adherents to each of the views complaining that I have not included every possible argument or Bible verse that they might use in the defense of their viewpoint. Having read the best sources I can get my hands on for each viewpoint, I endeavored to cull all of the strongest arguments, and to clearly and sympathetically present the ones that the proponents seem to regard as the best. The bibliography will direct interested readers to the more detailed defenses of each position. I could not include every minor argument, due to the fact that each position is given only one chapter of its own, and I have been forced to summarize, in so small a space, the strengths of each view, which many other writers have defended in book-length treatments.

4. Some readers may feel that, of the three views, it is the traditional view that is undermined more than the alternative viewpoints. In the nature of the case, it seems unavoidable that a tradition that has dominated the field without significant challenges for centuries might feel "attacked" when arguments for alternative viewpoints suddenly receive attention. In fact, it is not difficult to document from the literature that many traditional authors seem offended even at the suggestion that alternative views on this subject may be viable and have always existed among Bible-believing Christians.

I have not intended to attack tradition. It is my assumption that good traditions can (and ought to) hold their own against rivals, on the basis of their biblical arguments, rather than merely by default. I am of the opinion that the Reformers would have defended such an attitude.

Evangelical New Testament scholar Craig Blomberg, in discussing an entirely different evangelical doctrine, wrote wisely: "In sum, no Christian should shrink from interacting with any critique of traditional opinion. If the critique is valid, he or she should want to know about it and reassess the tradition, however associated with orthodoxy it may be in his or her mind or community. If it is invalid, careful study and analysis should sooner or later reveal that fact, and faith ought to be strengthened for having been tested and refined."[12]

I have attempted to provide the very best biblical arguments that I can find in the literature defending each viewpoint, including the traditional one. If any one view comes out sounding more credible than another as a result, I trust it may not be due to any prejudicial treatment by this author, but only to the fact that its biblical arguments are more sound and unassailable.

---

12. Craig Blomberg, *The Historical Reliability of the Gospels* (Downers Grove, IL: InterVarsity Press, 1987), 11–12.

CHAPTER 1

HELL HAS FEW FRIENDS

There is one very serious defect to my mind in Christ's moral character, and that is that He believed in hell. I do not myself feel that any person who is really profoundly humane can believe in everlasting punishment.

— *Bertrand Russell (atheist)*[1]

Even the most ardent advocates of eternal punishment must confess shrinking from the idea of hell as continuing forever. It is only natural to harbor the hope that such suffering may be somehow terminated.

— *Dr. John Walvoord (traditionalist)*[2]

H ell, as traditionally conceived, has few friends, it seems. Atheists find the doctrine to be a strong deterrent to their belief in the God of Christianity. Charles Darwin, a former theology student who turned agnostic, cited this doctrine as one of his reasons for rejecting Christianity. Darwin wrote, in his autobiography: "I can indeed hardly see how anyone ought to wish Christianity to be true; for if so the plain language of the text seems to show that the men who do not believe, and this would include my Father, Brother

---

1. Bertrand Russell, *Why I Am Not a Christian* (New York: Simon and Schuster, 1957), 17.
2. In William Crockett, ed., *Four Views on Hell* (Grand Rapids: Zondervan, 1992), 12.

and almost all my best friends, will be everlastingly punished. And this is a damnable doctrine."[3]

Darwin's biographer, Gertrude Himmelfarb, commenting on the above remark, wrote: "There may be more sophisticated reasons for disbelief, but there could hardly have been a more persuasive emotional one."[4]

Darwin speaks for many, no doubt, who would concur that the traditional doctrine of hell is a compelling emotional reason for disbelief. Defenders of the doctrine imply that the severest possible view of hell must provide the best incentive for the conversion of unbelievers. On the other hand, we may never know how many people's conversions have been *prevented* by their reaction to the doctrine. Many react negatively to the doctrine from a conviction that any God who could concoct such a monstrous "remedy" for evil does not qualify as either good or just. Randy Klassen wrote: "It is claimed that Nietzsche, Marx, and Lenin are among those whose revolt against the establishment and the church was in part based on the teaching of hell."[5]

Some Christians might be tempted to write off the objections of unbelievers as being due to their hostility toward God or their lack of sympathy for God's revealed sentiments. Such a cavalier dismissal, however, would fail to take into account the fact that many fervent Christians, who love God and acknowledge His wisdom and justice, also express the very same distaste for the doctrine. For example, the following statements all come from adherents to traditionalism:

> No evangelical, I think, need hesitate to admit that in his heart
> of hearts he would like universalism to be true. Who can take

---

3. Charles Darwin, *The Autobiography of Charles Darwin 1809–1882*, ed. Nora Barlow (London: Collins, 1958), 78.

4. G. Himmelfarb, *Darwin and the Darwinian Revolution* (Garden City, NY: Doubleday Anchor Books, 1959), 22.

5. Randy Klassen, *What Does the Bible Really Say about Hell?* (Scottsdale, PA: Pandora, 2001), 104.

pleasure in the thought of people being eternally lost? If you want to see folk damned, there is something wrong with you!

—*J. I. Packer*[6]

The saddest day of my life was the day I watched my grandmother die. When that EKG monitor flatlined, I freaked out. I absolutely lost it! According to what I knew of the Bible, she was headed for a life of never-ending suffering. I thought I would go crazy. . . . Since that day, I have tried not to think about it. It has been over twenty years. Even as I write that paragraph, I feel sick. I would love to erase hell from the pages of Scripture.

—*Francis Chan*[7]

There is no doctrine I would more willingly remove from Christianity than [hell], if it lay in my power . . . I would pay any price to be able to say truthfully: "All will be saved."

—*C. S. Lewis*[8]

The thought of hell, then, can carry no inherent attraction to the balanced and coherent human mind.

—*Sinclair B. Ferguson*[9]

As seen in these quotations, many staunch defenders of the traditional doctrine of hell also express the revulsion they feel toward the doctrine—though they also feel compelled, from the way that they have understood Scripture, to affirm and defend it.

Even stronger objections to the doctrine are raised by evangelical

6. Cited in Kenneth Kantzer and Carl F. H. Henry, *Evangelical Affirmations* (Grand Rapids: Zondervan, 1990), 107–108.

7. Francis Chan and Preston Sprinkle, *Erasing Hell* (Colorado Springs: David C. Cook, 2011), 13f.

8. C. S. Lewis, *The Problem of Pain* (London: Geoffrey Bles, 1940), 94.

9. Sinclair B. Ferguson, in Christopher W. Morgan and Robert A. Peterson, eds., *Hell Under Fire* (Grand Rapids: Zondervan, 2004), 220.

spokesmen who have abandoned traditionalism in favor of some alternative view. John R. W. Stott wrote: "Emotionally, I find the concept [of eternal torment] intolerable."[10] Similar sentiments were expressed by Stott's fellow conditionalist, John Wenham:

> Unending torment speaks to me of sadism, not justice. It is a doctrine which I do not know how to preach without negating the loveliness and glory of God. From the days of Tertullian it has frequently been the emphasis of fanatics. It is a doctrine which makes the Inquisition look reasonable. It all seems a flight from reality and common sense.[11]

Another critic of traditionalism, Dr. Grady Brown, expressed his disapproval in the following manner:

> The doctrine of "endless punishment" has for centuries been the "crazy uncle" that the Church, with justifiable embarrassment, has kept locked in the back bedroom. Unfortunately, from time to time, he escapes his confinement, usually when there are guests in the parlor, and usually just at the time when we are telling them about a loving God who gave His Son to die for their sins. It's no wonder that the guests run away never to return.[12]

Even traditionalist John Gerstner, whose book on hell reveals very little in the way of misgivings about the doctrine, at one point exhibits the familiar double-mindedness of many evangelicals. Like other writers, he feels he must give the obligatory disclaimer: "No conservative wants to seem to rejoice in eternal torment. . . . It breaks

---

10. David L. Edwards and John Stott, *Evangelical Essentials* (Downers Grove, IL: InterVarsity Press, 1988), 314.
11. John Wenham, *Facing Hell: The Story of a Nobody* (Carlisle, Cumbria: Paternoster Press, 1998), 254.
12. In Gerry Beauchemin, *Hope Beyond Hell* (Olmito, TX: Maltista Press, 2007), 4.

his heart to see people perish by the thousands around him daily, even though it never comes near his own soul."[13]

On the other hand, he added: "[The evangelical] holds tenaciously to the doctrine for one essential reason: God's Word teaches it. . . . If the evangelical will hold to God, he knows he must hold to hell. . . . If he loves God, he must love hell, too. . . . When Christ asks, 'Do you love Me?' He is asking also 'Do you love hell?'"[14]

This, then, is the awkward position into which the traditional doctrine of hell seems to place believers. On the one hand, the truth is to be embraced and loved, but on the other, it is universally viewed as repugnant!

Some traditionalists even affirm that God Himself hates hell. Charles Spurgeon wrote: "Beloved, the eternal torment of men is no joy to God."[15] More recently, Dr. J. P. Moreland wrote: "And it's important to understand that if the God of Christianity is real, he hates hell and he hates people going there . . . God says he takes no pleasure in the death of the wicked."[16]

As J. I. Packer said, "If you want to see folk damned, there is something wrong with you!" What could we think of any man who wished to see his personal rivals tortured without relief for millions of years? We might be able to find men on earth possessing such vindictive hatred as this, but, if we did, we could hardly believe them to have the Spirit of Christ.

Yet, if the traditional concept of hell is correct, we might be forced to describe such an implacably vengeful man as very "Godlike"—since God Himself, in such a case, would have conceived and deliberately engineered just such a destiny for those who have insulted His own majesty. This statement might be somewhat

13. John Gerstner, *Repent or Perish* (Morgan, PA: Soli Deo Gloria Publications, 1990), 31.
14. Ibid., 31–32.
15. Charles Haddon Spurgeon, "The Great Need—Or the Great Salvation," in *Metropolitan Tabernacle Pulpit*, Sermon #610.
16. Quoted in Lee Strobel, *The Case for Faith* (Grand Rapids: Zondervan, 2000), 172.

mitigated by the caveat that God does not desire such things for any of His creatures, but that He has been forced to this expedient, due to an element in His creation—human free will—that has seemingly gotten out of His control, forcing Him ultimately to adopt a policy of eternal hostility toward those whom He would have preferred to love.

The traditional doctrine of hell sits uneasily alongside that other prominent doctrine of the Christian faith—the one that affirms God's love for the world and His grace toward sinners, which was exemplified most vividly in God's self-manifestation in Jesus Christ. Christians who stand by both of these traditional beliefs (eternal torment and God's loving nature) have had to find satisfactory ways in which to keep the two concepts from seeming to cancel each other out.

TWO STRATEGIES FOR HARMONIZATION

One solution is found in Calvinist doctrine. This view holds that God does not really love all men redemptively, nor does He truly desire to save them. God is sovereign, and can save whomever He chooses. However, He *chooses* to save only *some*, while passing over others, whom He could just as easily have included among the elect, had He wished to do so. It is difficult to say that God loves those whom He has not chosen to save—especially if this neglect of choosing them means that they will endure eternal torment, from which He could have easily delivered them, as well as the others. No contradiction must be assumed to exist between God's vindictive wrath for the one group and His sacrificial love for another. God loves His elect, and demonstrates His love in saving them; but He hates the non-elect (Rom. 9:13), and makes that fact unmistakably clear by consigning them to eternal torment.

If this view is taken, it becomes difficult to affirm with Scripture that "God is love," apart from the addition of some caveat—that is, God is love to those whom He chooses to love. To the rest, He is apparently as unforgiving and vengeful as is the most graceless character on earth. A being whose personality is about equally divided between extreme love and extreme hatred may well exist, but one could hardly explain why such a bipolar entity would be admired for His grace and His loving character, when the very opposite of love burns in Him toward the majority of the unfortunate people whom He has not chosen to love, even though (unfortunately for them) it was He who chose to bring them into existence.

Those on the fortunate side of that ledger could be thankful to be among the few who escaped this default attitude of wrath, and, when thinking only of His conduct toward themselves (which is how people often think), might regard the God who saved them as a loving and gracious being. This would seemingly require blocking out of the mind the fact that multitudes of others, including many of their own loved ones, were denied that same grace, by a God who could as easily have given it to them, at no extra cost to Himself, had He simply been willing to extend His infinite grace more broadly.

What Calvinism gains in terms of affirming God's prerogatives, it seems to lose in terms of God's character. The Calvinist sees God's anger as being visited upon rebels whose rebellion was divinely ordained, and who are thus being eternally punished for living in bondage to forces they had no power to resist, and from which God did not choose to deliver them when He could have. If anything about this scenario seems morally objectionable, the Calvinist has one answer ready at hand: "O man, who are you to reply against God?" (Rom. 9:20).

The Arminian has an alternative solution to the difficulty of harmonizing God's love for sinners with the concept of eternal torment. In this view, God loves everybody and wishes to save them all. Tragically, His universal love is thwarted by the free will of some who stubbornly choose to resist Him all their life long. He loves them and would save them, if He could, but He cannot save them against their will, and He leaves the final outcome to the individual's own prerogative.

This view may solve the conundrum of why a loving God might not save everyone (namely, *He can't*), but it leaves entirely unaddressed the question of why a loving God, knowing from the beginning that He would lose most of those whom He loved, and that He would be obliged to punish them, would choose *endless torment* as the punishment of choice, given the availability of other options.

Among earthly governments there are humane criminal justice systems, which would never contemplate endless torture as either a necessary or tolerable consequence for any crime. In setting up the most ideal penal system that He could contrive, and being the most compassionate of all sovereigns, God might have been expected to adopt the most humane form of punishment for lawbreakers that justice would allow.

Arminian traditionalists bear the burden of explaining how their system allows for the omnibenevolence of God while retaining the most cruel (rather than the most loving) of all possible penalties for sinners.

SHOULD WE CONSIDER ALTERNATIVES TO THE TRADITION?

The ever-quotable G. K. Chesterton famously quipped: "Tradition means giving a vote to the most obscure of all classes, our ancestors. It is the democracy of the dead."[17] As a Roman Catholic, Chesterton might have been expected to give his ecclesiastical forebears (i.e., "tradition") a vote in determining theological questions, alongside Scripture itself. Protestants have generally espoused quite opposite

---

17. G. K. Chesterton, *Heretics/Orthodoxy* (Nashville: Thomas Nelson, 2000), 207.

commitments, namely, to uphold the sovereignty of Scripture over all other authorities—no matter how many of them may be "voting" against it. It is easily documented that, in every academic community—whether of theologians, historians, scientists, or anyone else—the majority have very often been mistaken, and their "votes," in their day, often stood in the way of progress toward more perfect understanding of the truth. Truth has never been determined by a majority vote.

The Protestant ideal, as stated by many theologians and clergymen, is to be "reformed and always reforming." This is an ideal more easily affirmed than followed, since intellectual inertia is often strong, and the tradition is often embraced by those whose approval has some impact upon our social acceptance, our finances, our reputations, and our careers. To be "always reforming" is an excellent way to guarantee that we shall offend the maximum number of our conservative friends.

It is the heritage of Protestantism to cross-examine longstanding traditions by appeal to Scripture, when necessary. Where Scripture and tradition fail to align, it is our acknowledged duty to stand with the Scriptures against the traditions. Staunch traditionalist J. I. Packer rightly articulated the Protestant ideal: "We are forbidden to become enslaved to human tradition . . . even 'evangelical' tradition. We may never assume the complete rightness of our own established ways of thought and practice and excuse ourselves the duty of testing and reforming them by Scripture."[18]

The late John R. W. Stott, who was once, arguably, the leading evangelical voice of Great Britain, confirmed this sentiment, namely, that "the hallmark of an authentic evangelicalism is not the uncritical repetition of old traditions but the willingness to submit every tradition, however ancient, to fresh biblical scrutiny and, if necessary, reform."[19]

---

18. James I. Packer, *Fundamentalism and the Word of God: Some Evangelical Principles* (Grand Rapids: Wm. B. Eerdmans, 1970), 70.

19. John R. W. Stott, interviewed in "Basic Stott," *Christianity Today*, January 8, 1996, 28.

There are a number of reasons that a thinking Christian would wish to know whether the traditional doctrine of hell is really true or whether there is something more humane than this taught in Scripture.

One reason, of course, would be the comfort this knowledge might allow us to extend to others (and ourselves) concerning the fate of loved ones who have died without having come to Christ. Paul says that Christians do not grieve the loss of their dead in the same way as do others "who have no hope" (1 Thess. 4:13). However, not all of the believer's loved ones are Christians themselves, and, if the traditional doctrine of hell is true, then Christians can have no more hope or comfort at the loss of their unsaved friends and family members than an unbeliever has. In the case of being bereaved for our unsaved loved ones, our faith has not positively transformed our experience of loss, as Paul suggested. If anything, our faith serves to make such loss more intolerable for us than for the unbeliever, who may be oblivious to the hell into which their deceased friends and family members descend. Our loved ones' hell becomes *our* hell, as well, in our believing that they will be endlessly tortured.

Another reason to discover whether the traditional view is really true or not is that it has presented the largest stumbling block to sensitive unbelievers (and believers as well) who are not as ready as some to see as a tolerable mystery the dichotomy of a God who is universally loving but nonetheless willing to endlessly torment His foes. To many, it is no "mystery" but simply "nonsense." As Dr. Brown noted above, the doctrine may be seen as the "crazy uncle" of evangelicalism, flying in the face of our declarations of the love of God for sinners. To this, many evangelicals may simply say, "We are not obligated to accommodate the objections of those who are God's enemies. They are bound to stumble at the offense of the cross, and there is little we can do to prevent that!"

Yet, if the traditional doctrine were, perhaps, demonstrated not to be true to the Scriptures, then its repugnance could not be bundled with the "offense of the cross"—and may actually place Christians who teach it in the position of those who are unnecessarily placing a stumbling block before those who otherwise would embrace the true God of Scripture who loves and pursues them despite their straying. We should not take lightly Christ's warning that being cast into the sea with a millstone around one's neck would be a fate more to be desired than that which awaits those who place such stumbling blocks before others (Matt. 18:6).

But there is one reason more important than all others that we must be sure we are not misrepresenting the truth of this matter. More than any other consideration, our view of hell determines our assessment of the character of God. As Douglas Jacoby pointed out: "If we predicate such a sternness of God and it turns out not to be true, would we not be impugning his character?"[20]

Christians should wish to know God as He really is and are obligated to portray Him correctly to the world. If He is a God who has chosen to torment His enemies endlessly as a punishment for a finite period of rebellion, then He is entitled to do so. He is, in that case, also a God whose sentiments seem to be in conflict with a number of Christ's teachings—not least, His teaching that we must love our enemies, bless those who curse us, and do good to those who hate us, so that we can resemble God's conduct in this respect: "But love your enemies, do good . . . and you will be sons of the Most High. For He is kind to the unthankful and evil. Therefore be merciful, just as your Father also is merciful" (Luke 6:35–36).

The force of Christ's teaching would seem to be considerably diminished if God, in fact, has none of these attitudes or behaviors toward His enemies that Christ here enjoins.

If Scripture clearly affirms the traditional view of hell, then so be it. We must accept it and factor it into our view of God. However, if the traditional view is merely that—*traditional*, and not demonstrably

---

20. Douglas Jacoby, *What's the Truth about Heaven and Hell?* (Eugene, OR: Harvest House, 2013), 107.

the teaching of Scripture—then some other view may better present the true case, and our propagation of the tradition may amount to little else than the sin of bearing false witness against the Almighty.

It is important that we consider clearly what it is that we are contemplating here. In assuming the traditional view to be correct, we are suggesting that God, under no duress from anyone, made a sovereign decision to torment billions of humans endlessly, because they were foolish enough to neglect Him during their brief lifetimes. This conscious punishment is eternal and unrelenting. It is not redemptive, in that it allows no opportunity of repentance to the sufferers (though God, if He wished, could have allowed this); nor does it bring about a final solution to the problem of sin in the universe, since the sufferers remain rebellious for eternity, and have no hope even of their finding ultimate relief through death (which God could have permitted, had He wished to do so).

Thus, the traditional view describes a final solution that does not obviously resolve anything—accomplishing no end, other than the venting of God's eternally unrelenting wrath. Yet, the Scriptures frequently seem to deny that such a permanent hostility is a part of God's nature:

> The LORD is merciful and gracious,
>> slow to anger and abounding in steadfast love.
> He will not always chide,
>> nor will he keep his anger forever. (Ps. 103:8–9 ESV)

> For I will not contend forever,
> Nor will I always be angry;
> For the spirit would fail before Me,
> And the souls which I have made. (Isa. 57:16)

> For the Lord will not cast off forever.
> Though He causes grief,

Yet He will show compassion
According to the multitude of His mercies.
For He does not afflict willingly,
Nor grieve the children of men. (Lam. 3:31–33)

If any religious tradition would warrant a critical cross-examination from Scripture, it would seemingly be one that, *prima facie*, denied the character of God as revealed in Scripture and in Christ. Rather than risking the possibility of being found affirming libelous ideas about God, and grievously misrepresenting Him to others, a full and careful investigation of such a tradition would seem warranted. If the traditional view of hell has few friends, it might conceivably turn out, upon investigation, that it actually *deserves* few.

GOD DOES EXACTLY WHAT HE WANTS TO DO

In his book-length defense of the traditional view of hell, Francis Chan reminds us that "God has the right to do WHATEVER He pleases."[21]

Chan is surely correct in this observation. God undoubtedly has the right to do whatever He pleases. The question is, do we have an adequate scriptural basis for affirming that the most horrendous scenario imaginable is, of all possible alternatives, the one that most pleases God? If tormenting men for eternity is what God really does, we cannot escape the conclusion that this is what He is pleased to do, and, try as we may to dodge it, this must inevitably inform our perception of His character.

Some may feel that the perception of God's character that would

---

21. Francis Chan and Preston Sprinkle, *Erasing Hell* (Colorado Springs: David C. Cook, 2011) (capitalization in the original), 17.

make Him the author of eternal torment of sinners might reasonably reopen the question of whose Son Jesus actually was. Jesus sometimes said that His identity as the Son of God could be discerned by the fact that He behaved just as His Father does.[22] The Son is the express image of His Father.[23] Yet, the Son scandalized the religious by behaving like a "friend of . . . sinners" (Matt. 11:19).

Jesus seemed to possess in Himself nothing of such malice toward His detractors as some theologians attribute to His Father. He wept when He contemplated the holocaust His enemies were soon to suffer at the hands of the Romans.[24] When Judas was in the very act of betraying Him, Jesus addressed him as "Friend" (Matt. 26:50). He also healed the severed ear of one who was participating in His arrest.[25] While on the cross, He forgave those who cursed and those who killed Him,[26] and, in the instructing of His disciples, He required that they adopt the same policy as His own, so that they might truly resemble their Father in heaven.[27]

If Christ's Father is implacably determined to consign those who offend Him to an eternal chamber of horrors, as some affirm, then we can hardly avoid wondering how it is that the divine "Apple" fell so very far from the "Tree."

CAN OUR VIEW OF HELL DEHUMANIZE US?

One general criticism that is brought against non-traditionalists is that they *sentimentalize* the love of God, so as to remove from His personality profile any adequate "justice" component. Larry Pettegrew,

---

22. e.g., John 5:16–21; 10:37; 14:7–11.
23. Hebrews 1:3; John 14:9.
24. Luke 19:41–44.
25. Luke 22:51.
26. Luke 23:34.
27. Luke 6:35–36; Matthew 5:44–48.

for example, wrote: "Their emphasis on God's nature to love disregards His many other attributes such as holiness, justice, truth, grace, and omnipotence and thereby sentimentalize[s] God's love."[28]

In the same vein, Kenneth Kantzer said that "the biblical answer [to the question of human destiny] does not satisfy our wishful sentiments. It is a hard and crushing word, devastating to human hope and pride."[29]

No doubt, the danger of interpreting God's love in sentimental terms exists and must be avoided, but there would also seem to be the opposite danger of interpreting love in overly clinical, non-emotional terms. While love, in the biblical sense, is often measured more by what one does than by what one feels (e.g., Matt. 7:12; John 15:13), it is difficult (and inappropriate) to imagine that love would lack in the emotions of sympathy and compassion. It violates our intuitions to believe that infinite love can coexist in the same heart with implacable wrath. Those who see God's nature as an amalgam of these disparate traits may well seek, thereby, to justify possessing both of these characteristics in themselves.

This is not a hypothetical suggestion. Historical examples abound of deeds of outright cruelty being committed in the name of God under the justification that God hates His enemies and will torment them forever. Islam embraces a view of hell (which they call "Jahannam"—derived from the Greek word *Gehenna*) which is very similar to the hell of our tradition. It cannot be denied that, for some jihadists, this doctrine has served as the justification for terrorism against "infidels." Why should anyone have compassion upon those whom God Himself deems worthy of eternal misery?

Sadly, we find the same phenomenon in Christian history. Queen Mary I of England ("Bloody Mary") allegedly justified her

---

28. Larry D. Pettegrew, "A Kinder, Gentler Theology of Hell?" *The Master's Seminary Journal* 9/2 (Fall 1998), 203–217.

29. Kenneth S. Kantzer, "Troublesome Questions," *Christianity Today*, March 20, 1987.

cruel persecution of Protestants by appeal to this very doctrine, proclaiming: "As the souls of heretics are to be hereafter eternally burning in hell, there can be nothing more proper than for me to imitate the divine vengeance by burning them on earth."[30]

Protestants, too, have been guilty of similar cruelty against "heretics." Though harsh, Gerry Beauchemin's assessment is no doubt correct when, recalling the burning of accused heretic Michael Servetus in Calvin-controlled Geneva, he wrote: "Such an act reflects the character of the God Calvin believed in."[31] Randy Klassen explained: "In years past, cruelty and injustice may well have found support in the traditional understanding of hell. The Crusades and the Inquisition certainly did. Failing to understand that God's judgments were meant to bring about repentance, the church justified hellish actions by claiming God's name in their heinous deeds. Blindness to God's justice and mercy can only lead to terrible injustice among humans."[32]

Beauchemin, with some credibility, blames belief in the traditional doctrine of hell for much of the cruelty historically done in the name of Christ, observing: "Believers can be just as brutal and cruel in the name of *Yahweh* as other religious extremists are in the name of their god."[33]

Most of those who embrace the doctrine of eternal torment certainly would not resort to the persecution or torture of unbelievers as a result of this belief. However, the doctrine may inadvertently have an impact on our view not only of God but of the lost as well.

It seems likely that few who hold to the traditionalist view actually spend much time thinking hard about the ramifications of this viewpoint. The doctrine is admittedly unpleasant in the extreme,

---

30. Cited by Lee Salisbury, "Eternal Punishment: Is It Really of God?," https://tentmaker.org/articles/EternalPunishment-IsitReallyofGod.html.

31. Gerry Beauchemin, *Hope Beyond Hell* (Olmito, TX: Malista Press, 2007), 150.

32. Randy Klassen, *What Does the Bible Really Say about Hell?* (Scottsdale, PA: Pandora, 2001), 86.

33. Gerry Beauchemin, *Hope Beyond Hell* (Olmito, TX: Malista Press, 2007), 151.

and it is easier to relegate it to the margins of our consciousness than to retain such stark prospects at the forefront of our minds. To do the latter would overwhelm the believer with despair and continual grief. In their book *Every Knee Shall Bow*, Thomas Allin and Mark T. Chamberlain express doubts that most Christians really do consciously believe the traditional view:

> No one lives as if he really believes that all around him are millions of people heading for eternal hell without a chance of escape without hearing and accepting the message that he possesses! It is impossible! Who would dare so much as to smile if he really believed that a member of his household was headed for a place of unending, unspeakable anguish and pain? . . . To perpetuate the human race would be to perpetuate endless misery for millions of souls. If people really believed in everlasting hell, the world would be a madhouse![34]

Gerry Beauchemin added: "Hell is a horrifying thought. Millions have been terrorized by it. Some have even killed their children to spare them such a fate. If we would truly grasp the horror of it, we would go insane."[35]

Take the following case: Your neighbor is a kindly widow, selflessly raising two difficult grandchildren by herself. Despite the burdens of her situation, she consistently acts with kindness and generosity toward you and the others in her life. You have shared the gospel with her, but she somehow does not seem to "get it." There is a mental block there, and she does not understand the danger her soul is in, nor does she grasp the nature of the grace of God to save. She is, by traditional definitions, on the road to a hell of eternal misery and torment. Do you believe this about her? Every time you see or

---

34. Thomas Allin and Mark T. Chamberlain, *Every Knee Shall Bow* (Oxnard, CA: self-published by Mark T. Chamberlain, 2005), 42.

35. Gerry Beauchemin, *Hope Beyond Hell* (Olmito, TX: Malista Press, 2007), 16.

think about her, do you vividly picture her spending endless ages in the torments of hellfire? Probably not. In all likelihood, entertaining such thoughts would keep you in a continual state of deep depression, and reduce you to tears whenever you saw her face. Most likely, in order even to function, you must somehow, at least temporarily, dampen such reflections, putting them largely out of your mind. The only alternative coping strategy to this would be to somehow train your heart to be less sympathetic—less sensitive to the ramifications of her unbelief. Some such self-protective strategy would seem necessary in order to be able to live a stable emotional life yourself in the midst of friends and loved ones who you believe will be tormented for eternity. Even if this viewpoint has the effect of motivating you to evangelize, there will still be many unresponsive to your efforts, with whose state you must somehow cope emotionally.

John R. W. Stott commented on the ramifications of this situation: "I find the concept [of eternal conscious torment] intolerable, and do not understand how people can live with it without cauterizing their feelings or cracking under the strain."[36]

If we believe that the doctrine of eternal torment is true, then, whether we choose to live in denial or we adopt a mind-set of uncomfortable acquiescence, the result must be the desensitization of our hearts. In a worst-case scenario, it may even cause us to hate sinners, because we cannot avoid concluding that God Himself hates them, given His plans to torment them eternally. Though this is not what Christianity is supposed to do to us, some feel there are few alternatives if we are convinced of the traditional doctrine of hell. In fact, some have argued that the very joyfulness that characterized the early Christian communities[37] proves that they had not yet adopted this horrendous view of the fate of the lost.[38]

---

36. David L. Edwards and John Stott, *Evangelical Essentials: A Liberal-Evangelical Dialogue* (Downers Grove, IL: InterVarsity Press, 1988), 314–15.

37. Acts 2:46; 8:8; 13:52; 15:3; Romans 14:17; 15:13; 2 Corinthians 8:2; 1 Thessalonians 1:6; 1 Peter 1:8; 1 John 1:4.

38. e.g., John Wesley Hanson, *Universalism: The Prevailing View of the Christian*

Of course, even with annihilationism and restorationism, hell is a horrendous place, greatly to be avoided. However, these alternatives to the tradition, by making hell serviceable to some good end, retain the credibility of the compassion of the God who created such a system. If God's hell does not represent as compassionate an outcome as divine justice will permit, then insensitivity to human suffering would seem to be an attribute of God, which in some measure will be emulated by those who are obliged to become like Him.

Church During Its First Five Hundred Years (Boston and Chicago: Universalist Publishing House, 1899), 32ff.

CHAPTER 2

WHY HELL?

The anger of the LORD will not turn back
Until He has performed and carried out the purposes
    of His heart;
In the last days you will clearly understand it.
                                    —*Jeremiah 23:20 NASB*

For centuries, Western Christianity has affirmed that, after death, every person faces one of two possible destinies. Colloquially, these destinies have been termed "heaven" and "hell." Though the technical correctness of these terms actually needs to be (and will be) reconsidered in the following pages, most Christians think of the former as being synonymous with "eternal life in God's presence," while the latter is viewed as "eternal separation from God," characterized by endless, conscious torment—usually in flames.

While enjoying pride of place among evangelicals, the common view of hell has never actually commanded universal acceptance among the followers of Christ. It has not always been even the majority opinion, if certain authorities are correct in their assessment.[1] From the earliest Christian times until today, alternative views of hell have been advocated by competent biblical scholars.

---

1. e.g., George T. Knight: "Many other theologians believed in Universal salvation; and indeed the whole Eastern Church until after 500 A.D. was inclined to it" (*The New Schaff-Herzog Encyclopedia of Religious Knowledge*, ed. Samuel Macauley Jackson,

In the early years of my own ministry, I paid little regard to any philosophical and theological difficulties associated with the traditional view of hell. I knew the doctrine was despised by many, but I was always prepared to bear "the offense of the cross" in the face of worldly scorn, and to champion the traditional doctrine for the simple reason that its scriptural support was, to my mind, clear and convincing.

Both in personal witnessing for Christ and as a Christian radio talk-show host dealing directly with the perplexing questions of skeptics and Christians on a daily basis, I frequently have been in the position to present a defense for the traditional doctrine, having learned long ago the standard answers to the most common challenges:

Q. Why would a loving God send anyone to hell?

A. Though God is a God of love, He is also a God of justice. Like any judge on the bench, God is obliged to balance the scales of cosmic justice.

Q. How could it be considered "just" to punish people eternally for temporal sins committed in a finite lifetime?

A. The magnitude of a crime, and the punishment it warrants, are wholly unrelated to the time it actually takes to commit the crime. The most heinous crimes can be committed in an instant, yet may deserve prolonged punishment.

Q. But how could any finite act carry with it an infinite measure of guilt?

A. Every sin of man is committed against an infinite God, and is, therefore, infinite in magnitude.

---

vol. 12 [New York, London: Funk and Wagnalls Company, 1912], 96); see also J. W. Hanson, *Universalism: The Prevailing Doctrine of the Christian Church During Its First Five Hundred Years* (Boston, Chicago: Universalist Publishing House, 1899).

Q. But why would a loving God even create people whom He knew would end up in hell?

A. Who are you, O Man, to answer against God?

Since the primary purpose of writing the present book is to explore three different views of God's purpose in creating hell, it is clear that the reality of hell is presupposed by this author, and the alternatives that will be included for consideration will be those that acknowledge the existence of a real hell of torment, but who differ from one another, primarily, in their perception of hell's *raison d'être*—that is, of God's rationale for allowing hell to exist.

In hosting a daily radio talk show, I have frequently been asked about the nature of hell. From the 1990s onward, I felt compelled to inform inquirers that I was aware of three credible views concerning hell. I would then survey primary arguments for the respective views, inevitably falling back on the traditional view as my default. My parting shot would usually go something like this:

There have been many respectable, Bible-believing Christians in each camp. Having read their books, it seems to me that each view can marshal significant scriptural arguments in its favor. I have even come to the conclusion that none of the views can claim a greater degree of scriptural support than all of its rivals. Many of those in each camp are my superiors in biblical scholarship, and, possibly, in Christian piety and virtue. Therefore, I must consider the possibility that the truth may possibly lie elsewhere than in the view I have always advocated. The knowledge that a "kinder, gentler" view of hell may ultimately prove to be true is comforting, though, in the absence of absolute certainty, I think it safest to maintain the most pessimistic position. I think it better to prepare myself, and others, for the worst-case scenario. If I were to do otherwise, I might be guilty of under-preparing my hearers for what could be a far worse fate than what the alternative views anticipate. On the other hand, if I am prepared, and preparing others, to anticipate the most undesirable of the options, and if it turns out not to be so, then we can all be relieved, rather than disappointed.

For years, this seemed to me to be the only responsible way to address this topic. In assuming the traditional view as a default, however, I now believe that I was not making a sufficiently responsible inquiry into a matter that now seems to me more important than merely that of which view might best prepare one emotionally to cope with grim discoveries after death.

The approach that evaluates a teaching merely from the standpoint of human reactions to it is inferior, in that it is man-centered. To be authentic, Christian theology must be God-centered. Whatever hell may turn out to be will be a reflection on God's character and God's purposes. Until we have considered hell adequately in terms of its harmony with God's character, we are likely merely to be playing at the game of "Beat That Text," in debating the theological options, without ever really making sense of our theological affirmations.

The matter has been well distilled by Robert K. Johnson, professor of theology and culture at Fuller Theological Seminary: "How can I formulate a biblically informed perspective on hell 'that is morally consistent with the character of God as revealed in Jesus Christ'? If God is not limited even by death, for example, could there be the possibility of a final salvation for all? If the goal of God's justice is closure, not torture, could 'annihilationism' be a more biblically consistent doctrine of judgment than eternal torment?"[2]

---

2. In the foreword to Randy Klassen, *What Does the Bible Really Say about Hell?* (Telford, PA: Pandora Press, 2001), 12.

HELL AND THE PURPOSE OF GOD

We may safely assume that whatever God does, He does with some purpose, or end, in view. God is intelligent and purposeful. He has a plan and He is continually working His plan.[3] We need to inquire as to what specific purpose God had in creating hell.

For years, I assumed that immortality was simply a necessary and natural aspect of having been created in God's image, and that those who did not choose to spend their immortal lives in God's presence had but one option—one over which even God Himself did not have control—and that was to spend an immortal existence consciously separated from God. I assumed that hell was not so much a place that God had designed and constructed as it was banishment from all that God had prepared for those who love Him—a condition from which He purposed to deliver all, but was thwarted by the stubborn free will of most people.

It never occurred to me to ask how it was that God had found Himself in such a predicament—burdened with the heartache of knowing that He could only do so much to prevent the loss of so many of His beloved creatures, and forced helplessly to watch them go into unthinkable horror, which He would never have willingly allowed, if only He had more power to save. I obviously was not thinking clearly.

One thing we are not at liberty to assume is that hell is a reality that God would have liked to leave out of the picture altogether. God's sovereignty in designing the universe can hardly be affirmed if we assume that the majority of the people He intended to save must end up, against His wishes, eternally lost to Him in a place that He never intended to exist. The wisdom and foresight of a sovereign being who engineered a system that must necessarily result in his own eternal disappointment might well be questioned.

---

3. e.g., Ephesians 1:9, 11; Isaiah 14:24, 27.

More consistent with the biblical picture of the sovereign and purposeful God is the recognition that, in His setting up of the cosmos, He has provided for every contingency, so that nothing will ultimately prove to be His undoing. Even hell, whatever it is like, was "prepared" by God for something.

Jesus said that "eternal fire" was "prepared for the devil and his angels" (Matt. 25:41 NASB). *Prepared* by whom? Surely by God Himself! God established hell as a suitable place for the ultimate punishment of Satan and fallen angels. Yet, this verse affirms that certain people will also be cast into the same place.

So God has prepared eternal fires, knowing full well that many—perhaps most—people will eventually enter that place. With this in mind, He certainly must have prepared the conditions in hell that would best suit whatever purpose He desired to see accomplished there. But what functions, in God's purposes, do such eschatological "fires" fulfill?

It was very common in both Testaments for writers to employ the imagery of fire to represent both God's temporal and His ultimate judgments. Fire could have had a number of associations in the minds of the original readers:

To consume, destroy, and do away with unwanted materials. One obvious effect of fire is that it consumes most physical objects as fuel. Buildings, forests, fouled clothing—even dead bodies—are soon reduced to ashes when consigned to the flames.[4]

To separate gold and silver from their dross. Gold and silver were the currency of daily transactions for ancient people. Everybody knew that precious metals were not generally found lying around on the ground. They had to be mined from shoals of ordinary rock, and separated from other minerals through a refining process. Fire was the most expedient medium for this process.[5]

---

4. e.g., 2 Kings 1:10, 12; Psalms 37:20; 106:18; Jeremiah 9:12; Ezekiel 23:47; Matthew 3:12; Luke 9:54; Hebrews 12:29; 2 Peter 3:10.

5. e.g., Job 23:10; Isaiah 1:25; Ezekiel 22:18; Zechariah 13:9; Malachi 3:2–3; 1 Peter 1:7.

To express the painfulness of burning flesh. Though not frequently mentioned in Scripture, it is commonly known that living
human flesh, when burned, experiences great pain. To imagine being
thrown alive into fire would be a painful thought. The prospect of
being burned slowly, so that the reprieve of death is not instantaneous, is almost as gruesome a means of torture as can be imagined.[6]

What, then, is being suggested by the metaphor of unquenchable
fire when applied to hell?

Of the three aspects of judgment by fire surveyed above, the first
is the most common in Scripture. This idea lies at the root of the
annihilationist (or conditionalist) view—the main point being that
hell serves a necessary purpose: it rids the universe of those unfit to
inhabit it.

This view does not necessarily preclude a season of suffering
and misery, preceding destruction, such as one's degree of guilt may
require. Therefore, it may be "more tolerable . . . in the day of judgment" for one criminal than for another (Matt. 11:22, 24). Though
unrepentant sinners may receive proportionate punishment, whether
"few stripes" or "many stripes,"[7] as justice may require, none will be
tormented infinitely or eternally. Ultimately, all will perish and be
no more. The permanent removal of human debris from the presence
of the divine Majesty is not an unworthy conclusion to the drama
of the ages, and might well be considered the intended purpose for
which the fires of hell were ordained.

The second most common of the metaphorical uses of fire,
listed above, is that of purging or purification. This is regarded as
hell's purpose by those who espouse the universal reconciliation
view. Like the annihilationist alternative, this view also sees hell
as accomplishing the permanent and complete removal of sin from
every realm, and the establishment of an order in which every knee

---

6. e.g., Luke 16:24; Revelation 20:10 (cf. 1 Corinthians 7:9).
7. Luke 12:47–48.

shall bow and every tongue will gladly confess that Jesus Christ is Lord.

The obvious difference between this view and the annihilationist view is that annihilation brings about this desired end by destroying those who could never be reformed or made to embrace such a righteous order. Universal reconciliation obtains the same end, not by the destruction, but by the conversion, of every last rebel.

This view assumes that all men are *ultimately* as winnable to Christ as were those of us who have already been converted. Some of us remained in rebellion longer than others before surrendering to God's claims. Some may remain in rebellion until death. Those for whom seventy years was not long enough to be broken, might find one hundred years, or two hundred years, or one thousand years (who knows?) long enough to accomplish this. On this view, every man has his limit, and, however foolish and rebellious some may be, none are infinitely foolish and rebellious. Finite man does not possess infinite powers. Unlike man, God has all the time in the world (and perhaps beyond) to wear down His opponent's resistance. The fires of hell (much like the fiery trials of this present life) are thus viewed as having a corrective intention—a purpose consistent with God's desire that all people be saved.

The least common metaphorical use of fire in Scripture is as an image of searing pain—which is the idea that the traditional view of hell sees as central to the purpose of hell. Retributive justice, pure and simple, is the purpose of hell fires. God is a God of justice. The lost get only what they deserve. If it were not so, there would be no ultimate justice in the universe—which would be unacceptable, both to God and to the consciences of good men and women.

Though this view has seemed acceptable to the majority of biblical theologians for many centuries, a minority of evangelical authorities has suggested that the view is problematic on several points:

1. While we may agree that severe punishment is rightly deserved by those who die in their sins, we who are Christians do not deserve it less than do other sinners, and it is no more inappropriate that God should show mercy to them than to us. "Who makes you differ from another?" (1 Cor. 4:7). We have been fortunate enough to have been brought to repentance before death. Others die prior to repenting. While less fortunate, they are no more deserving of judgment than are we. It is sometimes heard among Christians that, if the lost are not tormented eternally, justice will have been outrageously violated. Do these same objectors feel that justice was violated in their case, since, in the mercy of God, they have escaped the punishment they deserved?

2. Though some wish to settle the score with sinners, there is nothing in Scripture or logic that would suggest that eternal torment is the only just penalty that God could reasonably authorize. It is arguably not the most just or equitable (nor certainly the most merciful) means that God might count among His options for settling a dispute with His detractors. Nor would anything but malice authorize a more serious punishment than was necessary, either to remedy the situation or to satisfy strict justice. According to Scripture, the announced penalty for sin is always said to be "death."[8] God would seem to have no moral obligation to go beyond this, in punishing sinners.

3. The fact that pain is one of the effects of living flesh being cast into fire does not necessarily require the conclusion that pain is an end in itself. A man burned at the stake feels pain, but it is only one step in the direction of the goal intended by his executioners—his death. It is a painful way to die, but it remains just that—a way to die. The pain is real, but not

---

8. Genesis 2:17; 3:22; Deuteronomy 30:15, 19; Ezekiel 18:4; Romans 6:23; 8:13.

unending. Likewise, pain can be a form of discipline to bring about remorse and reformation. All chastening is said to be painful, but afterward it yields desirable results.[9] Pain that is a transition into nonexistence (and thus cessation of pain) has something in common with pain that reforms: they both lead to positive outcomes. By contrast, if pain is endless, it precludes both relief and reformation—meaning it can have only one imaginable purpose: the eternal ventilation of an infinite desire for vengeance.

4. Far from fulfilling the demands of justice, a punishment that never reaches an end can only guarantee that justice will never finally prevail. Unless the sinner's sin actually *deserves* infinite punishment, such punishment must be inherently unjust; whereas, if sin does indeed warrant eternal punishment, then there will never come a future point at which it can be said, "Justice has been served!" Instead, at any theoretical point in the eternal future, there will still be "unfinished business" in that the punishment for sin will not ever be complete. Judgment for sin will be *in process* endlessly, and thus God will never have a moment in the future at which time He can take a relieved sigh and say, "It is done!"

It must be acknowledged that all these considerations are the reasonings of mere men—but what other reasoning is at our disposal? We might say that God's reasoning so far transcends ours as to render it fruitless even to attempt to make sense of eternal torment. We should simply take it by faith ... but faith in what? "Faith comes by hearing, and hearing by the word of God" (Rom. 10:17). The primary question that needs to concern us is whether the Word of God has declared a thing to be so or not. This is the very question with which we will concern ourselves in the following chapters.

---

9. Hebrews 12:11.

HELL AND THE CHARACTER OF GOD

It is the sincere aim of this study to conduct a fair-minded and responsible investigation into the respective biblical bases for each of the three alternative views of final punishment. There is more at stake in this inquiry than the mere satisfaction of morbid curiosity. The greatest point at issue is nothing less than finding the most correct understanding of the character of God. Whatever hell may prove to be, it will be what God, in His good pleasure, created it to be. His character is revealed in all of His acts. Thus, we learn about what kind of God He is by what He has made and what He does.

If God finds it tragically necessary to eliminate unrepentant and irredeemable rebels from existence by annihilating them (analogous to putting down a beloved, but rabid, dog), this cannot be regarded as contrary to either compassion or justice. Nothing in God's character is impugned.

Alternatively, if God exploits unavoidable human suffering as a means to a worthwhile end (analogous to a parent disciplining a child to correct self-destructive behavior), then He may easily be viewed as entirely benevolent, despite the severity of His remedies. This would not compromise His justice, since He has already made provision, through Christ, for the reconciling of the whole world to Himself.[10] Whatever remains, for Him, may be mere administrative detail.

However, if God has created a hell of torment that serves no constructive end but merely to take endless vengeance on utterly pitiable (though technically "deserving") creatures, then He will tend to be viewed through an entirely different lens.

If hell turns out to be a means toward a good end, then one need find no conflict between belief in hell and the character of a God who everywhere declares Himself to be full of both justice and

---

10. Romans 5:18; 2 Corinthians 5:19; Colossians 1:20; Hebrews 2:9; 1 John 2:2.

compassion.[11] Contrariwise, if hell serves no purpose other than eternally to ventilate a vindictive and insatiable wrath, then the idea that the Creator loves all of His creatures is definitely a harder "sell."

Clark Pinnock made a good point when he wrote: "Of course, it is not our place to criticize God, but it is permitted to think about what we are saying. The traditional view of the nature of hell does not cohere well with the character of God disclosed in the gospel."[12]

If the traditional doctrine is true, then we must, of course, accept this "God of vengeance" as He is, since there is no other. However, if God is not like this, and we misrepresent His character to the world, we may be guilty of grievous slander. It is possible that we could further alienate sinners from One to whom they might more readily have been drawn, had He been presented to them more accurately.

---

11. Exodus 34:6–7; Psalm 103:8–18; James 2:13.
12. Clark Pinnock, "The Conditional View," in William Crockett, ed., *Four Views on Hell* (Grand Rapids: Zondervan, 1992), 149.

CHAPTER 3

PUTTING HELL IN ITS PLACE

Exactly how important is the doctrine of hell? What role does it play in providing an incentive for conversion, for holy living, for service, for missions? How central is it to the Christian message, and how urgent is the need to understand its nature and purpose?

In 2011, Rob Bell (then pastor of Mars Hill Bible Church, in Grandville, Michigan) sparked an uproar in evangelical circles with his book *Love Wins*, in which the traditional thinking about hell was challenged, and a more universalistic understanding was entertained. *Time* magazine ran a cover story entitled "What if Hell Doesn't Exist?"[1] celebrating the release of the book.[2] The mere rumor that the book was going to be published caused online blogs and chat rooms to be abuzz with severe critiques of Pastor Bell, as if he had been the first evangelical to deviate from traditional paradigms of the final punishment. Even before its publication, a number of evangelical leaders, not yet having seen the book, publicly declared *Love Wins* to be "heresy." Reformed pastor and theologian John Piper caused a cyber-storm when he tweeted the message, "Farewell, Rob Bell"[3]—as if to dismiss him from the Christian fold.

Bell's view of hell is certainly a kinder, gentler view than that of the traditionalists, of which one could not wish for a more

---

1. A misleading headline, since the *existence* of hell is not what is being questioned in this debate.
2. *Time*, April 14, 2011 (cover).
3. https://twitter.com/JohnPiper/status/41590656421863424.

uncompromising example than that of Jonathan Edwards, in his famous sermon "Sinners in the Hands of an Angry God":

> Tis everlasting wrath. It would be dreadful to suffer this fierceness and wrath of Almighty God one moment; but you must suffer it to all eternity. There will be no end to this exquisite horrible misery. When you look forward, you shall see a long for ever, a boundless duration before you. . . . You will know certainly that you must wear out long ages, millions of millions of ages, in wrestling and conflicting with this almighty merciless vengeance; and then when you have so done . . . you will know that all is but a point to what remains. So that your punishment will indeed be infinite.[4]

Some traditionalists may find Edwards's words uncomfortably direct, but he does not express anything other than what their conviction affirms. While an increasing number of Christians seem to be uncomfortable with this view, there are others who insist that nothing less than this is found in the teachings of Jesus Himself. John Gerstner, for example, wrote: "He is an angry God. . . . So when Jonathan Edwards preached about 'Sinners in the Hands of an Angry God,' he was only echoing His Lord."[5]

Many, in reading the life and teaching of Christ, come away with an impression of God quite different from that of Edwards and Gerstner. There is wrath expressed toward some (e.g., the Pharisees), indeed. However, the average "sinners"—common tradesmen, shepherds, synagogue rulers, centurions, tax collectors, adulteresses, prostitutes—did not seem to find Jesus to be an angry person. They did not, to our knowledge, come under the wrathful denunciations that Jesus reserved, primarily, for the religious scoundrels who misled the common people about the loving character of their God.

---

4. Cited from Myra Jehlen and Michael Warner, eds., *The English Literatures of America, 1500–1800* (New York: Routledge, 1997), 625.

5. John Gerstner, *Repent or Perish* (Morgan, PA: Soli Deo Gloria Publications, 1990), 18.

THE PLACE OF HELL IN THE BIBLE

Many Christians, as we shall document in future chapters, believe that the traditional view of hell is one of the very pillars of the Christian faith, without which the death of Christ itself would be rendered meaningless. If this pillar is removed or undermined, the whole gospel message, they feel, becomes destabilized, and in danger of collapse.

Yet, when we delve into the scriptural teaching about hell, what we will find most striking is the infrequency of its being mentioned in Scripture.

Hell, conceived as a place of future judgment, is not found in the Old Testament at all.[6] This represents more than three-quarters of the biblical material, covering a period of four thousand years of divine revelation. What we find here is, essentially, silence.

In the New Testament, the Epistles contain the occasional mention of a final judgment and some sort of punishment of the lost, but the place of this punishment is never specified. As a place of human destinies, hell is never mentioned by name.

In some translations, James and 2 Peter contain the English word "hell" (once in each), but these books do not use the term as a reference to the destiny of human beings.[7]

Most of the references to hell and the final destiny of the lost are restricted to the teachings of Jesus. In thirty-nine recorded days of Jesus's ministry, we do not find the topic of hell mentioned on more than half a dozen occasions (possibly less[8]), and as near as we can judge from the book of Acts, the subject never came up in apostolic preaching.

---

6. With the possible exceptions of Isaiah 66:24 and Daniel 12:2, to be examined later.

7. James speaks of the tongue as being "set on fire by hell" (Gr. *Gehenna*; James 3:6); and Peter speaks of the fallen angels (not humans) being incarcerated in "hell" awaiting the final judgment (Gr. *Tartarus*; 2 Peter 2:4).

8. The count will depend upon decisions concerning the translation of the word *Gehenna* (see chapter 5).

Though Jesus and the biblical writers evidently believed something about hell, the topic does not seem to have been a "front-burner" concern in their thoughts or writings. They must have found something other than terror to motivate them to obedience and service.

THE PLACE OF HELL IN SALVATION

Traditionalist Sinclair Ferguson has written: "While by no means the central theme of the New Testament, [hell] receives considerable emphasis as the context in which the gospel is set and the destiny from which it delivers us. It is written into the warp and woof of the tapestry of God's revelation in Jesus Christ. It is that from which salvation delivers us."[9]

While many Christians seem to think of salvation primarily (or even exclusively) as a divine rescue of the sinner from hell, the Scriptures actually present salvation as God's addressing a broader range of concerns. In Scripture, salvation is represented primarily as deliverance not from hell in a future life, but rather from present conditions that are the result of the sinner's alienation from God. This alienation from God is viewed as man's primary predicament.[10] While Peter, Paul, or other primitive preachers never specifically said that Jesus came to save people from "hell" (it is, no doubt, implied), they do tell us that Jesus came to save us from the following:

1. This present evil age (Gal. 1:4)
2. Our present alienation from God (2 Cor. 5:19–20; Eph. 2:12–19)

---

9. Sinclair B. Ferguson, "Pastoral Theology: The Preacher and Hell," in Christopher W. Morgan and Robert A. Peterson, eds., *Hell Under Fire* (Grand Rapids: Zondervan, 2004), 221.

10. e.g., Isaiah 59:1–2; Jeremiah 2:5, 13; Ephesians 2:12.

3. An aimless and hopeless life (Eph. 2:12; 1 Peter 1:18–19)
4. Bondage to sin (Matt. 1:21; Luke 4:18; John 8:31–36; Acts 3:26; Rom. 6:22)
5. The fear of death (1 Cor. 15:54–55; Heb. 2:14–15)

Additionally, "salvation" is seen as a rescue from "the wrath to come" (Matt. 3:7; Rom. 5:9; 1 Thess. 1:10; 5:9), though what form this wrath may take remains obscure. It does not necessarily refer to postmortem destinies. Though frequently mentioned in the Old Testament,[11] God's "wrath" is never clearly identified there with circumstances of the next life, but with severe temporal judgments upon nations or individuals.

Likewise, in the New Testament, "wrath" is said to be a present reality resting upon, and revealed against, sinners while they live on the earth.[12] There are three passages that speak of believers being saved from "wrath."[13] While there is the possibility that this expression was seen as equivalent to postmortem "hell," the biblical writers chose not to clarify this.

While we recognize that the failure to obtain salvation will bring dire consequences upon the sinner, the sinner's loss is not central to the concerns addressed by biblical salvation. If the rebel is not recovered, God suffers loss. God saves the sinner not for the sinner's sake but for His own. Paul said in Titus 2:14 that Jesus "gave Himself for us, that He might redeem us from every lawless deed and purify *for Himself His own special people*, zealous for good works." John confirmed this in his first epistle: "I write to you, little children, because your sins are forgiven you *for His name's sake*" (1 John 2:12).

We need to be frequently reminded that the universe does not revolve around us—our needs, our wants, our happiness, our eternal

---

11. e.g., Exodus 15:7; 22:24; Numbers 11:33; 1 Samuel 28:18; 2 Kings 22:17; Psalms 59:13; 78:31; Isaiah 9:19; Jeremiah 32:37; Ezekiel 21:31; etc.

12. John 3:36; Romans 1:18; 1 Thessalonians 2:16.

13. Romans 5:9; 1 Thessalonians 1:10; 5:9.

well-being. God is the true center of reality, and therefore of biblical concern—*God's* glory, *His* prerogatives, *His* pleasure. Like all other things Christian, biblical salvation is God-centered, not man-centered. Participation in salvation requires a reorientation that is brought about by genuine repentance (which means a change of the mind). The first step toward Christ is that a man "deny himself" (Matt. 16:24).

Jesus came to seek and to save that which was lost. We must not forget that those who are lost have been lost to their owner. God is our owner: "It is He who has made us, and not we ourselves; we are His people and the sheep of His pasture" (Ps. 100:3).

God's heart for the recovery of the lost is illustrated in the three great parables in Luke 15. In each case, there is great rejoicing on God's part due to the recovery of something He had lost.

We may tend to think of how much the lost sheep benefits from being found (Luke 15:1–7), forgetting that the same sheep may become the shepherd's main course shortly after it is brought back home. A shepherd seeks a straying sheep because its disappearance from the flock represents an economic loss to the shepherd, and its recovery is the shepherd's boon.

The same lesson is found in the parable of the lost coin (Luke 15:8–10). The coin itself certainly had no interest in being found. The woman's search was launched in order to recover something of value to *her*. She was not motivated by the thought that the lost coin was suffering or in danger of harm to itself. The coin was the woman's wealth, and she rejoiced to regain it.

The case of the prodigal son (Luke 15:11–32) is more complex, due to the fact that the lost son was a human being (with whom we can sympathize), suffering for his foolish choices, and stood much to gain personally by being reconciled to his father. However, the rejoicing of the father was not over the recovery of just any unfortunate fellow coming into a better circumstance, but it was in regaining his own son. He belonged to his father's family, but had been lost. It was a loss to the son, to be sure, but what occasioned such joy on the part of the father was not merely the opportunity to assist a miserable man, but the regaining of a lost family member.

Certainly, being saved means, for us, that we are better off and no longer have reason to dread eternity, but its more important significance is that we have ceased to deprive God of what is His own. Our salvation means that He ceases to be robbed by our continuing rebellion. In saving mankind, God has recovered what He has created, purchased, and rightfully owns. "Do you not know that . . . you are not your own? For you were bought at a price; therefore glorify God in your body and in your spirit, which are God's" (1 Cor. 6:19–20).

THE PLACE OF HELL IN EVANGELISM

For many people, Jonathan Edwards's "Sinners in the Hands of an Angry God" serves as the benchmark for assessing powerful preaching and a faithful representation of the "good news" to sinners. "Folks need to hear the 'bad news' before they will be ready to accept the 'good news,'" goes the standard reasoning. Robert A. Peterson, in his book *Hell on Trial: The Case for Eternal Punishment*, lamented: "Few Christians speak of the destiny of the lost when they share the gospel with unsaved people."[14]

If we wish to criticize the reticence of modern preachers to place an emphasis on hell in their evangelism, we must first account for the same reticence found in the preaching of the apostles and evangelists of the early church. If we are accustomed to thinking that threats of hell are essential to faithful gospel preaching, it is a startling thing to examine the examples of apostolic evangelism recorded in the book of Acts, where references to hell are conspicuous only by their

---

14. Robert A. Peterson, *Hell on Trial: The Case for Eternal Punishment* (Phillipsburg, NJ: Presbyterian and Reformed Publishing Company, 1995), 240.

absence. Never do we find hell mentioned in any of the evangelistic sermons of the preachers that are recorded in the Bible. And this is true not only of the sermons in Acts but even in the Epistles, as traditionalist author Douglas J. Moo noted: "Paul never . . . explicitly uses hell as a means of stimulating unbelievers to repent."[15]

We are often told that Jesus spoke more on the topic of hell than did any other person in the Bible. This would not be difficult for Him to do, since almost all the biblical authors were silent on the subject. When Jesus and His disciples preached the gospel to unbelievers, there was little attempt to turn the listeners' thoughts to matters of the afterlife. While the eternal ramifications of turning to, or away from, God were not entirely out of view, they did not comprise a central thrust of their message.

Jesus seldom spoke of hell—probably on less than six or seven occasions out of about forty recorded days of His ministry. He also seldom spoke of heaven, conceived as a place where people go when they die. Unlike our modern preaching, Jesus's message was not about going to heaven after death.[16]

Jesus compared His movement, which He called "the kingdom of God," to a small seed, or a pinch of leaven, which was destined to expand and to permeate its environment (the earth).[17] Disciples were taught to pray not that they might go to heaven when they die, but that this kingdom would come here, resulting in God's will being done "on earth as it is in heaven" (Matt. 6:10). It was concern for this kingdom "on earth," not for a postmortem heavenly home, that was the focus of the majority of His parables,[18] and remained the burden

---

15. Douglas J. Moo, "Paul on Hell," in Christopher W. Morgan and Robert A. Peterson, eds., *Hell Under Fire* (Grand Rapids: Zondervan, 2004), 109.

16. The expression "kingdom of heaven" (found only in Matthew's Gospel) does not refer to heaven; rather, it is Matthew's synonym for "the kingdom of God," the term used by the other New Testament writers referring to Christ's messianic movement, which was, in the person of Christ Himself, and the company of those who embraced Him as King, launching an offensive against the devil's domain (e.g., Matt. 3:1; Mark 1:14–15; Luke 10:9–11; 16:16; 17:20–21; Acts 17:7; Rom. 14:17; Col. 1:13).

17. Matthew 13:31–33.

18. e.g., Matthew 13:10–11, 24, 31, 33, 44, 47; 22:2; Mark 4:26, 30, etc.

of His teaching to the disciples, even after His resurrection.[19] The same is true of the apostolic preaching in the book of Acts.[20]

The gospel that must be preached in all the world as a witness to all nations is the good news "of the kingdom" (Matt. 24:14). Judging from the samples of evangelistic preaching found in Acts, we would have to conclude that the main elements of this message were as follows:

1. Long ago, God made promises to the patriarchs and to David that a King of David's lineage would be permanently enthroned in David's place—one called the "Messiah," or "Christ."[21]
2. These promises have been fulfilled in Jesus of Nazareth, the Promised One, whom God publicly endorsed by working acts of power through Him before many witnesses.[22]
3. Jesus had enemies who crucified Him, but God restored Him to life, after which He was seen by witnesses, prior to ascending to His throne at the right hand of God.[23]
4. Since Jesus has been enthroned, it is incumbent upon all people to acknowledge His royal prerogatives (or "lordship"), and to repent of their rebellion against Him. To those who do this—embracing Him as Lord and Messiah (King)—He will graciously grant amnesty for all past rebellion.[24]

It is evident that the gospel, as preached by Jesus and His apostles, had an entirely different focus from that which has become standard evangelistic fare in American evangelism. Modern presentations

---

19. Acts 1:3.
20. Acts 2:30–36; 8:12; 14:22; 19:8; 20:25; 28:23, 31.
21. Acts 2:16–21, 25–31; 3:18, 22–25; 4:11; 10:43; 13:27, 29, 32–35; 26:22.
22. Acts 2:22; 3:13, 16; 10:38–39; 13:23.
23. Acts 2:23–24, 32–35; 3:14–15, 26; 4:10; 5:30–32; 10:39–41; 13:28–35; 17:31; 26:23.
24. Acts 2:36–39; 3:19–20; 4:12; 5:31; 10:43; 13:26, 34, 38–39; 17:30–31; 26:23.

are commonly directed to the self-interest of the hearers ("Come to Christ so you can escape from the punishment you deserve in hell"). By contrast, the biblical sermons appealed to God's interests, namely, the crown rights of Christ and the duty of man to surrender, here and now, to His lordship and to become a part of His expanding kingdom. Primitive preaching focused on giving Christ the place that He deserves, rather than on sinners escaping from the place that they deserve. The subtext of postmortem ramifications of compliance or noncompliance may have been *assumed* in the preaching, but they were not generally mentioned.[25]

Probably our modern methods do manage to attract more respondents of a particular mentality, but Jesus never encouraged self-centered multitudes to follow Him without first denying themselves and bearing a cross.[26] His evangelistic methods chased people away who were not willing to come on His terms.[27]

Jesus has never been desperate for friends. He is not compelled to "settle" for shallow and insincere companions, or an apathetic bride who will only agree to marry Him for advantage, rather than for love. He is the King of kings and the Lord of lords. Those who come to the table intending to negotiate the best deal for themselves with God have simply not yet come to terms with *who* it is they are dealing with—and neither He nor His apostles ever offered inclusion in His kingdom on any terms other than unqualified surrender to His lordship.[28]

The gospel is not so much an invitation as an ultimatum. God "commands all men everywhere to repent" (Acts 17:30). This is a divine summons to submit to a King whose kingdom is righteousness,

25. It is true that we don't have the complete sermons of all the apostles recorded in Acts. However, it seems that Luke has endeavored to preserve the germ of their messages. For us to suggest that any particular element was present in their preaching that is nowhere recorded in Scripture would be a case of our importing our own ideas of what we think they ought to have said, and assuming they agreed with us.

26. e.g., Matthew 16:24.

27. e.g., Matthew 19:21–22; John 6:60–66.

28. Matthew 19:21; Luke 14:33; John 14:15; 15:14; Acts 2:36; Romans 10:9.

58

peace, and joy in the Holy Spirit,[29] and into which all true disciples have entered at the time of their conversion.[30]

Whatever value there may be in informing unbelievers about hell, it cannot be claimed that any particular view of the subject is central to the biblical message that the church has been commissioned to preach to the world. The gospel is the good tidings of the reign of the righteous King Jesus. The message that the church is commissioned to preach has never been about hell, but about Christ.

For many centuries, sinners have been told by Christians that hell is a place of eternal torture in flames. This message has not prevented most of those who have heard it from ignoring the claims of Christ and continuing in their self-centered lifestyles. If people don't believe in hell, or do not take it seriously, it will make little difference which view of hell they may be disbelieving.

Ironically, the preaching of the traditional view may be one of the main reasons that modern unbelievers do not take our message seriously. The apparent injustice of infinite and endless suffering, in the minds of many, must certainly seem too bizarre—too surreal—to be believed. How many times have we heard unbelievers say something like, "I could never believe in a God who would torture little old ladies and naughty children forever in hellfire"?

When we preach, on the one hand, that God loves sinners and sent Jesus to die for them, and, on the other, that He is also the merciless Tormentor of all who would have the effrontery to slight Him, this must sound, to all but the convinced believer, like a hopeless contradiction, indicating that Christians must be wrong about one or another of those propositions—and perhaps about everything else too!

I know a devout and mature Christian man whose testimony is that he could not become a Christian (that is, he could not love God) until he actually came to disbelieve in the traditional doctrine of hell.

---

29. Romans 14:17.
30. Colossians 1:13.

He was not able to find God lovable while thinking of Him in terms of the traditional hell. His studies of Scripture finally disabused him of (what he now regards as) a slanderous misrepresentation of God, and he was then able to embrace and submit himself to Christ for the first time. This believer may or may not be correct in his abandoning the traditional doctrine of hell, but his story illustrates that its presentation may be more of a hindrance to evangelism than a boon to it. Certainly, we should not cling to the tradition merely in the hopes of retaining what we imagine to be the most effective soul-winning device.

In 1989, Gregory Boyd began a three-year season of correspondence with his skeptical father Edward concerning the latter's intellectual and moral questions which had prevented his acceptance of the Christian faith. This correspondence produced a series of 29 letters from Edward, and the same number of responses from his son, dealing with specific Christian issues that often are barriers to faith for intelligent and sensitive unbelievers. Greg's answers were respectful, well-informed, and well-argued. The entire correspondence was published, in 1994, under the title *Letters from a Skeptic: A Son Wrestles with His Father's Questions about Christianity*, after the elder Boyd's conversion. More than two years into this dialogue, the matter of hell remained a nagging problem. Edward did a good job of articulating the common objections with which thinking unbelievers (and some believers) wrestle when contemplating this subject. He wrote:

> So I need to kick around this hell business a little more. If I can make some sense out of this, I feel like I will have gone a long way toward making Christianity more plausible to me . . .
>
> Now tell me, what the hell (excuse the pun) would be the purpose of torturing someone eternally? What's the point? Obviously there's no "lesson" to be learned. This isn't corrective punishment. The person in hell has no hope of ever improving his character or situation. So this is sheer vengeance, pure retribution,

unadulterated anger, with no motive other than the pure, divine delight of inflicting horrifying pain on a person!

... Related to this is another point. I don't see how heaven can go on as heaven while hell is burning down below. Wouldn't the knowledge that there are billions of people boiling in hot lava down below you throughout eternity kind of dampen the "party spirit"? It seems as if this would present a problem, especially for an all-loving God who is supposedly in love with all these poor, tortured souls.[31]

In his response, Greg indicated that this is not the only view of hell that can be defended from Scripture, and laid out the case for one of the alternatives discussed in this book. After three years of honest questioning, and receiving good answers from his son, the older man finally came to the point of surrender, and came to Christ. In afterward writing to his son, he acknowledged the role that an alternative view of hell played in removing the final barriers to his faith:

Looking back on it, it seems that things really began to change for me when you convinced me of the Bible's inspiration and helped me make sense out of hell. I'm not sure why, but I think it was at that point that I really started to "see the light." Around this time I began to get the distinct impression that my case for skepticism was ultimately a lost cause.[32]

This is yet another example of how the traditional view of hell may be more of a barrier to the gospel than a help.

In 2004, Antony Flew, widely regarded as the preeminent atheist of the late twentieth century, shocked the world by announcing that he had been converted to belief in God. Sadly, this was not a belief

---

31. Gregory A. Boyd and Edward K. Boyd, *Letters from a Skeptic: A Son Wrestles with His Father's Questions about Christianity* (Colorado Springs: David C. Cook, 2008), 194f.
32. Ibid., 232.

in Christianity, but to Deism—the view that there was an intelligent Designer-God, who, after creating the universe, retreated from the creation and has never since interacted with what He made. In his 2007 book *There Is a God: How the World's Most Notorious Atheist Changed His Mind*, he gave his reasons for the move from atheism to Deism, which was based on the scientific discoveries made in his lifetime, including the "Big Bang," the incredible complexity of the cell, the "fine-tuning" of the universe, and the recently acquired awareness of the "information content" that forms the basis of life.

Flew (who is now deceased) did not embrace any religion, but stated that, if he were to do so, he judged that Christianity would be the most rational option available. He even allowed a Christian scholar, N. T. Wright, to include an appendix in his book, in which Wright defended the resurrection of Christ!

So why did Antony Flew move so far toward Christianity, but not commit to believing in it? An article first published in the *Christian Research Journal* answers this question:

In affirming belief in an Aristotelian God, Flew stresses that he has not come to believe in the God described by Islam or by Christianity. In both of these religions, Flew is troubled by teachings on hell—which he rejects as incompatible with God's holiness—and on what he describes as God functioning like a despot, demanding to be feared and obeyed.

"Even the greatest monsters of our time—like Hitler, Lenin, and Mao Zedong—might be subjected to a few millennia of hard labor, but not to an eternity of torture," Flew told the *Journal*. "If my argument is wrong, then I ought to be much more concerned about my fate in the universe, which is apparently in the hands of this monster [God]."[33]

---

33. Douglas LeBlanc, "Atheists and Theists Analyze Anthony Flew's Newfound Deism," *Christian Research Institute*, June 11, 2009, https://www.equip.org/articles/atheists-and-theists-analyze-anthony-flews-newfound-deism/.

We have already observed that the traditional understanding of hell prevented Charles Darwin from believing in Christianity. We can now see that the same objection prevented the world's most notorious atheist, in his journey toward faith, to stop short of embracing Christ.

Clark Pinnock, responding to another theologian's claim that belief in the traditional hell serves as a spur to evangelism, wrote: "This just confirms my suspicion that people hold to this teaching about hell for pragmatic and not biblical reasons—hell is the ultimate big stick to threaten people with. I would turn it around the other way: It is more likely that this monstrous belief will cause many people to turn away from Christianity, that it will hurt and not help our evangelism."[34]

We mustn't allow pragmatism to drive our message. Our message must be the truth. Any deviation from what the Bible really teaches may produce undesirable and unforeseen consequences. That God will judge unrepentant sinners, and that it will be horrible for them, is clearly affirmed in Scripture. We needn't shrink from telling them so, when appropriate. However, the details are actually left somewhat hazy in Scripture. Whether the horrors of hell are endless for the condemned, or whether they only last for an undesignated, torturous period and eventually accomplish something desirable, it is hard to imagine how anyone taking any view of hell seriously could fail to be interested in avoiding it. How many minutes of torture would be necessary to motivate any reasonable person to seek to avoid it?

The good news is not the story of God's judgment on sinners. Jesus, who understood the gospel best of all, immortalized its key theme in His story of the prodigal and his father. The message of the gospel is that Jesus has come to restore us to a proper relationship with our estranged Father, to whom all must return (repent), humbly and without agendas. This Father is waiting to get His hands on us not to punish us but to embrace us, and to restore us to the privileges

---

34. Clark Pinnock, "The Conditional View," in William Crockett, ed., *Four Views on Hell* (Grand Rapids: Zondervan, 1992), 39.

of full sonship. It was not fear of his father's wrath, nor threats of his punishment, that converted the prodigal in the far country. It was the memory of the goodness of his father toward his servants (Luke 15:17). As Paul wrote: "The goodness of God leads you to repentance" (Rom. 2:4).

THE PLACE OF HELL AS A MOTIVATOR FOR CHRISTIANS

Many believe that a diminishing of either hell's severity or its duration in our theology would remove the Christian's chief motivation for serving God and evangelizing sinners. If hell is not endless torment, say some, then what motive would remain to induce people to fight the good fight of faith and to lay down their lives to win others to Christ? Paul answered this question directly: "For the love of Christ compels us, because we judge thus: that if One died for all, then all died; and He died for all, *that those who live should live no longer for themselves, but for Him who died for them* and rose again" (2 Cor. 5:14–15).

Presumably, "the love of Christ" and the conviction that people "should live no longer for themselves, but for Him who died for them," would have motivated Paul to obey and serve Christ, regardless what he believed about the nature of divine judgment. As the staunch traditionalist Charles H. Spurgeon preached: "[The child of God] can boldly say, 'I have never done a right thing since I have followed Christ because I hoped to get to heaven by it,' or 'I have never avoided a wrong thing because I was afraid of being damned.' . . . For if a man has done what is called a virtuous action because he hoped to get to heaven or to avoid hell by it, whom has he served? Has he not served himself?"[35]

---

35. C. H. Spurgeon, "The Fatherhood of God," in *Sermons of Rev. C. H. Spurgeon of London*, vol. 5 (New York: Robert Carter and Brothers, 1883), 101f.

The idea that hell is the best motivator for doing what is right betrays a mentality that looks only to personal advantage, and fails to appreciate 1) the intrinsic value of God Himself, 2) His right to be glorified in His creatures, and 3) the incalculable and undeserved honor of being in a right relationship with Him, quite apart from any specific benefits He may offer us.

When I was a young man, a preacher challenged me, saying, "If Jesus Himself were to appear to you, and inform you that there really is no heaven and no hell after this life, would you still serve Him?" It was startling to hear the matter put in this manner, but it required only a moment's reflection to know the answer. Of course! Christians do not serve God for their own advantage, but for His glory! We serve Him because He *deserves* our love and obedience, and we have decided to cease and desist from our life of rebellion, through which we have previously deprived God of His rightful claims over us. In the story of Job, it was the devil who argued that the godly serve God only for their own advantage. God disagreed. Job's testing vindicated God's claim.

It would appear that many of the Old Testament saints had little or no conception of what awaited them after death, but they served God for the delight of knowing Him and of pleasing one whom they loved for His own worthiness. David desired "one thing" as his sole pursuit in life: "To behold the beauty of the LORD, and to inquire in His temple" (Ps. 27:4).

It would be unwarranted to assume that the threat of divine judgment played no role in motivating godly lives or divine service in either the Old or the New Testament, but there are higher reasons given there to seek God and to find that "fullness of joy" and "pleasures forevermore" that are said to be found in His presence (Ps. 16:11). *God alone is enough* for those who seek and find Him. He is the "rewarder of those who diligently seek *Him*" (Heb. 11:6)—thus He is Himself the reward of the quest. Who could require additional motivation for seeking Him than this?

CHAPTER 4

LAZARUS AND THE
RICH MAN

All that stuff I was taught about evolution . . . is lies
straight from the pit of hell.

— *Georgia Rep. Paul Broun[1]*

War is Hell.

— *General Wm. T. Sherman*

Osama bin Laden is burning in hell.

— *Anonymous*

I n popular parlance the English word "hell" is used many ways,
some theological, and some only colloquial. Consider the various
uses of "hell" in the quotations above.

In the first instance, when Congressman Broun spoke of evolution as a doctrine from "the pit of hell," he was using a fairly common idiom, speaking as if hell is a place from which evil influences
emerge, rather than a place to which people go. The idiom may have
been inspired by the concept of the *abyss* from which demons emerge

---

1. Quoted by Matt Pearce in "U.S. Rep. Paul Broun: Evolution a lie 'from the pit of
hell,'" *Los Angeles Times*, October 7, 2012, http://articles.latimes.com/2012/oct/07/nation/la
-na-nn-paul-broun-evolution-hell-20121007.

(Rev. 9, 11, 20), but which is not properly identified with what we commonly think of as hell.

The quotation from General Sherman employs another common idiom, which speaks of any terrible ordeal as a sort of hell. Along the same lines, people often may be heard to say, "I went through *hell* in my last marriage." This is a figure of speech, merely. It does not really express the speaker's theological convictions about the nature of a postmortem human destiny.

The final citation reflects an actual theological conviction of many Christians, who think of hell as a place where people like Osama bin Laden and Adolf Hitler find themselves after they die. Such people may be confusing postmortem habitations with another belief (which they probably also hold) of hell as a place where the wicked, after the judgment, will burn eternally. Biblically, no one is actually sent to their final or eternal destiny until after the last judgment, occurring at the second coming of Christ (as described in Matthew 25:46 and Revelation 20:15). Where people go in the intermediate time, between death and the final judgment, is a separate question.

While one may find a biblical basis for placing the lost in Hades immediately after death, this is not to be confused with the eventual place of the final judgment. Hades, as we shall see, is not eternal, nor is its population demographically limited to unbelievers. It is, thus, not what most people think of when they speak of "eternal hell."

The idea of persons immediately going to Hades after death can be found in only one New Testament passage, in which a miserly rich man is described as being "in torments in Hades" (Luke 16:23). Since his brothers are described as still living on the earth (v. 28), we know that this is a description not of the man's eternal fate, following the final judgment, but of his immediate condition after death. Since the King James Version uses the word "hell" for this intermediate place, it has inspired expressions like "Bin Laden is in *hell* today."

Too often, even Christian preachers and teachers have become accustomed to using the term "hell" carelessly, without indicating which place they have in mind. This is largely due to the unfortunate decision, on the part of the earliest English translators, to use one word, "hell," in translating multiple biblical terms: *Sheol*, *Hades*, *Tartarus*, and *Gehenna*. Since these four terms do not all speak of the same place or concept, the use of the same English word to render all of them was unfortunate, and has led to much confusion and inconsistency in the way we have come to understand and speak about "hell." Let's briefly consider the different scriptural terms:

1. **SHEOL.** Whenever the word "hell" occurs in the Old Testament, it is always translating the Hebrew word *Sheol*. Occasionally, this word is also translated "the grave" or "the pit." Sheol refers to the place where all the dead—both the righteous and the unrighteous—go at the end of this life. Though the KJV frequently translated Sheol as "hell," there is no exact English equivalent, and most scholars believe that it conveys the concept of an undifferentiated place of the dead. This word was treated, by the Septuagint (the Greek translation of the Hebrew Old Testament) and by New Testament writers, as the functional equivalent of the Greek word *Hades*, though the Greek word had somewhat different connotations in the pagan usage.

2. **HADES.** This Greek word is found eleven times in the New Testament,[2] where, in most cases, the writer or speaker is rendering Old Testament references to Sheol.[3] It always refers to the place of the dead (including the righteous) *prior to* the resurrection. It only occurs on three occasions in the recorded teaching of Jesus.[4]

   The three views of hell that we are examining in this

---

2. Matthew 11:23; 16:18; Luke 10:15; 16:23; Acts 2:27, 31; 1 Corinthians 15:55; Revelation 1:18; 6:8; 20:13, 14.

3. Matthew 11:23; Luke 10:15 (Isaiah 14:15); Matthew 16:18 (Job 17:16; Isaiah 38:10); Acts 2:27, 31 (Psalm 16:10); 1 Corinthians 15:55 (Hosea 13:14).

4. Matthew 11:23; Luke 10:15 (parallel); Matthew 16:18; Luke 16:23.

study do not concern themselves directly with the temporary or intermediate state of the dead, but with final destinies. Passages that speak of Sheol, or Hades, will not have much bearing, therefore, upon our inquiry. Hades itself is destined to be cast into the lake of fire (Rev. 20:14), so it obviously is not the same thing as the lake of fire!

3. **TARTARUS.** This is another Greek word that is translated as "hell," in some English Bibles. It occurs only once in the New Testament,[5] but was earlier used in Greek mythology to describe the place where the Titans were sent for punishment. In the New Testament, we are told nothing about Tartarus, except that it is the temporary abode of the fallen angels, where they remain chained while they await their final judgment. There is nowhere any suggestion of humans going there. Thus, Tartarus is not really what we think of as "hell" either. Even for the fallen angels it is not the final place of judgment, nor are we given any reason to believe that any, other than angels, will ever be there.

Considering the actual meanings of Sheol, Hades, and Tartarus, it seems clear that Christian parlance should never have adopted the English word "hell" for these terms—unless some entirely different term was to be adopted to represent the entirely different concept of final destiny of the lost. The most suitable term for the latter concept may be "the lake of fire," an expression found only in the book of Revelation—but that is a whole phrase, not a word.

According to Revelation 20:15, those whose names are not found written in the Book of Life will be thrown into the lake of fire—not as soon as they die, but after the final judgment at the end of the world. This is generally thought to be the same fate elsewhere referred to as a "furnace of fire"

---

5. 2 Peter 2:4.

(Matt. 13:42, 50), "everlasting [Gr. *aionios*] fire" (Matt. 18:8; 25:41), and "outer darkness" where there will be "weeping and gnashing of teeth" (Matt. 8:12; 22:13; 25:30).

4. **GEHENNA.** Most Christians throughout history have identified this final place of judgment with the Greek word *Gehenna*, the examination of which will be a focus of our next chapter.

THE ENIGMA OF ENOCH

Jewish thought in Jesus's time was heavily influenced by a literary work whose author identifies himself as the biblical Enoch, though scholars agree that it was written only a century or two before Christ—more than two thousand years after Enoch's day. The book of 1 Enoch belongs to the category of intertestamental literature which scholars label *pseudepigrapha* (a Greek word meaning "falsely subscribed"). What we might call "writing under a pen name" was a common practice of Jewish writers, especially in the two centuries prior to the coming of Christ. Some of these books—especially 1 Enoch—were highly regarded in both Jewish and Christian circles. Some Christians even favored its inclusion in the canon of Scripture, but the criteria for accepting books as canonical rightly excluded pseudepigraphal works. Craig Evans wrote: "The materials in I Enoch range in date from 200 B.C.E. to 50 C.E. I Enoch contributes much to intertestamental views of angels, heaven, judgment, resurrection, and the Messiah. This book has left its stamp upon many of the NT writers, especially the author of Revelation."[6]

According to Gerhard Kittel: "Under the influence of Persian and Hellenistic ideas concerning retribution after death the belief arose that the righteous and the godless would have very different

---

6. Craig A. Evans, *Noncanonical Writings and New Testament Interpretation* (Peabody, MA: Hendrickson, 1992), 23.

fates, and we thus have the development of the idea of spatial separation in the underworld, the first instance being found in Enoch."[7]

We read in *The International Standard Bible Encyclopedia*: "In the intertestamental period the idea of the afterlife underwent some development. In Jewish apocalyptic literature Hades was an intermediate place (1 En. 51:1) where all the souls of the dead awaited judgment (22:3f.). The dead were separated into compartments, the righteous staying in an apparently pleasant place (v. 9) and various classes of sinners undergoing punishments in other compartments (vv. 10–13)."[8]

And in *The Zondervan Pictorial Encyclopedia of the Bible*: "Enoch . . . includes the description of a tour supposedly taken by Enoch into the center of the earth. . . . In another passage in Enoch, he sees at the center of the earth two places—Paradise, the place of bliss, and the valley of Gehinnom, the place of punishment. The above illustrates that there was a general notion of compartments in Hades that developed in the intertestamental period."[9]

Anyone acquainted with mainstream evangelical notions of the state of the dead will recognize a great similarity—even identity—between these ideas introduced by Enoch into Judaism and those held by many modern Christians. It is not customary for evangelical Christians to look to intertestamental Jewish sources for their doctrine, and these ideas about the state of the unsaved dead probably would never have made the transition into Christianity from the influence of pre-Christian Enoch alone. Given the frequent references by Jesus and Paul to the dead as "sleeping,"[10] it is not likely that this concept of souls being tortured in the intermediate state would be

---

7. Gerhard Kittel, *Theological Dictionary of the New Testament*, vol. 1 (Grand Rapids: Wm. B. Eerdmans, 1964), 147.

8. Geoffrey W. Bromiley, ed., "Hades," in *The International Standard Bible Encyclopedia*, vol. 2 (Grand Rapids: Wm. B. Eerdmans, 1988), 591.

9. Harry Buis, "Hades," in Merrill C. Tenney, ed., *The Zondervan Pictorial Encyclopedia of the Bible*, vol. 3 (Grand Rapids: Zondervan, 1975), 7.

10. e.g., Matthew 9:24; John 11:11; 1 Corinthians 15:20, 51; 1 Thessalonians 4:14–15.

accepted as a Christian idea at all, if not for Christ's own use of this
motif in His famous story of the rich man and the beggar Lazarus.

LAZARUS AND THE RICH MAN

When seeking for clues in the Bible concerning the postmortem
state of the lost, there is really nowhere else to go than to Jesus's
story about the beggar Lazarus and the ungenerous rich man (Luke
16:19–31). In the story, both men die and find themselves in separate
compartments of Hades, exactly as Enoch had previously described
things. We find that the rich man, getting the worst of the deal,
appeals to Abraham—in whose bosom the beggar is comforted—
first crying out for relief, and then requesting the favor of sending
Lazarus back to the world of the living to warn his unprepared
brothers about this fate. Abraham replies that these men should heed
the Law and the Prophets, and that they need no messenger to come
to them back from the grave.

Here, and only here, in the teaching of Jesus, do we find any
description of the intermediate state of the dead. A great burden
is therefore placed upon this one story, in evangelical discussions
of hell, to provide information about what Jesus thought about the
afterlife. Yet, the applicability of this story to the topic is questionable, for several reasons.

First, scholars seem incapable of reaching a consensus as to
whether the story is a true story, or one of Jesus's parables, or something else. Its ability to speak helpfully to the topic of the state of the
dead depends upon the manner in which Jesus expected His hearers
to understand its genre.

Scripture does not identify the story as a parable, and Jesus,
in mentioning the proper names of two individuals (Lazarus,
Abraham), introduces a feature not found in any other of Jesus's
recorded parables. These factors have inclined many to conclude that

this is not one of Jesus's parables, but that He is relating an actual case of two real men who died.[11]

A second view is that this is indeed a parable, though it may exhibit unique characteristics (like named individuals) not found in other parables. The main characters may be fictional, it is argued, but the scenario is realistic. While none of Jesus's parables are stories of actual cases, all of them do employ true-to-life settings—a man sowing seeds, a woman making dough, two debtors being forgiven different amounts and exhibiting different degrees of gratitude, and a rebellious son being welcomed home by his father. Even if the story of Lazarus and the rich man is a parable (so goes the argument), we would expect that it nonetheless presents an accurate portrayal of the real world of the dead.

On either of these first two views, Jesus would be placing His *imprimatur* upon the pagan notions of the afterlife that originated among the Greeks and entered Judaism through 1 Enoch.

A third approach to this story, which has gained support from increased rabbinical studies, is the suggestion that it was, indeed, a parable—or at least a fictional account to make a spiritual point—but that the story, in its major features, did not originate with Jesus, nor would He, by telling it, necessarily have been understood to be advocating a literal scenario for the afterlife. It has been observed by scholars that many of the features of the story, while not agreeing with anything specifically taught in the Old Testament, nonetheless do echo 1 Enoch, as well as themes commonly found in tales told by the rabbis of Jesus's day.

For example, references to the dead being "carried by angels" to "Abraham's bosom," and to the dead communicating among themselves and being able to see across the gulf between Paradise and the place of flames, are all found in the Talmud.[12]

---

11. It should be noted that, even if this story is a true one, it does not involve the same Lazarus of Bethany, of whose death we read in John 11—one notable difference being that Bethany's Lazarus was a righteous man, whom Jesus raised back to life, whereas this Lazarus was a beggar, and not raised to life again. Though the request that this should happen is made by the rich man, the request is denied.

12. See examples cited in J. W. Hanson, *The Bible Hell* (Boston: Universalist Publishing House, 1888), 43.

These Jewish ideas seem to have been derived from earlier pagan concepts, both Greek and Egyptian, which were given their own Jewish flavor by 1 Enoch and the rabbis. The Scottish Presbyterian commentator James MacKnight affirmed the pagan origin of this rabbinic imagery:

> It must be acknowledged . . . that our Lord's descriptions (in this parable) are not drawn from the writings of the Old Testament, but have a remarkable affinity to the descriptions which the Grecian poets have given. They, as well as our Lord, represent the abodes of the blessed as lying contiguous to the region of the damned, and separated only by a great impassable river, or deep gulf, in such sort that the ghosts could talk to one another from its opposite banks. The parable says the souls of wicked men are tormented in flames; the Grecian mythologists tell us they lie in Phlegethon, the river of fire, where they suffer torments.[13]

Since these features of the afterlife were not revealed by God to Moses or the Prophets, and they seem to be rabbinic speculations, based upon the common Greek template of Hades, many scholars have concluded that Jesus was telling a rabbinic story familiar to His hearers, and placing His own spin on it to drive a point home. As Craig Blomberg wrote:

> One of the most misinterpreted of Jesus' parables is the story of the rich man and Lazarus (Luke 16:19–31), which has been used repeatedly to provide in great detail a realistic depiction of life after death. In fact, the picture of the rich man in Sheol and Lazarus in Abraham's bosom separated by a chasm but able to call to each other across it is paralleled by popular Jewish and

---

13. William G. T. Shedd, *The Doctrine of Endless Punishment* (1885; repr., Carlisle, PA: Banner of Truth, 1986), 60.

Egyptian folk tales. Jesus may have simply adopted well-known imagery but then adapted it in a new and surprising way.[14]

The International Standard Bible Encyclopedia confirms this idea: "This parable follows a story common in Egyptian and Jewish thought."[15]

The *New Commentary on the Whole Bible* also suggests that the rabbinic story was "possibly derived from an Egyptian source."[16] Douglas Jacoby has also said: "Scholars have discovered parables with a similar message in earlier Egyptian and Jewish texts. A doctoral dissertation at the University of Amsterdam identified seven versions of the parable circulating in the first century. The fortunes of a rich man and a poor man are reversed in the afterlife. As often happens in the Bible, a preexisting story is adapted to present a theological truth."[17]

Did Jesus, by Use of This Story, Confirm the Rabbinic Picture of Hades?

Would it necessarily follow that Jesus was endorsing the view of the afterlife employed as the backdrop for the story? Probably not any more than if a modern preacher were to begin a sermon illustration thus: "So this guy dies, and meets Saint Peter at the Pearly Gates . . ." His audience would easily recognize, in the reference to Saint Peter at the Pearly Gates, an allusion to popular religious folklore—and no one would mistakenly think that the preacher was actually affirming his own buy-in to such an afterlife scenario.

There would be nothing objectionable in Jesus's taking something from Jewish folklore and teaching from it. A modern preacher

---

14. Craig Blomberg, *The Historical Reliability of the Gospels* (Downers Grove, IL: InterVarsity Press, 1987), 22–23.

15. Bromiley, *International Standard Bible Encyclopedia*, vol. 3, 94.

16. J. D. Douglas, gen. ed., *New Commentary on the Whole Bible* (Carol Stream, IL: Tyndale House Publisher, September 1991), based on the classic commentary of Jamieson, Fausset, and Brown.

17. Douglas A. Jacoby, *What's the Truth about Heaven and Hell?* (Eugene, OR: Harvest House, 2013), 38.

might similarly employ ideas from *The Pilgrim's Progress*, *The Chronicles of Narnia*, or other well-known religious fiction, without for a moment suggesting that he regarded any of those stories to be historically true or set in an environment resembling the real world.

Many of the modern writers on hell, whose works I have researched in writing this book, make use of illustrations from C. S. Lewis's classic (and admittedly fictional) descriptions of heaven and hell in *The Great Divorce*, and frequently cite Lewis's metaphor, from *The Problem of Pain*, affirming that "the doors of hell are locked from the inside."[18] In employing these famous images, our Christian writers, as well as the preachers who quote them, do not mean to imply that they literally believe in a heaven that is periodically visited by busloads of hell's curious occupants, nor that hell has doors with locks that can be opened from the inside by the inhabitants if they wish. But they still find such imagery useful and may employ it in making some legitimate point or another. Though an adamant traditionalist, Robert Morey wrote:

> The rabbinic literature before, during, and after the time of Christ is filled with parables which built imaginative stories around real historical characters. There are multiple examples in the Talmud and Midrash of parables in which Abraham had dialogues with people such as Nimrod, with whom he could never have spoken literally. Everyone understood that these parables and dialogues did not literally take place.... Therefore, it does not bother us in the least to say that Christ used a rabbinic story and dialogue in Luke 16:19–31 which was not "true" or "real" in the sense of being literal.[19]

For Jesus to take something from rabbinic tradition and to turn it back upon the rabbis would not be unprecedented. In fact, He did this very thing on another occasion, when the Pharisees accused

---

18. C. S. Lewis, *The Problem of Pain* (1940; repr., New York: HarperOne, 1996), 130.
19. Robert A. Morey, *Death and the Afterlife* (Minneapolis: Bethany House, 1984), 85.

Him of casting out demons "by Beelzebub, the prince of demons" (Luke 11:15; Matt. 12:24 NIV). In Old Testament times, Ba'al-zebul (meaning "Ba'al the prince") was the name of one of the imaginary deities whom the Philistines worshipped at Ekron. In rabbinic tradition, this name had deliberately been morphed into the pejorative *Beelzebub* ("lord of the flies"), regarded as the "chief of the demons." When Jesus turned their statement back upon the Pharisees, saying, "If I cast out demons *by Beelzebub*, by whom do your sons cast them out?" (Matt. 12:27), He was not necessarily accepting their tradition about Beelzebub as true. This would be an example of Jesus's use of one kind of *ad hominem* argument ("On the basis of your own premises . . ."). Jesus used this kind of argument on more than one other occasion.[20]

In employing a traditional story about Hades for His purpose, Jesus is not unlike Paul, who also wrote as if he believed the notion (from rabbinic tradition) that the water-yielding rock literally *followed* the children of Israel through the wilderness,[21] and (when among Greeks) cited statements about Zeus, found in the writings of the Greek philosophers, and applied them to Yahweh.[22]

Jude and Peter[23] both alluded to Jewish stories about fallen angels, drawn from the book of 1 Enoch—and Jude also cited a (possibly mythical) encounter between Michael and Satan from the intertestamental apocryphal book *The Assumption of Moses*.[24]

If Jesus did not tell the story of Lazarus and the rich man in order to affirm Jewish notions about the afterlife, then what was the lesson He intended for His hearers—the Pharisees—to take away from the story? There are, no doubt, two separate lessons, corresponding to the early and the later portions of the story, respectively:

---

20. John 10:34–35; Matthew 12:3–7.
21. 1 Corinthians 10:4.
22. Acts 17:28. Paul alludes to the Cretan philosopher, poet, and prophet Epimenides, and cites the *Phaenomena* of Aratus.
23. 2 Peter 2:4; Jude 6.
24. Jude 9.

1. The story begins by introducing its two main characters: a rich Jew in circumstances that the Pharisees regarded as evidence of God's favor and blessing upon a man—and a poor beggar, whose circumstances would be interpreted by the Jews as indicating God's disfavor upon him. Both men died, and, in the afterlife, found their circumstances reversed (v. 25). This drives home the first obvious lesson of the story, namely, that God does not judge as man judges, and that those who are poor in this life may be rich toward God, while others may be rich in this life, but "not rich toward God" (Luke 12:21). This lesson is an oft-repeated theme of Christ's teaching (e.g., Matt. 19:23–24; Luke 6:20, 24; Rev. 2:9; 3:17).[25]

2. The second part of the story focuses on the rich man's request for Lazarus to be sent back to the realm of the living to warn the rich man's brothers, giving them the opportunity to avoid a like fate. Abraham replies that they have adequate warning, in the writings of Moses and the Prophets, to steer them the right direction, and that even a man returning from the realm of the dead will not convince those who are already rejecting the Scriptures. The message here seems to be that even the spectacle of a man rising from the dead (i.e., Jesus) would not impress those who have already hardened themselves against God's prior revelation. His point: the apostasy of the Jews, seen in their rejection of Moses and the Prophets, can only result in their rejection of Himself, even once He has risen (cf. John 5:46–47).

---

25. A number of commentators spiritualize the rich man's "riches," seeing them as a reference to the spiritual benefits given to the Jewish people through the Law and the Prophets, while the beggar represents the Gentiles, languishing without such knowledge. While a rebuke of Jewish snobbery toward Gentiles may have been justified, such a point would hardly be *in sync* with any major emphasis in Jesus's public teaching elsewhere, as would the lesson about material wealth and poverty—one of His principal themes.

Traditionalist Robert Yarbrough wrote: "It is widely accepted that this story is parabolic and not intended to furnish a detailed geography of hell."[26] Likewise, N. T. Wright confirmed: "The parable is not, as often supposed, a description of the afterlife, warning people to be sure of their ultimate destination."[27]

Douglas Jacoby added: "The literal interpretation of the parable was common in the Middle Ages, but it has been largely abandoned in more recent theological articles."[28]

The conclusion of many, that the imagery of the story was not necessarily intended to teach anything about the real nature of hell, nor to confirm popular lore on the subject, seems reasonably justified. The purpose of the parable was not to reveal the nature of the afterlife, but to teach entirely unrelated lessons. I once heard a preacher make an excellent point from the Greek myth of Ulysses and the Island of the Sirens, but I am pretty sure he did not actually believe such an island existed. In similar fashion, Jesus may simply have borrowed a template of the afterlife from the Jews' own mythology, in order to provide a framework for His story.

Not all evangelicals are willing to accept this explanation, but let us consider the consequences of rejecting it. If we insist that Jesus's description of Hades, in this story, corresponds to the actual state of the dead, we are left to conclude that the Egyptians and Greeks (from whom, apparently, the rabbis derived some parts of their visions of hell), lacking divine inspiration, somehow guessed accurately about unseen matters that could only be known by God or by revelation from God. Jesus would then be seen as placing His stamp of approval on the mythical speculations of the pagan religions. While this is possible, it is a thesis both improbable and unnecessary.

---

26. Robert W. Yarbrough, "Jesus on Hell," in Christopher W. Morgan and Robert A. Peterson, eds., *Hell Under Fire* (Grand Rapids: Zondervan, 2004), 74.

27. N. T. Wright, *Christian Origins and the Question of God*, vol. 2, *Jesus and the Victory of God* (London: SPCK, 1996), 255.

28. Douglas A. Jacoby, *What's the Truth about Heaven and Hell?* (Eugene, OR: Harvest House, 2013), 39.

CHAPTER 5

TWO KEY WORDS TO DEFINE: *GEHENNA* AND *AIONIOS*

In arguing for one or another view of hell, writers often lean heavily upon passages that employ either the word *Gehenna* or the word *aionios*. As mentioned in the previous chapter, *Gehenna* is one of the Greek words traditionally translated "hell," while *aionios* is a Greek word usually translated "eternal" or "everlasting." The meanings of these words are often assumed to be understood and agreed upon by all, prior to the commencement of the discussion. Yet, there are controversies concerning the precise import of these words—controversies that render arguments based upon them more tenuous than many acknowledge. Those who wish to make informed decisions about the nature of hell should consider how alternative meanings of these two important words may impact one's assessment of the relevance of key passages in the debate.

GEHENNA: IS IT HELL, OR JUST A LOCAL CREMATORIUM?

In Scripture, the word *Gehenna*, as a place of judgment, is used only by Jesus, and only in the Synoptic Gospels. That it is synonymous with Revelation's "lake of fire" (as is commonly assumed) is quite possible, but the two are not explicitly identified with each other in any place in Scripture. The identity of the concepts would have to be established exegetically before being affirmed. There is another possibility, which will be considered presently.

Gehenna is a Greek word, of which the English word "hell" is not a translation, but an interpretation. The term's literal meaning is "the Valley of Hinnom." This valley was and is an actual place on the face of the earth, not in the next world. It is the valley southwest of, and adjacent to, the old city of Jerusalem, where one can walk today upon green grass. References to this literal valley occur in the Old Testament, but, in the intertestamental period, the term took on an entirely new connotation in the speculative eschatology of the rabbis. Christ's use of *Gehenna*, seemingly, must be traced either to its use in the Old Testament, or else to its use by the rabbis of His own day.

In the Old Testament, this valley was known by a number of names. It was usually called the "Valley of the son of Hinnom,"[1] or, sometimes, simply the "Valley of Hinnom,"[2] or "Tophet."[3] Figuratively (because of the number of war dead to be deposited there), it is sometimes called the "Valley of Slaughter."[4]

Gehenna, or the Valley of Hinnom, was the place where the Jews, when apostate, worshipped the pagan god Molech, even burning their children alive in the arms of the idol,[5] a practice the Bible refers to as causing one's sons to "pass through the fire."[6] In the days of the God-fearing King Josiah, Molech-worship was abolished, and the Valley of Hinnom was (according to some accounts) turned into Jerusalem's common garbage dump, where perpetual fires consumed the offal of the city.[7]

---

1. e.g., Joshua 15:8; 18:16; 2 Chronicles 28:3; 33:6; Jeremiah 7:31, 32; 19:6; 32:35.
2. Nehemiah 11:30.
3. e.g., Isaiah 30:33; Jeremiah 7:31, 32; 19:6, 11–14.
4. Jeremiah 7:32; 19:6.
5. 2 Kings 23:10.
6. Leviticus 18:21; 20:2–5; Jeremiah 32:35.
7. There is no early evidence that this valley was used as a garbage dump in the time of Christ. Some sources claim that this oft-repeated tradition was first mentioned in a rabbinic writing around the year 1200.

Shortly before the time of Christ, certain Jewish writings (e.g., 1 Enoch) used the term *Gehenna* as a reference to the place of judgment for the wicked in the next world. The term never bore this meaning in the canonical Scriptures. Following the apocryphal writings, the rabbis began to speculate about the judgment of the damned, using *Gehenna* as the term for what we would call "hell." By the time of Christ, the term commonly carried this connotation, and was probably associated with this concept in the minds of many of Jesus's hearers.

Even so, there was no unanimity among the rabbis as to the ultimate destiny of the wicked in Gehenna. Some thought that sinners who had not led others into sin would go to Gehenna for only twelve months, as a purging experience, after which they would go to the throne of God (*Babylonian Talmud* RH64). Thus, "[a]ll that descend into Gehenna shall come up again, with the exception of three classes of men: those who have committed adultery, or shamed their neighbors, or vilified them (*B. M.* 58b)."[8] Others thought that the outcome, after a time in Gehenna, would be annihilation (*R. H.* 17a; comp. *Shab.* 33b).

A third view, championed by the apocryphal book of Judith, insisted that the totally wicked would burn forever in torment, though the word *Gehenna* is not used there (Judith xvi. 17). In other words, just like the early Christians, some Jews were annihilationists, some were restorationists, and some taught eternal torment. These were all variant opinions about the judgment of Gehenna.

There is little reason to credit any of these views with divine inspiration, since they have no basis in the Old Testament and are not the product of inspired writers.

Gehenna is found twelve times in the Greek New Testament. James used it one time, and Jesus used it the other eleven times. James's usage does not contribute to our knowledge of the subject,

---

8. JewishEncyclopedia.com.

since he simply said that the human tongue (figuratively) "is set on fire by [Gehenna]" (James 3:6). What James may have pictured to be the actual nature and character of Gehenna we are not told.

Though we have eleven occurrences of this word in the New Testament from the lips of Jesus, some of them are in parallel statements occurring in different gospels. It is probable that Jesus only used the term on four occasions:

1. In the Sermon on the Mount (Matt. 5:22, 29, 30)
2. In warning the disciples not to fear men (Matt. 10:28; Luke 12:5)
3. In the discourse on relationships (Matt. 18:9; Mark 9:43, 45, 47)
4. In His denunciation of the scribes and Pharisees (Matt. 23:15, 33)

Of the various biblical words translated as "hell" in our Bibles, only *Gehenna* can possibly refer to the ultimate place of judgment for the wicked. Yet, all that Jesus tells us about Gehenna is restricted to these four occasions. We are told almost nothing about it in these places, except that bodies[9] can be thrown into "everlasting" and "unquenchable" fire there,[10] resulting in a fate worse than mere mutilation or martyrdom, involving the destruction of soul and body.[11]

If Gehenna is to be identified with the eternal fate of all who are unsaved, this would be a seemingly important doctrine. It is surprising, therefore, to find it mentioned so seldom in Scripture—and, usually, without any descriptive detail.

Even the mention of "fire," associated with Gehenna, is not very informative. In biblical imagery, the use of fire as a metaphor for divine judgment (whether temporal or eschatological) is so common

---

9. Matthew 5:29, 30; 18:9; Mark 9:43, 45, 47.
10. Matthew 18:8; Mark 9:43, 45, 48.
11. Matthew 10:28.

as to have acquired the status, almost, of an apocalyptic cliché.[12] The fire mentioned in various judgment passages may involve real fire—as with Sodom and Gomorrah, or the burning of Jerusalem—but actual fire is not necessarily implied, since it is often God's wrath, not His chosen medium of judgment, that is likened to fire.[13]

In the Old Testament, where the majority of this imagery is found, such a "fiery" judgment almost always refers to a national judgment occurring in history (to Babylon, Assyria, Edom, Israel, etc.), not to an eschatological or postmortem punishment. This is true even when the fire is said to be "unquenchable," as is often the case.[14]

In view of the rabbinic convention of using *Gehenna* as a reference to ultimate punishment after death, it may seem reasonable to identify Gehenna with Revelation's "lake of fire," and this has, in fact, been the most common identification made by Christian theologians. However, there is reason to inquire into the possibility that Jesus used the word literally, as did the Old Testament, rather than in the innovative sense that the rabbis had adopted.

That is, Jesus may not have been speaking of a fate beyond the grave that can figuratively be *likened to* the Valley of Hinnom, but of the earthly Valley of Hinnom itself. This would be the most literal understanding of the term He used, and should not be rejected prior to investigation.

A growing number of evangelical scholars have been acknowledging that the message of Jesus (and of His predecessor, John the Baptist) was presented in a particular, pivotal historic milieu. The end of Second Temple Judaism was coming upon those to whom

---

12. e.g., Job 15:34; 20:26; 22:20; 31:11–12; Psalms 11:6; 18:7–8; 21:9; 50:3; 78:21; 80:16; 97:3; Isaiah 9:19; 10:16; 29:6; 42:25; 47:14; Jeremiah 11:16; 15:14; 21:14; Ezekiel 15:6–7; 19:12; 28:18; 30:8; 38:22; Amos 1:4, 7, 10, etc.

13. e.g., Psalms 79:5; 89:46; Isaiah 30:27; 66:15; Jeremiah 4:4; 21:12; Lamentations 2:3; Ezekiel 21:31; 22:21, 31; 36:5; 38:19.

14. e.g., 2 Kings 22:17; 2 Chronicles 34:25; Isaiah 1:31; 34:10; Jeremiah 4:4; 7:20; 17:27; 21:12; Ezekiel 20:47, 48; Amos 5:6.

Jesus referred as "this generation." It was not a minor transition that was about to take place. God was inaugurating the new messianic order, one consequence of which would be the violent destruction of the older Mosaic order—abolishing the temple, its sacrifices, and the corrupt Jewish State.

John the Baptist had said that the population of Israel was about to be divided into two groups, which would suffer two separate fates: the faithful remnant (likened to fruitful trees and wheat) would be spared, but the apostate in Israel (likened to fruitless trees and chaff) would be relegated to "unquenchable fire."[15] The imagery of "unquenchable fire" was commonly used in the Old Testament when speaking not of hell, but of temporal judgments upon wicked nations. Jeremiah had employed the terminology as an image of God's wrath coming upon Jerusalem in the Babylonian conquest.[16] The words of John make it unmistakable that the judgment threatened was impending (not eschatological) and his prophecy was literally fulfilled, because apostate Jerusalem fell to Rome in a gory massacre, in the year AD 70. The Judean Christians, the faithful remnant, fled from Jerusalem before the siege, and so escaped.[17]

Many of Christ's teachings specifically predicted the events of AD 70 as the great calamity that would befall the apostates in Israel in that very generation.[18] Is there a possibility that His references to Gehenna might fall into this category as well? Strange and unfamiliar as this suggestion may seem to us, some argue that this would be the most literal understanding of Christ's language, and the Old Testament provides a striking precedent for speaking of the Valley of Hinnom precisely in this way.

In the early sixth century BC, Judah and Jerusalem were on the verge of being invaded and conquered by the Babylonians, led

---

15. Matthew 3:10–12.
16. Jeremiah 4:4; 7:20; 17:27; 21:12.
17. Eusebius, *Ecclesiastical History*, Book III, ch. 5.
18. Matthew 23:33–36; 24:1–2, 34; Luke 13:3, 5; 19:41–44.

by Nebuchadnezzar. This disaster came to pass in 586 BC, and resulted in a Jewish holocaust, accompanied by the burning down of Jerusalem and its temple, and the deportation of survivors into the regions beyond the Euphrates. Prior to this, God had sent prophets to Judah, who had warned the people that this crisis was coming upon them as a punishment for their unfaithfulness to God.

Jeremiah was the principal prophet of Yahweh preaching to Judah throughout that time of judgment. His message was dominated by tearful appeals and warnings of impending doom. At least twice, Jeremiah made reference to the Valley of Hinnom (or Gehenna), as the place outside the city where the corpses of those slain by the invaders would be cast off (Jer. 7:32–33; 19:6–9).

Whether the language was intended literally or impressionistically, Jeremiah's warnings provide a biblical precedent for seeing Gehenna as an emblem of the horrible fate of Judah and Jerusalem, which they suffered at the hands of ruthless Babylonian invaders. There is no reference to "hell" in Jeremiah's use of the term, but only of a horrendous national disaster brought on by Judah's sins.

The Roman conquest of Jerusalem, in AD 70, was almost the exact replay of that which befell the Jews at the hands of the Babylonians, in Jeremiah's day. Like Jeremiah and his generation, Jesus's generation faced an impending national crisis. Israel was about to be invaded by a flood of Roman armies, who would ultimately slaughter much of the Jewish population; destroy the cities and villages throughout Galilee, Samaria, and Judea; and burn Jerusalem and its temple to the ground, just as the Babylonians had done six centuries earlier. John the Baptist and Jesus both warned their listeners of this looming crisis, and presented their messages as God's final appeal to an apostate nation facing God's judgment.

Biblical scholarship usually commends the practice of reading passages in the light of their historical settings and circumstances. But *which* historical precedent should inform our understanding of Jesus's use of *Gehenna*—the rabbinic usage current in His time, or that of the canonical prophets?[19] Commentators often assume without question that Jesus accepted the rabbinic convention in His use of *Gehenna*, rather than following the precedent found in the Old Testament. We have already noted that John borrowed Jeremiah's imagery in warning of the impending judgment. What would be more natural than for Jesus to do the same?

It is possible that the failure to appreciate the historical context of Christ's ministry to His own generation has caused later readers of the Gospels to universalize the warnings that He directed specifically to the people of His time. While we recognize that there are passages wherein Christ and the biblical writers do describe a future, universal judgment of the world, He also indisputably spoke of the impending national crisis on several occasions, and may have done so in His remarks about Gehenna as well. In Matthew 23:33, 36, He specifically associated Gehenna with the crisis that would come upon Jerusalem in His hearers' own generation. "Serpents, brood of vipers! How can you escape the condemnation of [*Gehenna*]? . . . Assuredly, I say to you, all these things will come upon this generation."

The faithful remnant in Jerusalem, Christ's followers, actually escaped the disaster that came upon the nation, as the historian Eusebius informs us.[20] Therefore, Christ's Jewish audience literally were faced with two alternatives: Christ or Conquest, the kingdom of God or Gehenna. They could surrender to the call of the Messiah, or they could face the prospect of having their corpses tossed by Roman conquerors into the mass crematorium that was the Valley of Hinnom.

Seeing *Gehenna* as a reference to the slaughter of the Jews in AD 70 also provides a satisfying explanation to the otherwise

---

19. I say "prophets" (plural) because I believe that we will find Isaiah (in addition to Jeremiah) also speaking of *Gehenna* in this manner.

20. "The whole body, however, of the church at Jerusalem, having been commanded by a divine revelation, given to men of approved piety there before the war, removed from the city, and dwelt at a certain town beyond the Jordan, called Pella" (*Ecclesiastical History*, Book 3, Chapter 5).

perplexing fact that the fate of Gehenna is not threatened in any passage addressed to people other than first-century Palestinian Jews. If Gehenna refers to a postmortem judgment of sinners, generally, why didn't Peter or Paul ever make mention of it to those living outside Israel?

OBJECTIONS TO *GEHENNA* AS A REFERENCE TO THE JUDGMENT IN AD 70

While most of what Jesus said on this subject can be harmonized with the above thesis, two objections arise to the idea that *Gehenna* may be identified with nothing more than that historical disaster.

The first objection is that Jesus spoke of both "soul and body" being destroyed in Gehenna (Matt. 10:28). Thus, it is argued, Gehenna must be more than the earthly Valley of Hinnom, since only bodies—not souls—would be consumed in those earthly fires.

An answer to this objection might be that the destruction of "both soul and body" is elsewhere used as an idiom simply meaning to "destroy thoroughly," without reference to any postmortem fate. We find this precedent in Isaiah 10:18, where God's judgment on Israel (apparently) is described as a devastating wild fire burning down a forest—with people being likened to trees. The military conquest of the people is envisaged: "And it will consume the glory of his forest and of his fruitful field, *both soul and body . . .*"

What is striking is the exactness of the parallel to the phrase Jesus used (even in the counterintuitive placing of "soul" before "body"), so that it would appear Jesus is quoting the very expression from Isaiah—an expression describing a national (not postmortem or eschatological) judgment in terms of the destruction of a forest by fire. The imagery of a forest, in any case, does not encourage the interpretation of the word "soul" in this idiom as meaning some immaterial aspect that survives physical death.

This raises the additional question as to why Jesus, if not referring to some further penalty after death, would refer to Gehenna as a fate far worse than mere physical death. Why would one kind of death be regarded as so much worse than another?

To the Jewish hearer, having one's corpse cast into the Valley of Hinnom, rather than honorably buried, would suggest a dishonorable death under the judgment and displeasure of God. This would be a matter of greater concern in a shame/honor-based culture, like that of ancient Israel, than it would be among us.

Jesus's exhortation about not fearing those who can only kill the body is given in the context of their facing persecution and martyrdom at the hands of ungodly men. Those dying in this way are assumed to be dying honorably for their faithfulness to God. By contrast, being cast into Gehenna suggests a disgraceful death suffered under God's judgment. Jesus would then be saying that it is better to let others kill you because of your faithfulness to God than to have God kill you because of your apostasy. In the latter case, you lose your soul (possibly your good name, or honor) as well as your body.

There might be, in the statement, the unstated subtext of further troubles to come after death, but it would not be equating Gehenna itself with those further troubles. It would simply mean that those who would die, in the coming judgment on Jerusalem, would be cast off physically (and even spiritually, by God) like so much garbage, in the mass pyre of the Valley of Hinnom. To this, being killed by men who persecute you for Christ's sake is much to be preferred. Such an explanation would remove any need to identify Gehenna as a place where the immaterial soul is separately destroyed, subsequent to physical death—that is, as Revelation's lake of fire.

A second objection is that Jesus described Gehenna as a place where the "worm does not die and the fire is not quenched" (Mark 9:44). Doesn't this speak of a place of eternal torment?

A "fire that is not quenched" is not synonymous with that of a fire that never goes out. A fire that man could not "quench" (or "put out") would nonetheless be expected to burn out eventually. In the ancient world, any forest fire, or other large conflagration, would fit this description. There are numerous Old Testament references to God's temporal judgments upon nations, which are described (figuratively) as raging fires that shall "not be quenched" (Jer. 7:20; 17:27; Ezek. 20:47, 48), that "no one shall quench" (Isa. 1:31), that "no one can quench" (Jer. 4:4; 21:12), or for which there will be "no one to quench" (Amos 5:6). All of these passages refer to historical disasters brought upon earthly cities as judgments from God. The image of "unquenchable" fire, while not speaking of eternal burning, does seem to refer to the fire of God's wrath, which no human power would be able to extinguish or resist.

Thus, when Jesus said that the fire of Gehenna "is not quenched," He was employing a common Old Testament figure, which does not speak of eternally burning flames. In fact, the specific joining of "the worm does not die" and the fire that is "not quenched" is a direct quote from an Old Testament passage—the closing words of the book of Isaiah:

> And they [the righteous] shall go forth and look
> Upon the corpses of the men
> Who have transgressed against Me.
> *For their worm does not die,*
> *And their fire is not quenched.*
> They shall be an abhorrence to all flesh. (Isa. 66:24)

Commentators often assume without question that Isaiah is here presenting a vision of a place of eternal torment. Though there is actually nothing in the passage itself, or its context, to encourage this idea, their sole reason for doing so would seem to be a desire to harmonize the passage with Jesus's words in Mark 9 that also (perhaps too hastily) are applied to hell. A comparison of Isaiah 66:24 with Mark 9:43 confirms that both passages are talking about Gehenna, and it is at least possible that both passages have in view the Valley of Hinnom and the AD 70 judgment upon Jerusalem. If Jesus had this in mind, then Isaiah (whom Jesus was quoting) probably did as well. We might at least be skeptical of the suggestion that Isaiah was describing anyone experiencing torment in fire, since it is clear that the inhabitants of the place he described were not living, conscious people, as the traditional view of hell would have them. They are specifically referred to as "corpses." Furthermore, they are said to be in a place where the righteous, apparently, may view and walk among them.

Furthermore, a closer look at the context of this passage from Isaiah (specifically chapters 60–66) shows us that it seems to be speaking of the establishment of the new covenant order under Messiah, and the consequent obliteration of the old order (the temple system). In fact, this section specifically mentions Jerusalem and the temple being burned, as in AD 70.[21] That these events have a first-century fulfillment was the view of the New Testament writers, who often quoted from this section, invariably applying its statements to their own times.[22]

Therefore, it remains plausible, even in the light of these strange phrases of immortal worms and unquenchable flames, to see *Gehenna* as a reference to the impending judgment coming upon Jesus's contemporaries, from which they could escape only by embracing His kingdom.

A FINAL VERDICT ON GEHENNA

This raises legitimate doubts as to whether translators should ever have translated *Gehenna* as "hell," or whether they should have left

---

21. Isaiah 64:10–11.
22. e.g., Isaiah 61:1–2 with Luke 4:18; Isaiah 61:11 with Mark 4:28; Isaiah 65:1–2 with Romans 10:20–21; Isaiah 65:13–14 with Luke 6:20–25; Isaiah 66:1–2 with Acts 7:49–50; Isaiah 66:20 with Romans 15:16.

the word untranslated (as many translations now do with *Sheol* and *Hades*)—or, perhaps, *translated* it (instead of interpreting it) as "the Valley of Hinnom."

The Valley of Hinnom had one significance to Jeremiah and Isaiah, and a very different one to the rabbis of Christ's day. In seeking to identify the backstory behind Christ's use of *Gehenna*, our choice must weigh the respective likelihood of Christ taking His verbal cues from the Pharisees, on the one hand, or from the Prophets, on the other.

Are we to assume that the uninspired speculations of uninspired Jewish teachers actually discovered inaccessible mysteries of the afterlife that were hidden even from the canonical prophets? Jesus would seem to be affirming this, if He agreed with the rabbinic use of *Gehenna*. On the other hand, if He used the term the way that the prophets before Him had used it, there is no such difficulty to explain.

AIONIOS: DOES "ETERNITY" LAST FOREVER?

All three of the views of hell under our present consideration foresee a sentence of misery for the unrepentant, lasting for some duration, following the final judgment. The traditional view makes that duration endless, and gains a large measure of its *prima facie* credibility from passages that speak of the fire, the torment, or the separation from God as "eternal" or "everlasting." Verses that merely speak of *some* punishment, *some* misery, or *some* regret are not helpful in establishing the superiority of one of the three views over the others, since all three posit some measure of suffering in the "lake of fire" for the lost.

Much hangs on the meaning of the Greek words underlying our English terms "eternal," "everlasting," and "forever." With the exception of two verses unrelated to our topic,[23] there are only two words (closely related to each other) translated in this manner in the New Testament. One is the noun *aion* (which generally conveys the concept of an age, or period of time), and the other is its related adjective, *aionios* ("pertaining to" or "enduring for" an *aion*).

In Scripture, these words modify many concepts besides those related to the fate of the wicked. The list of things described in Scripture as *aion* (usually translated "forever") or *aionios* (translated "eternal" or "everlasting") would include things that are truly eternal (e.g., God Himself, the life given to the believer, the reign of Christ, God's glory, God's kingdom) as well as things that are not eternal (e.g., the hills, Jerusalem's doors, certain human relationships). In passages about final judgment, the same words describe fire (Matt. 18:8; 25:41), judgment (Heb. 6:2), destruction (2 Thess. 1:9), condemnation (Mark 3:29), punishment (Matt. 25:46), ascending smoke (Rev. 14:11), and the devil's torment (Rev. 20:10).

If "eternal," "everlasting," and "forever" are truly the English concepts that best correspond to the Greek terms used, then the case for never-ending suffering is greatly enhanced. It is easy to see that very much rides upon the meanings of these two words.

THEORIES CONCERNING THE MEANING OF *AIONIOS*

The most common meaning given for this adjective, according to many lexicons, is "eternal." However, if we equate the word "eternal," as we commonly do, with the idea of "endlessness," then this English word seems inadequate to address every case of its occurrence.

The ancient translators of the Greek Old Testament, the Septuagint, regularly used *aion* and *aionios* to translate *olam*, a

---

23. The two exceptions are Romans 1:20 and Jude 6, which have no bearing on our present subject.

Hebrew word that is also often translated "eternal" or "forever." Yet, Hebrew scholars do not necessarily associate *olam* with "endlessness," but merely with the quality of "having no end in sight." *Olam* is said to speak of that which extends beyond the horizon of sight, or the vanishing point. That which is described as *olam* is not necessarily everlasting, but its end cannot be seen from here. *Strong's Concordance*, in agreement with other authorities,[24] defines *olam* as follows: "Olam [5769]: From 5956; prop. *concealed*, i.e., the *vanishing* point; gen. time *out of mind* (past or fut.), i.e. (practically) *eternity* . . . or lasting, long (time), (of) old (time), perpetual . . ."

Many times *olam* is used simply to denote a lengthy period, whose end is undesignated and out of view. For example, in Isaiah 34:10, the period of *olam* is parallel to the phrase "generation to generation," and in Isaiah 60:15, *olamic* gladness is parallel to "a joy of *many generations.*"[25]

So, do the Greek words carry the same meaning as *olam*?

R. Laird Harris, Gleason J. Archer Jr., and Bruce K. Waltke think so:

> The lxx [Septuagint] generally translates *olam* by *aion* which has essentially the same range of meaning. That neither the Hebrew

---

24. James Strong, *Strong's Exhaustive Concordance*. Other authorities confirm: "First, in a few passages [*olam*] means 'eternity' in the sense of not being limited to the present. . . . Second, the word signifies 'remotest time' or 'remote time.' In 1 Chron. 16:36, God is described as blessed 'from everlasting to everlasting' (KJV, 'for ever and ever'), or from the most distant past time to the most distant future time. . . . In Isa. 42:14, the word is used hyperbolically meaning 'for a long time.' . . ." (Merrill F. Unger and William White Jr., eds., *Nelson's Expository Dictionary of the Old Testament* [Nashville: Thomas Nelson, 1980], 117) and: "Probably derived from *alam* . . . 'to hide,' thus pointing to what is hidden in the distant future or in the distant past. . . . Though *olam* is used more than three hundred times to indicate indefinite continuance into the very distant future, the meaning of the word is not confined to the future. There are at least twenty instances where it clearly refers to the past. Such usages generally point to something that seems long ago, but rarely if ever refer to a limitless past." R. Laird Harris, Gleason J. Archer Jr., and Bruce K. Waltke, *Theological Wordbook of the Old Testament*, vol. 2 (Chicago: Moody Press, 1980).

25. As noted by G. K. Beale, a supporter of the traditional view of hell, "The Revelation on Hell," in Christopher W. Morgan and Robert A. Peterson, eds., *Hell Under Fire* (Grand Rapids: Zondervan, 2004), 118.

nor the Greek word in itself contains the idea of endlessness is shown both by the fact that they sometimes refer to events or conditions that occurred at a definite point in the past, and also by the fact that sometimes it is thought desirable to repeat the word, not merely saying "forever," but "forever and ever." . . . Both words came to be used to refer to a long age or period.[26]

George Milligan and James Hope Moulton said that *aionios* "depicts that of which the horizon is not in view, whether the horizon be at an infinite distance . . . or whether it lies no farther than the span of a Caesar's life."[27] This is essentially identical to the meaning of the Hebrew *olam*, and obviously does not require that the thing, of which the end is beyond our vision, must necessarily go on into endless eternity. It might, but it needn't.

Addressing the use of *aionios* in Revelation 20:10, where Satan, the beast, and the false prophet are cast into the lake of fire, Gregory Beale, who defends the traditional view of hell, wrote: "Strictly speaking, even the expression 'they will be tormented *forever and ever*' is figurative, since the phrase *eis tous aionas ton aionon* literally can be rendered 'unto the ages of the ages.' At the least, the figurative point of the phrase connotes a very long time. The context of the passage and of the book must determine whether this is a long but limited time or an unending period."[28]

Authorities also note that in "later poetry and prose [*aionios*] is also used in the sense of 'lifelong' or 'enduring,' in accordance with the basic meaning of [*aion*]."[29] Douglas Jacoby said: "Few are so bold as to claim that the Greek adjective aionios always suggests

---

26. Harris, Archer Jr., and Waltke, *Theological Wordbook of the Old Testament*.

27. James Hope Moulton and George Milligan, *The Vocabulary of the Greek Testament Illustrated from the Papyri and Other Non-Literary Sources* (London: Hodder & Stoughton, 1914), 16.

28. Gregory K. Beale, in Christopher W. Morgan and Robert A. Peterson, eds., *Hell Under Fire* (Grand Rapids: Zondervan, 2004), 128.

29. Gerhard Kittel, *Theological Dictionary of the New Testament*, vol. 1 (Grand Rapids: Eerdmans, 1964).

'infinity in time'—such thinking has been rejected by most modern exegetes."[30]

That it is a mistake to assume *aionios* must only refer to endlessness is seen in the variety of its occurrences. For example, in the Septuagint, Isaiah 32:14–15 predicts that Judah will become desolate, forsaken, and deserted "forever" (Gr. *aion*) . . . but this is only to continue "until the Spirit is poured upon [them]"! In other words, the "eternal" desolation only lasts *until it ends* with the outpouring of the Spirit. It is *aionios*, to be sure, but it is neither permanent nor endless.

F. F. Bruce concurs with the concept of an "indeterminate" or "indefinite" (but not necessarily "endless") duration as the meaning of *olam*, *aion*, and *aionios*: "these in themselves express indefinite duration, but the context or the inherent sense may make the indefiniteness more explicit."[31]

Among scholars, at least four possible explanations have been advocated for the usage of *aion* and *aionios*, when applied to the ultimate punishment of sinners:

1. The Thing Described Is Everlasting, Eternal (Literal or Hyperbole)

This meaning works with the majority of occurrences of *aionios*, though, even when it does, it is likewise possible to suggest one of the other interpretations (see below) for the same cases. When modifying such words as "God," "life," "salvation," and the like, it poses no difficulty to understand the word *aionios* as meaning never-ending. This is not so much the case in certain other occurrences of the word. Whether *aionios* conveys this meaning when applied to such things as "punishment," "destruction," "fire," and the like would be less obvious, without other modifiers or factors present to inform us.

---

30. Douglas Jacoby, *What's the Truth about Heaven and Hell?* (Eugene, OR: Harvest House, 2013), 16.

31. F. F. Bruce, *Answers to Questions* (Grand Rapids: Zondervan, 1972), 202.

Even allowing for the definition "eternal," of course, biblical scholars are aware that the writers of Scripture used hyperbole (exaggeration for the sake of emphasis) a great deal—perhaps as much as we moderns do. This means that, even if the Greek words' primary meanings were best rendered as "forever" or "eternal," they might sometimes be used non-literally, as when we say, "He and I have been friends *forever!*" or "It's been an *eternity* since I saw you!"

The editors of *Nelson's Expository Dictionary of the Old Testament* wrote: "In Isa. 42:14, the word is used hyperbolically meaning 'for a long time.' ..."[32]

2. The Thing Described Lasts for an Age, or a Long Time (Long-Enduring)

This meaning is easily demonstrated by a simple appeal to the occurrences of this term in the Bible and other literature. It was well summarized by Marvin Vincent, D.D., Baldwin Professor of Sacred Literature at Union Theological Seminary, New York, in his *Word Studies in the New Testament*: "Neither the noun [*aion*] nor the adjective [*aionios*], in themselves, carry the sense of endless or everlasting. They may acquire that sense by their connotation. ... Aionios means 'enduring through' or 'pertaining to a period of time.' Both the noun and the adjective are applied to limited periods. ... Out of the 150 instances in LXX, four-fifths imply limited duration."[33]

The *Rotherham Emphasized Bible* translates these words "age-abiding," and *Young's Literal Translation* renders them "age-during" (that is, "age-enduring"). In one place, the first-century Jewish historian Josephus spoke of the imprisonment of the tyrant John as "perpetual" (*aionios*). It was an imprisonment that lasted three years.[34]

---

32. Merrill F. Unger and William White Jr., eds., *Nelson's Expository Dictionary of the Old Testament* (Nashville: Thomas Nelson, 1980), 117.

33. Marvin Vincent, *Word Studies in the New Testament* (Grand Rapids: Wm. B. Eerdmans, 1973), 58f.

34. Flavius Josephus, *Wars of the Jews*, Book 6, Section 434.

3. The Thing Described Pertains to a Given Age, or to "the Age to Come"

Edward Beecher wrote: "As *aion* denoted an age, great or small, so the adjective *aionios* expressed the idea pertaining to or belonging to the *aion*, whether great or small."[35] Gregory MacDonald elaborated:

> The translation of *aionios* has been the subject of numerous studies in recent years, but there seems to be a strong case for maintaining that it means "pertaining to an age" and often refers not just to any age but to "the age to come" (cf. Heb 6:2; 9:12). Thus "eternal life" may be better translated as "the life of the age to come" and "eternal punishment" as "the punishment of the age to come." . . . but if this is so, then it is no longer obvious that the punishment is everlasting. True, the age to come is everlasting, but that does not necessitate that the punishment of the age to come lasts for the duration of that age, simply that it occurs during that age and is appropriate for that age.[36]

F. F. Bruce commented: "As for 'eternal life' (Gk. *zoe aionios*), that is probably an abridged way of saying 'the life of the age to come'—the life of the resurrection-age."[37]

If this view is correct, then *aionios* would often simply bear the meaning "eschatological." The adjective would address, in such cases, not the question of duration but the nature of the thing and its time of occurrence.

That *aionios* means "pertaining to an age" seemed to be taken for granted by Chrysostom in his sermon on the book of Ephesians,

---

35. Edward Beecher, *History of Opinions on the Scriptural Doctrine of Retribution* (New York: D. Appleton and Company, 1878), 142.

36. Gregory MacDonald, *The Evangelical Universalist* (Eugene, OR: Cascade Books, 2006), 148.

37. Bruce, *Answers to Questions*, 202.

where he said: "[Satan's] kingdom is *aionios*, in other words that it will cease with the present age."[38]

4. The Thing Described Is of Divine Origin—
Inherent in (or Proceeding from) the Eternal God

The destruction of Sodom and Gomorrah, according to Jude 7, was an example of "eternal (*aionion*) fire," given as a warning to future observers who might otherwise be tempted to live in an ungodly manner. Since this judgment of "eternal" fire is said to serve as a warning, it cannot be a reference to a postmortem judgment of the Sodomites. Such judgment could not be observed as a lesson for the living; furthermore, the Sodomites would not presently be experiencing their final punishment, which awaits the day of judgment and the lake of fire.

Why, then, does Jude refer to the temporary burning of Sodom and Gomorrah as their "suffering the vengeance of eternal fire"? Could it not be that the fire, being the fire of God—who is Himself a consuming fire (Heb. 12:29)—be regarded as *eternal* fire insofar as God Himself is *eternal*, and the fire proceeds from Him? The fire that consumed Sodom was, in fact, the fire of the eternal God, a momentary manifestation of His eternal wrath toward sin. It was *divine* fire.

William Barclay, author of *The Daily Study Bible Series*, wrote: "[*Aionios*] means more than everlasting, for Plato—who may have invented the word—plainly says that a thing may be everlasting and still not be *aionios . . . aionios* cannot be used properly of anyone but God; it is the word uniquely, as Plato saw it, of God. Eternal punishment is then literally that kind of remedial punishment which it befits God to give and which only God can give."[39]

According to David Hill, *aionios* sometimes suggests "quality of being, almost meaning 'divine' rather than enduring."[40]

---

38. Chrysostom's *Homily of the Epistle of Saint Paul to the Ephesians*, Homily 4.

39. Excerpted from *William Barclay: A Spiritual Autobiography* (Grand Rapids: Wm. B. Eerdmans, 1977), 65–67.

40. David Hill, *Greek Words and Hebrew Meanings: Studies in the Semantics of Soteriological Terms* (Cambridge: Society for New Testament Studies Monograph Series,

When *aionios* modifies words like "life," "glory," "righteousness," "salvation," "wrath," and "punishment," could it not be that the writers are simply speaking of these things as coming from God, and being manifestations of His character or attributes, which are eternal?

TENTATIVE CONCLUSIONS CONCERNING *AIONIOS* AND RELATED WORDS

Because of the admitted ambiguity of the words "eternal" and "everlasting" in the Greek and Hebrew text, it is not necessarily clear that "endless" suffering is actually what these words are threatening. William Crockett (traditionalist) has pointed out that among the Qumran sect members (contemporaries with the New Testament writers), "*aionios* torment" and "*aionios* damnation" were seen as concepts harmonious with "extinction" or annihilation. He cited "everlasting damnation by the avenging wrath of the fury of God, eternal torment and endless disgrace together with shameful extinction in the fire of the dark regions (1QS 4:12–13)."[41]

Advocates of all three views have managed to accommodate these terms in the relevant verses within their systems. In surveying the views of the church fathers, John Wesley Hanson wrote: "Barnabas, Hermas, 'Sibylline Oracles,' Justin Martyr, Polycarp, Theophilus and Irenaeus all apply the word *aionios* to punishment, but two of these taught annihilation, and one universal salvation beyond *aionion* punishment."[42]

In other words, among the early church fathers, some believed

---

no. 5, 1967), cited by Edward William Fudge, *The Fire That Consumes* (Lincoln, NE: iUniverse.com, Inc., 1982, 2001), 41.

41. William Crockett in William Crockett, ed., *Four Views on Hell* (Grand Rapids: Zondervan, 1992), 64.

42. John Wesley Hanson, *Universalism: The Prevailing Doctrine of the Christian Church During Its First Five Hundred Years* (Chicago, Boston: Universalist Publishing House, 1899), 150.

in eternal torment, some in annihilation, and some in universal reconciliation—but all of them were comfortable in speaking of "eternal [*aionios*] punishment." This suggests that those closest to New Testament times, for many of whom New Testament Greek was their native tongue, understood the word *aionios* to be sufficiently flexible to accommodate any of their positions. What this means for us is that it is irresponsible to try to settle the controversy over hell's duration and its purpose by the mere citation of verses containing the words "eternal" and "forever." Those who knew the Greek better than we do did not consider the question settled by such appeals. Francis Chan, while defending the traditional doctrine of hell, admitted the ambiguity of the word *aionios*: "The debate about hell's duration is much more complex than I first assumed. While I lean heavily on the side that says it is everlasting, I am not ready to claim that with complete certainty."[43]

---

43. Francis Chan and Preston Sprinkle, *Erasing Hell: What God Said about Eternity, and the Things We Made Up* (Colorado Springs: David C. Cook, 2011), 86.

CHAPTER 6

VIEWS OF THE
EARLY CHURCH

Consensus Is Evasive

In reading some authors, one gets the impression that the view that sinners face the prospect of endless suffering after the judgment has its roots in all the earliest fathers of the church, who regarded rival opinions as heretical—or at least "not mainstream." Richard Bauckham wrote: "Until the nineteenth century almost all Christian theologians taught the reality of eternal torment in hell. Here and there, outside the theological mainstream, were some who believed that the wicked would be finally annihilated. Even fewer were the advocates of universal salvation, though these few included some major theologians of the early church. Eternal punishment was firmly asserted in official creeds and confessions of the churches."[1]

Robert Morey minces no words: "The Universalists and the annihilationists have invaded the Christian Church just as the Philistines invaded Israel. It is once again necessary to defend the gospel truth that unbelief results in God's wrath (John 3:36) and that this wrath is eternal (Matt. 25:46)."[2]

---

1. Richard J. Bauckham, "Universalism: A Historical Survey," *Themelios* 4.2 (January 1979), 48.
2. Robert A. Morey, *Death and the Afterlife* (Bloomington, MN: Bethany House, 1984), 16.

The actual testimony of the church fathers seems much more ambiguous than these statements would suggest, and advocates of all three views of hell have found what they credibly regard to be support for their positions among important witnesses in the early church.

The earliest Christian writings, after the New Testament, were not explicit as to the precise fate that awaits sinners after the resurrection and final judgment. The earliest creeds make no mention of the subject, and the early authors do not speak unambiguously, until the latter part of the second century. Louis Berkhof, in *The History of Christian Doctrines*, wrote: "The earliest Church Fathers have very little to say about the last judgment, but generally stress its certainty."[3]

One of the reasons that traditionalists believe that they find support for their view in the writings of the early fathers is that these ancient Christians, in their descriptions of hell, used terms such as "eternal judgment," "eternal punishment," and "eternal fire, which shall never be quenched." To the traditionalist, these expressions speak of unending torment.

The problem with reaching conclusions from the use of these terms in patristic writings is that they are simply repetitions of the actual scriptural phrases. While this shows the fathers' fidelity to, and dependence upon, the Scriptures, it really does not provide much insight into their interpretation of those Scriptures. These very phrases are embraced without discomfort by all three views of hell today, and are quoted in their defense. An adherent to any view can assume that the early writers understood such scriptural expressions in accordance with his own system—and without more explicit statements than these to go on, no one could refute this.

One could as readily assume (and some do) that the fathers were conditionalists, since they frequently used the words "death,"

---

3. L. Berkhof, *The History of Christian Doctrines* (Grand Rapids: Baker Book House, 1937), 267.

"destruction," and "perish" when describing the fate of the wicked. What they meant by these terms is what remains disputed. If modern traditionalists, conditionalists, and restorationists can all comfortably use the same biblical terms, but mean different things by them, then it remains unclear, in many cases, which view was held by the early Christians when they used the same vocabulary.

All three views of hell claim to have been the "original" teaching of the church—and each can "prove" it by appeal to early church fathers. Obviously, since the three views contradict each other in their distinctive claims, they cannot all be true. However, they could all have been held by various leaders in the early church—for the same reasons that they can all be held by different church leaders today. Matthew Rose rightly noted: "Our knowledge of the early church comes from a limited amount of surviving material. What's more, advocates of the view that wins out in the end sometimes control the material that survives. It is perhaps surprising, then, that we have surviving material from this period in support of all three views. Indeed, the views under consideration were all supported by notable characters from the period in question."[4]

Edward William Fudge is likewise correct in saying: "Traditionalists and conditionalists alike claim the apostolic fathers for support. Anyone approaching the literature on final punishment in search of dogmatic statements or "authorities" to quote in proof of a position can find plenty—on both sides!"[5]

Then again, there are scholars like John Wesley Hanson, D.D., who have written well-documented volumes[6] defending the thesis that the dominant view of the early church (especially

4. Matthew Rose, *Hell: A Fresh Evaluation of the Nature of Hell Using the Wesleyan Quadrilateral as an Epistemological Guide* (unpublished thesis), 72.

5. Edward William Fudge, *The Fire That Consumes* (Lincoln, NE: iUniverse.com, Inc., 1982, 2001), 314.

6. e.g., John Wesley Hanson, *Universalism: The Prevailing Doctrine of the Christian Church During Its First Five Hundred Years* (Boston, Chicago: Universalist Publishing House, 1899), 189.

in the centuries immediately after Origen) was that of universal reconciliation.

Reading the fathers' own statements can definitely leave one with mixed messages on this topic. Each view can present a list of church fathers whose statements sound as if they are in his own camp. Some fathers can be cited in support of more than one view—possibly due to the fact that there was no official position held throughout the church, and individual leaders may have fluctuated in their beliefs over the course of their lifetime, as modern leaders often do.

SOUNDS LIKE CONDITIONAL IMMORTALITY

Some of the earliest testimony of the fathers on this subject seems to point to a belief in conditional immortality, or ultimate annihilation.

Barnabas (c. 70–130) spoke of "eternal death with punishment."[7] "Death" sounds like termination or end of life. If Barnabas meant death *preceded by* punishment, then this is also the view of most modern conditionalists.

In the *Letter of Mathetes to Diognetus* (c. 125–200), the writer speaks of "eternal fire," but then says that this fire "will afflict those who are committed to it even *to the end*."[8] This does not sound like a belief in eternal torment—since this writer speaks of an "end" of afflictions for the lost. It sounds like the doctrine of conditional immortality.

The language of Hermas (90–150) sounds like that of one who believed in temporary afflictions in hell, followed by extinction. He wrote: "Sinners shall be *consumed* because they sinned and did not repent."[9] When a thing has been "consumed" it has generally

---

7. *Epistle of Barnabas*, ch. 20.
8. *Letter to Diognetus*, ch. 10.
9. *The Shepherd of Hermas*, Book 3, Similitude 4.

ceased to exist (in contrast, for example, to the burning bush, which "burned," but was not "consumed" [Ex. 3:2]). Similarly, Hermas spoke of "death" as the end of the sinner's punishment, though some, he said, must experience more punishment than others prior to experiencing it: "They who have not known God and do evil are condemned to death; but they who have known God and have seen His mighty works, and still continue in evil, shall be chastised doubly, and shall die forever."[10]

If Barnabas, Mathetes, and Hermas were not advocates of ultimate annihilation, their choice of words to get across their beliefs was very infelicitous.

Both traditionalists and conditionalists claim Irenaeus (130–200) in support of their respective views of hell. The former depend upon his frequent references to "*aionios* fire" in his descriptions of damnation. As we have seen, this phrase is used comfortably by the advocates of every view of hell, and seems insufficient to demonstrate his adherence to one view or another. One could as easily claim that Irenaeus was a universalist, based upon his repeating Paul's prediction that "all things will be subdued unto Him . . . that God may be all in all."[11]

The writings of Irenaeus, on the whole, seem to reveal a belief in conditional immortality. He described the postmortem punishment of the lost as consisting of their being deprived of "length of days."[12] Eternal existence in hell would certainly be a "lengthening" of days. According to Irenaeus, the damnation of the lost means God's "cutting them off from life."[13] He spoke of the wicked being, like chaff, "consumed by fire."[14]

Henry Constable has noted a number of expressions used by Irenaeus in writing of the fate of the lost, such as sinners being

---

10. *The Shepherd of Hermas*, Book 3, Similitude 9, ch. 18.
11. Irenaeus, *Against Heresies*, Book 5, ch. 36:2, quoting 1 Corinthians 15:28.
12. Irenaeus, *Against Heresies*, Book 2, ch. 34:3.
13. Irenaeus, *Against Heresies*, Book 4, ch. 11:4.
14. Irenaeus, *Against Heresies*, Book 4, ch. 4:3.

"burned up as were Nadab and Abihu" by fire from the Lord; souls that perish, "punished with everlasting death"; those who "pass away" and "will not endure for ever"; and the wicked who will be "deprived of continuance for ever and ever."[15]

While Irenaeus never affirmed a belief in eternal torment, he regularly used terminology better suited to conditionalism. The suggestion that he should be included in that category, along with Barnabas, Hermas, and Mathetes, would be hard to refute from the content of his extant writings.

Justin Martyr (c. 160) sometimes wrote as if the sensate sufferings of the damned will continue perpetually and endlessly. Speaking of at least *some* period of consciousness beyond death for all men, Justin wrote: "Sensation remains to all who have ever lived, and eternal punishment is laid up."[16] He also affirmed his belief that the devil and those who follow him "would be punished for an endless duration."[17] But Justin, like the early tradition itself, seems to have been double-minded on this point, because he elsewhere spoke of a time when "the wicked angels and demons and men shall cease to exist."[18] It is difficult to know which view Justin would have championed, if pressed, or if he was ultimately undecided.

EARLY ATTITUDES TOWARD UNIVERSAL RECONCILIATION

In the late second century, two important theologians held very different views about the ultimate fate of those consigned to hell. Tertullian of Carthage (c. 197) was the father of Latin theology, and Clement (c. 195) was the head of the theological college in Alexandria.

---

15. Henry Constable, *Duration and Nature of Future Punishment*, 6th ed. (London: Edward Hobbs, 1886), 188.

16. Justin Martyr, *First Apology*, ch. 18.

17. Justin Martyr, *First Apology*, ch. 28.

18. Justin Martyr, *Second Apology*, ch. 7.

Both men, unlike the conditionalists, held to the innate immortality of human beings. Tertullian, following Justin, Tatian, and Athenagoras (see below), was explicit in his declarations that the suffering of the damned is "not merely long-enduring but everlasting."[19]

Clement, by contrast, believed in the possibility that the souls of the lost could be reformed and purged in hell, resulting in their repentance and restoration to God. Though not as well known for his advocacy of this view as was his successor Origen, Clement seems to have considered this possibility seriously. The following citations are illustrative of his view:

> For all things are ordered both universally and in particular by the Lord of the universe, with a view to the salvation of the universe . . . [N]eedful corrections, by the goodness of the great, overseeing judge . . . compel even those who have become more callous to repent.[20]

> So he saves all . . . but some he converts by penalties, others who follow him of their own will, and in accordance with the worthiness of his honor, that every knee may be bent to him of celestial, terrestrial and infernal things (Phil. 2:10), that is angels, men, and souls who before his advent migrated from this mortal life.[21]

> If in this life there are so many ways for purification and repentance, how much more should there be after death! The purification of souls, when separated from the body, will be easier. We can set no limits to the agency of the Redeemer; to redeem, to rescue, to discipline, is his work, and so will he continue to operate after this life.[22]

---

19. Tertullian, *Apology*, ch. 45.
20. Clement, *Stromata*, VII:2.
21. Clement, *Fragments: Comments on the First Epistle of John*.
22. Quoted by Neander and cited in Philip Gulley and James Mulholland, *If Grace Is True: Why God Will Save Every Person* (San Francisco: HarperSanFrancisco, 2003), 212f.

The view of Clement, that there is hope for conversion beyond the grave, was taken up by the most famous and influential leader of the Alexandrian school, Origen (185–254), who is often mentioned (with Augustine) as one of the two greatest theologians in the first quarter of Christian history. Origen's doctrine of *apocatastasis* takes its name from Acts 3:21, where Peter speaks of "the times of restoration [Gr. *apokatastasis*] of all things." This is the view of Christian universalism, which, though usually attributed first to Origen, obviously can be traced to Clement, and (arguably) to Clement's predecessor, Pantaenus—who founded and led the Alexandrian school from 180 to 190.

Irenaeus can credibly be claimed by traditionalists and conditionalists (but seemingly more so by the latter), yet, in writing *Against Heresies*, Irenaeus did not list among the false doctrines of his time the universalist view, which was found in the *Sibylline Oracles* (widely read by Christians of the time), and "he mentions [universalism] without disapproval in his description of the theology of the Carpocratians."[23] In fact, Irenaeus may, at times, have written very much like a universalist himself.[24] It is of Irenaeus that the traditionalist historian Philip Schaff wrote: "In the fourth Pfaffian fragment ascribed to him (Stieren I, 889) he says that 'Christ will come at the end of time to destroy all evil . . . and to reconcile all things . . . from Col. i:20—that there may be an end of all impurity.' This passage, like I. Cor. xv: 28, and Col. i:20, looks toward universal restoration rather than annihilation."[25]

John Wesley Hanson presents arguments indicating that, for some period (centuries?) after Origen's time, some form of restorationism

23. John Wesley Hanson, *Universalism: The Prevailing Doctrine of the Christian Church During Its First Five Hundred Years* (Boston, Chicago: Universalist Publishing House, 1899), 84.

24. Ibid., 87. Hanson wrote: "The different statements of Irenaeus are hard to reconcile with each other, but a fair inference from his language seems to be that he hovered between the doctrines of annihilation and endless punishment, and yet leaned not a little hopefully to that of restoration."

25. Ibid., 86.

(that is, universalism) may have prevailed as the majority belief of the Greek-speaking churches. During those centuries, other views existed alongside Origen's, but no one, in those days, spoke of anyone else's view of hell as heretical. Christian councils and the Roman Catholic Church, of much later centuries, would eventually anathematize all who did not affirm the eternal torment view.

In his discussion of the earliest councils of the church, in the first four centuries, Hanson pointed out: "It is historical (See Socrates's *Ecclesiastical History*) that the four great General Councils held in the first four centuries—those at Nice, Constantinople, Ephesus, and Chalcedon—gave expression to no condemnation of universal restoration, though, as will be shown, the doctrine had been prevalent all along."[26]

Even more surprising (given today's evangelical attitudes) is the fact that "Gregory Nazianzen presided over the council in Constantinople, in which the Nicean creed was finally shaped . . . and as he was a Universalist, and as the clause, 'I believe in the life of the world to come,' was added by Gregory of Nyssa, an 'unflinching advocate of extreme Universalism, and the very flower of orthodoxy,' it must be apparent that the consensus of Christian sentiment was not yet anti-Universalistic."[27]

One thing that can be said about the early fathers is that, although they differed from one another in their views on hell (as all three views were held through the first five centuries), they were not, like many church leaders of our time, contentious or condemning of those who differed from their own preferred positions. It was clearly not a matter to them over which to break fellowship with those of other views.

In modern evangelicalism, it is common to find the attitude expressed that views other than the traditional one are heretical. This was not the attitude of the church, during the first five centuries (prior to the rise of Roman Catholicism).

26. Ibid., 12.
27. Ibid., 11.

THE RISE OF THE TRADITIONAL VIEW

Statements sounding like advocacy of eternal torment begin to appear with Tatian (c. 170), the Christian apologist and disciple of Justin. He was a contemporary of Irenaeus (in whom we found evidences of conditionalism) and of Clement of Alexandria (who taught restorationism), but differed from these significant Christian authorities on this subject. Tatian wrote: "We, to whom it now easily happens to die, afterwards receive the immortal with enjoyment, or the painful with immortality."[28]

While Tatian spoke of immortality not as innate in human beings but as something people will receive as a special gift after death, Athenagoras (c. 175), writing around the same time, seemed to believe in innate human immortality when he contrasted men with animals. Unlike humans, he wrote, the animals "perish and are annihilated."[29] Constable and Fudge have described Athenagoras as "the first *explicit* advocate of the traditional view."[30]

The Western church eventually followed the influence of the Latin Fathers on this matter. Tertullian of Carthage (c. 160–240), who is generally regarded as the "Father of Latin Christianity," exceeded Athenagoras in his advocacy of the immortality of the soul. In dealing with passages about the judgment of the lost, Tertullian interpreted "'death' as *eternal* misery, 'destruction' and 'consume' as *pain* and *anguish*."[31] He gave the church such phrases as "perpetual life in hell" and "eternal killing"—terminology and concepts for which no clear equivalent exists in Scripture.

As influential as Tertullian may have been, even in the West, not

---

28. Tatian, *Address to the Greeks*, ch. 14.
29. Athenagoras, *A Plea for the Christians*, ch. 31.
30. Fudge, citing the opinion of Constable in *The Fire That Consumes*, 330f.
31. Leroy Edwin Froom, 951, cited by James Kenneth Brandyberry, "The Roots of Opposition to Conditionalism" from *Resurrection*, vol. 94:1, 2 (Winter and Spring, 1991), http://www.truthaccordingtoscripture.com/documents/death/history-of-opposition-to -Conditionalism.php.

all Christians accepted his doctrine. James Brandyberry reported: "As a late patristic voice, Lactantius of Nicomedia in Asia Minor (c. 250–330) addressed the Roman Emperor Constantine in the fourth century, vividly maintaining Conditionalism. Athanasius, bishop of Alexandria (c. 297–373) and most prominent theologian of his generation, championed certain aspects of Conditionalism. As such, he was virtually the last man of renown in his era to do so."[32]

A separate reaction against Tertullian's teaching of souls being eternally tormented was that of the Alexandrian school, whose restorationist doctrine, according to certain authorities, became a dominant teaching of much of the church for several centuries.

Another Latin father, Augustine (354–430), bishop of Hippo, is generally acknowledged to have been, for the Western church, the most influential theologian of all time. If Athenagoras and Tertullian seem to have originated the traditional doctrine of hell, it was Augustine whose advocacy of it caused it to become the "traditional" doctrine. As traditionalist Harry Buis pointed out: "Augustine (354–430) stood uncompromisingly for the doctrine of eternal punishment. As with many other doctrines, his advocacy of this position tended to cause it to become the accepted doctrine of the church for the centuries that followed."[33]

Many of the major doctrines of the Western church (whether papal or reformed) look to Augustine as the first either to formulate their teaching or at least to demolish all significant opposition to it. Frederick W. Norris, professor of Christian Doctrine at Emmanuel School of Religion, Johnson City, Tennessee, wrote of Augustine: "In many instances [the] shape of his later thought became the mark of orthodoxy in the West; the synod of Orange in 529 offered twenty-five canons intended to make Augustine's views primary."[34]

---

32. Brandyberry, "The Roots of Opposition to Conditionalism."

33. Harry Buis, *The Doctrine of Eternal Punishment* (Philadelphia: The Presbyterian and Reformed Publishing Company, 1957), 61.

34. Frederick W. Norris, *Universalism and the Doctrine of Hell*, ed. Nigel M. de S. Cameron (Grand Rapids: Baker Book House, 1992), 35.

James Brandyberry agrees:

> For [Augustine], eternal loss of life was an eternal life of loss. Significantly, he had written a book giving 16 reasons for the immortality of the soul *before* he became a Christian. This neo-platonism was never abandoned. . . . Augustine's crucial role in the development of theology—his advocacy of eternal torment—tended to cause it to become the accepted doctrine of the Church for the centuries that followed. His Platonic presupposition of the natural immortality of the soul erected a barrier to a clear exegesis and consequently set a similar standard for most of Christendom.[35]

It is chiefly in his book *The City of God* that Augustine presents his case for eternal torment. This book may have been the most elaborate philosophy of history ever penned. Book XXI of this work contains twenty-seven chapters expounding and defending the traditional doctrine of hell, in which he answers pagan critics who hold alternative viewpoints.

In *The City of God*, Augustine's defense of eternal torment was waged, largely, from an *a priori* acceptance of the immortality of the soul, rather than by vigorous exegesis. As a Latin father, Augustine confessed that he could not read Greek well, which may have limited his exegetical powers—especially in interpreting *aion* and *aionios*. Speaking of Augustine's defense of the traditional doctrine in that book, Brandyberry pointed out: "Largely, the subject is approached in a philosophical rather than scriptural discussion."[36]

While Augustine's views would eventually become dominant in the church of the West, they did not enjoy universal acceptance in his own times. He acknowledged that there were a very great number of Christians in his own day who disagreed with him on this matter. In his work *Enchiridion*, Augustine wrote: "It is in vain, then, that

---

35. Brandyberry, "The Roots of Opposition to Conditionalism."
36. Ibid.

some, indeed very many, moan over the eternal punishment, and perpetual, unintermittent torments of the lost, and say they do not believe it shall so be; not, indeed, that they directly oppose themselves to Holy Scripture, but at the suggestion of their own feelings, they soften down everything that seems hard . . . for 'Hath God,' they say, 'forgotten to be gracious? Hath He in anger shut up his tender mercies?'"[37]

Augustine acknowledged that he knew of "very many" Christians who did not "oppose themselves to the Holy Scripture," but who nonetheless rejected his doctrine of hell. Since Augustine's view of hell was not yet regarded as an established orthodoxy in his day, he found no occasion to anathematize those who challenged it. He clearly believed them to be mistaken, but did not regard them as heretical—nor even as opposed to Scripture. In *The City of God*, Augustine devoted a brief chapter to the "errors" of Origen and those who held views like his, or even unlike his, on the subject of restorationism. There he wrote: "I must now, I see, enter the lists of amicable controversy with those tender-hearted Christians who decline to believe that any, or that all of those whom the infallibly just Judge may pronounce worthy of the punishment of hell, shall suffer eternally, and who suppose that they shall be delivered after a fixed term of punishment, longer or shorter according to the amount of each man's sin."[38]

It is worthy of note that Augustine could not bring himself to condemn the Universalists. Only their beliefs about restorationism, he felt, needed correction. The rebuttal to their views, promised in these opening words of the chapter, is not a very thorough one. In fact, it consists of a single argument, resting on no particular Scripture. His argument is as follows: If it is a merciful thing for God to save all men, then it would be even more merciful for Him to save the devil and demons as well. If the latter seems unacceptable, it must

---

37. Augustine, *Enchiridion*, 112.
38. Augustine, *The City of God*, Book XXI, ch. 17.

not be thought that He will save all men either. In Augustine's own words: "Why does this stream of mercy flow to all the human race, and dry up as soon as it reaches the angelic? And yet they dare not extend their pity further, and propose the deliverance of the devil himself."[39]

Augustine acknowledges that Origen himself actually did not shrink from extending this mercy even to the fallen angels,[40] but says that Origen's views were rejected by the church. Origen was controversial for teaching a number of strange doctrines, including the preexistence of the soul and a notion of cycles of history that many thought resembled pagan ideas. However, his doctrine of universal restoration was never condemned in his own times, nor for almost three centuries following his death. Origen's unsympathetic contemporary Hippolytus (a traditionalist) wrote a treatise exposing thirty-two heresies of his time, but does not include universal reconciliation (a well-known doctrine at the time, from Clement and Origen) among them. Of this and similar cases, Hanson wrote: "What a force there is in the fact that not one of those who wrote against the heresies of their times ever name universal salvation as one of them!"[41]

A generation before Augustine, the respected church historian Eusebius spoke glowingly of Origen's life and work, and described him as highly regarded throughout the churches. In relating Origen's ministry after leaving Alexandria, Eusebius wrote of the great respect with which he was received by the churches in other lands. Referring to the Cappadocian bishop Firmilianus, Eusebius wrote:

---

39. Ibid.

40. Due to the loss of many of his writings, and "a virtual interpolation industry" that marked the history of document preservation, it is disputed as to whether Origen actually did teach the ultimate restoration of Satan. Jerome and Rufinus, in translating Origen's letters, agree that he rejected this doctrine (the original Greek of these letters is now lost).

41. John Wesley Hanson, *Universalism: The Prevailing Doctrine of the Christian Church During Its First Five Hundred Years* (Boston, Chicago: Universalist Publishing House, 1899), 189.

He was so earnestly affected toward Origen, that he urged him to come to that country for the benefit of the churches and moreover he visited him in Judea, remaining with him for some time, for the sake of improvement in divine things. And Alexander, bishop of Jerusalem, and Theoctistus, bishop of Caesarea, attended on him constantly, as their only teacher, and allowed him to expound the Divine Scriptures, and to perform the other duties pertaining to ecclesiastical discourse.[42]

It is clear that the church leaders of his own day, who knew him well, had not taken offense to his doctrines nor regarded him as a heretic. Augustine's own contemporary, the impeccably orthodox Athanasius, also spoke highly of Origen,[43] and never said a critical word about his well-known universalism.

There are historians who conclude that the "very many" in Augustine's day, who were too "tender-hearted" to embrace his views of eternal torment, actually constituted the *majority* of those in the churches. This cannot be proven beyond question, but it is clear that the majority of Christians in the century prior to Augustine had no serious objection to Origen's universalism. For example, Augustine's elder contemporary Gregory of Nyssa (330–395) was influenced by no teacher so much as by Origen, and was himself an outspoken universalist. Yet, his orthodoxy was considered exemplary. Gregory was asked, about 379, to come to Syria to solve a doctrinal schism there, and he played a leading role at the First Council of Constantinople (381). "Such was Gregory's fame that at the Seventh General Council [AD 787] of the church he was entitled 'Father of Fathers.'"[44] It is clear that his Origenist views of universal reconciliation, which were known to all, were not considered a blot on his orthodoxy.

---

42. Eusebius, *Ecclesiastical History*, Book 6, ch. XXVII.
43. Athanasius, "De Decretis" [of the synod of Nicea], 6, 27. See *Nicene and Post-Nicene Fathers*, 2nd series (repr. Grand Rapids, 1980), 4:168.
44. G. L. Carey, in J. D. Douglas, gen. ed., *The New International Dictionary of the Christian Church* (Grand Rapids: Zondervan, 1974, 1978), 436.

It is true that some of Origen's stranger views had been condemned prior to Augustine's time, in the century following Origen's death, but the specific belief in universal reconciliation was not among them. This particular belief had previously been promulgated by Clement, Origen's predecessor in the Alexandrian school, who likewise had never come under criticism for teaching this doctrine. Origen's belief in universal restoration would not be officially condemned until nearly three hundred years after his death, at the insistence of Emperor Justinian, in 543, and at the Fifth Ecumenical Council in 553.

It is often claimed that, of the six Christian catechetical schools existing in the fourth century and following, the majority taught some form of universalism. An article on universalism found in the *Encyclopedia of Religious Knowledge* asserts: "In the first five or six centuries of Christianity there were six theological schools, of which four (Alexandria, Antioch, Caesarea, and Edessa, or Nisibis) were Universalist, one (Ephesus) accepted conditional immortality; one (Carthage or Rome) taught endless punishment of the wicked."[45]

The objectivity of this statement might be called into question in view of the fact that the article was written by George T. Knight, a universalist teacher at a universalist seminary, Crane Theological School (part of Tufts University in Massachusetts). Yet, his article appears in an encyclopedia edited by a strong traditionalist who was an expert in church history (Philip Schaff). While it is possible, it seems unlikely that a reputable scholar like Knight would submit a statement like this, or that the editors would let it pass into print, were there not some measure of expertise behind it. One might as justly conclude, as many skeptics do, that the canonical gospels do not present reliable history because their authors were convinced Christians.

---

45. *The New Schaff-Herzog Encyclopedia of Religious Knowledge*, ed. Samuel Macauley Jackson, vol. 12 (New York, London: Funk and Wagnalls Company, 1912), 96.

The scholarly work by Edward Beecher, *History of Opinions on the Scriptural Doctrine of Retribution*, confirms and expands upon this information:

> What, then, was the state of facts as to the leading theological schools of the Christian world, in the age of Origen, and some centuries after? It was, in brief, this: There were at least six theological schools in the Church at large. Of these six schools, one, and only one, was decidedly and earnestly in favor of the doctrine of future eternal punishment. One was in favor of the annihilation of the wicked. Two were in favor of the doctrine of universal restoration on the principles of Origen, and two in favor of universal restoration on the principles of Theodore of Mopsuestia.[46]

In the pages following this summary, Beecher supports his claims by the appeal to the leading theological lights of each of these schools. Origen was clearly the leading theologian followed by the schools of Alexandria and Caesarea; Theodore of Mopsuestia (another major church father espousing restorationism) was the primary "interpreter" of Scripture for the schools in Antioch and Edessa; Irenaeus, whose conditionalism has been documented previously, came from the school of John, in Ephesus; and Carthage was the school influenced by Tertullian—who may be regarded as the first strong proponent of the traditional view, later championed by Augustine.[47]

> It is also true that the prominent defenders of the doctrine of universal restoration were decided believers in the divinity of Christ, in the Trinity, in the incarnation and atonement, and in the great

---

46. Edward Beecher, *History of Opinions on the Scriptural Doctrine of Retribution* (New York: Appleton, 1887). Chapter 22: "Early Theological Seminaries and Retribution," electronic version available at http://www.tentmaker.org/books/Retribution/retribution22.htm.
47. Ibid.

Christian doctrine of regeneration; and were, in piety, devotion, Christian activity, and missionary enterprise, as well as in learning and intellectual power and attainments, inferior to none in the best ages of the Church, and were greatly superior to those by whom, in after-ages, they were condemned and anathematized.[48]

We see, then, that all three views of hell were prevalent, existing side-by-side from the second century onward, and were regarded as acceptable for Christians to believe, at least for the first four or five centuries of the church. It may be that conditionalism was the earliest documentable view in the patristic writings, while restorationism may have been dominant at a slightly later period.

In any case, it was the influence of Augustine that ultimately overwhelmed the general acceptance of competing views of hell in the Western church. He could not have known, of course, that his writings would have such a profound influence upon later generations, but once his views were accepted, they continued to hold sway—possibly as much through the force of momentum as through exegetical superiority.

After praising Augustine for positive contributions made in other areas of theology, former Dutch Reformed pastor Jan Bonda wrote:

The question here is not what this great church father has meant for western Christianity. It is rather what posterity did with his defense of eternal punishment. By transmitting this defense, century after century, his followers have given these words a weight they did not possess in Augustine's own mind—the weight of the "church of the ages." The task of posterity was to compare these words with Scripture before handing them down to the next generations. There is ample reason to question whether posterity did what it should have done in this matter.[49]

---

48. Ibid.
49. Jan Bonda, *The One Purpose of God* (Grand Rapids: Wm. B. Eerdmans, 1993), 24–25.

Augustine's influence (following that of Tertullian) eventually secured pride of place for the eternal torment view of hell in the Latin church, from which arose Roman Catholicism. This position has continued, to this present day, to be regarded as orthodoxy among Roman Catholics and most Protestants. It was not until the Reformation times that freedom of thought reemerged in Western Christianity. Once it became acceptable to question Roman Catholic tradition, the cat was out of the bag. Many Christian theologians and Bible students soon were reconsidering the old alternatives to the Roman view of hell. This discussion is still very much alive today—and it should be. No one should be threatened by ongoing dialogue, nor should any condemn those who are still in the process of sorting the matter out, nor those who have done so and have embraced views other than our own. In the context of his appeal that an alternative view of damnation be allowed a place at the table, Rob Bell correctly wrote: "To shun, censor, or ostracize someone for holding this belief is to fail to extend grace to each other in a discussion that has had plenty of room for varied perspectives for hundreds of years now."[50]

---

50. Rob Bell, *Love Wins* (New York: HarperCollins, 2011), 111.

PART 2

FIRST, THE BAD NEWS

CHAPTER 7

THE CASE FOR TRADITIONALISM

SUMMARY OF THE BASIC POSITION

Human beings, among the creatures of earth, have been granted the unique opportunity to know and worship our Creator intelligently, to willingly glorify Him and enjoy Him forever. Having been created in His image, we have the potential of becoming like mature sons of a powerful and benevolent Monarch, and to inherit positions of authority in His universal kingdom.

Of course, privilege never comes without responsibility, and as we have the possibility of sharing in infinite glory, we also bear the burden of commensurate accountability. The best-case scenario will bring eternal joy and pleasures in the presence of God (Ps. 16:11); but a squandered opportunity carries with it consequences of eternal misery.

This is because we have sinned against infinite Majesty, and as criminals against the Crown, we are subject to the utmost penalties. Mercy and amnesty have been offered by the King, but the rejection of mercy necessarily means that the penalties cannot be avoided.

Man's sinfulness incurs the consequence of separation and alienation from God, and leaves the rebel subject to the wrath of God on the day of judgment. Scriptures speak equally of eternal life for believers and eternal punishment for the wicked. This seems to imply eternal consciousness—either with God or apart from Him. Since we must live somewhere forever, those who do not find forgiveness in this lifetime must spend their immortal eternities separated from God and all light, love, and blessing that is associated with His presence.

Such complete separation from God has never been fully known by anyone in this life. Even those who do not know God have, all their lifetimes, been beneficiaries of His general grace and mercy, "for He makes His sun rise on the evil and on the good, and sends rain on the just and on the unjust" and "He is kind to the unthankful and evil" (Matt. 5:45; Luke 6:35).

This kindness "to the unthankful and evil" has its limits, however. At the point of the unrepentant sinner's death, God's general grace and kindness give way to that other, more terrifying, attribute of the Deity—His holy hatred toward sin and wrath toward sinners. For one who has neglected salvation during this life, there is no place for mercy beyond the grave, and that rebel who finds him- or herself "in the hands of the living God" on the day of judgment will have nothing to which to look forward, other than indignation, wrath, torment, and regret for an endless, conscious tenure in the lake of fire.

Within the traditional pale, there is room for some variety of opinion on details. However, there is general agreement on the broad contours of certain beliefs.

1. The Soul Was Created Immortal

The Greek philosophers held that man is immortal by nature. There were some early theologians who accepted this concept, and it has been the default assumption of many in the rank and file of the Christian church ever since. For example, the Westminster Confession of Faith, chapter 32, reads: "The bodies of men after death return to dust, and see corruption; but their souls (which neither die nor sleep), having an immortal subsistence, immediately return to God who gave them . . . the souls of the wicked are cast into hell,[1] where they remain in torments and utter darkness, reserved to the judgment of the great day."[2]

Lehman Strauss similarly affirmed: "The Word of God assumes the eternal existence of every soul regardless of its destiny. Every man's soul is immortal and can never be annihilated."[3]

However, it is common, among other traditionalist theologians, to deny the innate immortality of human beings, and to recognize that the lost, as well as the saved, will be made immortal in the resurrection, and sustained eternally by the special providence of God. This seems to be the view put forward in the Belgic Confession, in Article 37: "The Last Judgment": "The evil ones . . . shall be made immortal—but only to be tormented in the eternal fire prepared for the devil and his angels."[4]

Robert Morey has expressed the view of most traditionalist writers today: "Man is always and absolutely dependent upon the Creator for this life as well as for the next life. Man should never be viewed as independent or autonomous. Life in this world and in the next must always be viewed as a gift from God."[5]

Of course, this view of things involves God in proactively sustaining, in a conscious state, persons in hell, who would without such intervention lapse into nonexistence. Of the lost in hell John Gerstner has affirmed: "Their suffering would be everlasting . . . because He could and would keep the impenitent sinner alive forever."[6]

---

1. It is clear that the Westminster divines were associating the word "hell" here with Hades, rather than with Gehenna.

2. Westminster Confession of Faith 32.1, https://www.apuritansmind.com/westminster-standards/chapter-32/.

3. Lehman Strauss, *Life after Death: What the Bible Really Teaches*, abridged from *We Live Forever* (Westchester, IL: Good News Publishers, 1979), 14.

4. Belgic Confession 37, https://www.apuritansmind.com/creeds-and-confessions/the-belgic-confession-circa-1561-a-d/.

5. Robert A. Morey, *Death and the Afterlife* (Minneapolis: Bethany House, 1984), 94.

6. John Gerstner, *Repent or Perish* (Morgan, PA: Soli Deo Gloria Publications, 1990), 71.

2. Fire May Be Literal or Figurative

Visions of hell differ among those who hold the view of eternal misery. Earlier Christian writers envisioned literal flames, such as we know here on earth. John Walvoord is a modern theologian who continues to hold to the view of literal fire: "The question is naturally raised as to whether the fire of eternal punishment is literal. However, the frequent mention of fire in connection with eternal punishment supports the conclusion that this is what the Scriptures mean (cf. Matt. 5:22; 18:8–9; 25:41; Mark 9:43, 48; Luke 16:24; James 3:6; Jude 7; Rev. 20:14–15)."[7]

By contrast, most modern writers (e.g., Morey,[8] Peterson,[9] Yarbrough,[10] Beale[11]) see the flames as metaphorical—representing some preternatural phenomenon of exquisite misery—whether physical, emotional, or spiritual—for which no exact parallel from earth can be drawn. Earthly flames provide only the best possible, though still inadequate, analogy of it. Some would picture hell as cosmic loneliness—isolated from all love and comfort in dense darkness. William Crockett, who himself defends the non-literal view, indicates that the fires of hell were understood literally for the first fifteen hundred years of the church, and that the idea that the fires are not literal has only been around since the sixteenth century.[12]

3. Repentance Will Be Unavailing or Nonexistent in Hell

Some traditionalists think that the lost in hell will be capable of regret, and even repentance, but that they will have missed their

---

7. John F. Walvoord, in William Crockett, ed., *Four Views on Hell* (Grand Rapids: Zondervan, 1992), 28.

8. Robert A. Morey, *Death and the Afterlife* (Minneapolis: Bethany House, 1984), 31.

9. Robert A. Peterson, *Hell on Trial* (Phillipsburg, NJ: Presbyterian and Reformed Publishing, 1995), 192.

10. Robert W. Yarbrough, in Christopher W. Morgan and Robert A. Peterson, eds., *Hell Under Fire* (Grand Rapids: Zondervan, 2004), 79–80.

11. Gregory K. Beale, in Christopher W. Morgan and Robert A. Peterson, eds., *Hell Under Fire* (Grand Rapids: Zondervan, 2004), 128.

12. William Crockett, "The Metaphorical View," in William Crockett, ed., *Four Views on Hell* (Grand Rapids: Zondervan, 1992), 63.

opportunity to find grace, and will benefit nothing from their belated remorse. Others assert that the rebellion and hatred toward God on the part of the damned will continue eternally, thus justifying the perpetual continuation of punishment. The disagreement hinges, in part, on what is meant by "weeping and gnashing of teeth" in several statements of Jesus about the judgment of the lost (Matt. 8:12; 13:42, 50; 22:13; 24:51; 25:30). It is possible to take these as expressions of grief (and thus remorse). Though Robert Peterson does not think there will be true repentance in hell, he does think that these expressions suggest remorse: "Weeping signifies sorrowful crying; the gnashing of teeth, 'extreme suffering and remorse.'"[13]

Alternatively, "gnashing of teeth" can be an expression of anger or hostility (as in Psalm 35:16 and Acts 7:54)—suggesting a continuing rebellious attitude against God. The idea that the sinning of the sinner continues in hell for all eternity is expressed by numerous authors. For example, Peterson also opined: "There is no hope in hell because there is no repentance there."[14]

This idea is expanded upon by W. G. T. Shedd: "[The] Bible teaches that there will always be some sin, and some death, in the universe. Some angels and men will forever be the enemies of God."[15]

4. The Saints' Happiness Will Not Be Compromised by the Damnation of the Lost

A question that often arises is what the saved will think and feel about the continuing torment of sinners in hell—which would include many of their own former friends and family members. Various answers have been suggested. Tertullian, Thomas Aquinas, Jonathan Edwards, and others believed that the saints will rejoice

13. Robert A. Peterson, *Hell on Trial* (Phillipsburg, NJ: Presbyterian and Reformed Publishing, 1995), 164f.
14. Ibid., 133.
15. W. G. T. Shedd, *The Doctrine of Endless Punishment* (1885; repr., Carlisle, PA: Banner of Truth, 1986), 159.

to see the justice of God vindicated in the torment of the lost.[16] Augustine wrote: "The unjust will burn to some extent so that all the just in the Lord may . . . look upon the punishments which they have evaded, in order that they may realize the more that they are richer in divine grace unto eternity, the more openly they see that those evils are punished unto eternity which they have overcome by his help."[17]

Others believe that there will be a somber appreciation for the fact that all injustice has been redressed, resulting in mere acquiescence—resembling God's own attitude. Still others have suggested that the promise of God's wiping "all tears from their eyes"[18] will require that He will erase from the minds of the saints all memory of lost loved ones.

Such is the variety of options that find a legitimate place within the range of traditional beliefs concerning hell. While there may be no consensus as to the exact nature of the suffering, all traditionalists share the conviction that there will be no end to the punishment of those who neglect the grace of God in this lifetime.

THE WEIGHT OF TRADITION

The case for eternal torment is based upon direct scriptural testimony, though it also has the weight of nearly two thousand years of tradition in its favor. While Protestants acknowledge the authority of Scripture above that of tradition, it remains true that tradition represents the beliefs of the majority of informed biblical scholars and clergy through the centuries. As Robert Yarbrough has warned:

---

16. Tertullian, in *De Spectaculis*, Chapter XXX; Thomas Aquinas in *Summa Theologica*, Third Part, Supplement, Question XCIV, "Of the Relations of the Saints Towards the Damned," First Article, "Whether the Blessed in Heaven Will See the Sufferings of the Damned . . ."; Jonathan Edwards, "The Eternity of Hell Torments" (Sermon), April 1739 & *Discourses on Various Important Subjects*, 1738.

17. Augustine, *On the Sacraments of the Christian Faith*, 2.18.2.

18. Revelation 7:17; 21:4.

"We should be skeptical of arguments that overturn age-old under-standings of Scripture on ultimately speculative grounds. . . . If our aim is to be faithful to Scripture, we must face what Jesus's teachings have been understood to assert by most biblical interpreters over many centuries, cutting across a wide assortment of confessional and denominational settings."[19]

William Crockett issued a similar warning: "When someone proposes to change a doctrine taught consistently since the inception of the church, it should make us wonder how everyone throughout the centuries could have been so terribly wrong."[20]

THE IMPORTANCE OF THE ISSUE

The traditional doctrine of hell should not be abandoned lightly, regardless how unpopular it may become for Christians to stand firmly by it. The matter is not a minor one, and the consequences of being wrong are not likely to be insignificant. As Francis Chan wrote: "When it comes to hell, we can't afford to be wrong. This is not one of those doctrines where you can toss in your two cents, shrug your shoulders, and move on. Too much is at stake. Too many people are at stake."[21]

Much as we may recoil at the thought of eternal torment, if it is what the Bible teaches, we cannot neglect to preach it. Sinners do not naturally know how much they need salvation, and without receiving full and accurate information concerning the consequences of reject-ing Christ, they are less likely to give Him serious consideration.

---

19. Robert W. Yarbrough, in Christopher W. Morgan and Robert A. Peterson, eds., *Hell Under Fire* (Grand Rapids: Zondervan, 2004), 71, 87.

20. William Crockett, "The Metaphorical View," in William Crockett, ed., *Four Views on Hell* (Grand Rapids: Zondervan, 1992), 62–63. After issuing this warning, however, he frankly acknowledges that his own view of metaphorical, rather than literal, fire is itself a modification of fifteen hundred years of tradition.

21. Francis Chan and Preston Sprinkle, *Erasing Hell* (Colorado Springs: David C. Cook, 2011), 14f.

If the message seems unloving, we must remember that no one was ever more loving (in the appropriate manner and degree) than was Jesus, and it is primarily through His teachings that we learn about hell.

As Shedd wrote, "The strongest support of the doctrine of Endless Punishment is the teaching of Christ, the Redeemer of man."[22] So also, Scot McKnight confirms: "What Christians have believed about hell has been constructed almost entirely out of what Jesus teaches in the Gospels."[23]

WHAT DID JESUS MEAN BY "GEHENNA"?

In chapter five, we explored the meaning of Jesus's usage of *Gehenna*, which is the word most frequently translated "hell" in Jesus's teaching. It was observed there that a case can be made for this being a reference to the valley into which corpses would be cast when the Romans conquered Jerusalem. However, since the rabbis of Jesus's day associated the word with the postmortem punishment of the wicked, most scholars are of the opinion that this is also what Jesus meant when using the term. Francis Chan said that, if Jesus was not using *Gehenna* in the popular manner of His times, He "would have had to go out of His way to distance Himself from these beliefs."[24] Robert Yarbrough, too, stands with the majority of scholars, who see Jesus as referring to a postmortem judgment, rather than the mere Valley of Hinnom: "The connotative meaning (sense) of Matthew 5:22 is primarily God's hell, not a Judean waste disposal site."[25]

---

22. W. G. T. Shedd, *The Doctrine of Endless Punishment* (1885; repr., Carlisle, PA: Banner of Truth, 1986), 12.

23. Scot McKnight, *A New Vision for Israel* (Grand Rapids: Wm. B. Eerdmans, 1999), 139.

24. Francis Chan and Preston Sprinkle, *Erasing Hell* (Colorado Springs: David C. Cook, 2011), 49.

25. Robert W. Yarbrough, in Christopher W. Morgan and Robert A. Peterson, eds., *Hell Under Fire* (Grand Rapids: Zondervan, 2004), 79. There are scholars who question

THE SCRIPTURAL CASE

Although Jesus is our primary source for the vision of hell, the concept is by no means confined to His teachings. The beginnings of the idea of eternal consequences for sinners is found in the beginning of the Old Testament, and continues to be confirmed and developed right through the last chapters of the New Testament. Let's look at some of the key texts:

Genesis 2:17: "For in the day that you eat of it you shall surely die."

In Scripture, often, the consequence for sin is said to be "death" (e.g., Gen. 2:17; Ezek. 18:4; Rom. 6:23). We may tend to think of death as a cessation of existence, or the absence of consciousness, but the true wages of sin extend far beyond physical death. Though John Gerstner's enthusiasm for the subject may take him beyond the actual wording of Scripture, he did not go beyond the general opinion of most scholars when he wrote: "What are the wages of sin? *Eternal* death (Rom. 6:23)."[26]

Since Adam and Eve did not physically die on the very day of their transgression, it is safe to assume that they incurred another kind of death through their sin. We find that they were cut off from the tree of life so that they might not live forever, and that they were driven from the presence of the Lord (Gen. 3:22–24). Death, therefore, is to be understood as separation from God and His blessings, not as a state of nonexistence or unconsciousness. This separation is the default state of all sinners (cf. Eph. 2:1; Col. 2:13),

---

the common idea that there was a garbage dump in the Valley of Hinnom in the times of Christ. "There is no convincing evidence in the primary sources for the existence of a fiery dump in this location" (Peter Head, "Duration of Divine Judgment," in *Eschatology in Bible and Theology*, ed. Kent E. Brower and Mark W. Elliott [Downers Grove, IL: InterVarsity Press, 1997], 223).

26. John Gerstner, *Repent or Perish* (Morgan, PA: Soli Deo Gloria Publications, 1990), 5 (italics added).

and continues perpetually into eternity, unless they find salvation and reconciliation to God through faith in Christ. Hell is simply the continuation of that separation into the endless future for those who do not find reconciliation in Christ during the present lifetime. William Crockett, not wishing to speculate too much concerning the exact experience of those in hell, wrote: "The most we can say is that the rebellious will be cast from the presence of God, without any hope of restoration. Like Adam and Eve they will be driven away, but this time into 'eternal night,' where joy and hope are forever lost."[27]

> **Daniel 12:2:** "And many of those who sleep in the dust of the earth shall awake, some to everlasting life, some to shame and everlasting contempt."

Few passages in the Old Testament employ such clear language, as does this one, concerning the future resurrection (a topic upon which the New Testament has far more to say than does the Old Testament). This is also the only Old Testament passage in which the term "everlasting life" is found. Not only is the "life" everlasting for many, but so also are the "shame" and the "contempt" for others. As Morey noted: "It is obvious that 'shame' refers to the inner turmoil of the wicked as they feel the 'contempt' of the righteous. The shame and contempt are personally felt by the wicked. . . . there is no way to escape the obvious grammatical contrast between the unending well-being of the righteous and the unending shame and contempt of the wicked. To limit the suffering of the wicked without limiting the bliss of the righteous is grammatically impossible."[28]

---

27. William Crockett, "The Metaphorical View," in William Crockett, ed., *Four Views on Hell* (Grand Rapids: Zondervan, 1992), 61.

28. Robert A. Morey, *Death and the Afterlife* (Minneapolis: Bethany House, 1984), 117f.

Isaiah 66:24: "And they shall go forth and look upon the corpses of the men who have transgressed against Me. For their worm does not die, and their fire is not quenched. They shall be an abhorrence to all flesh."

This is the passage from which Jesus drew His most graphic description of Gehenna. The references to undying worms and unquenchable fire convey the distinct impression of a punishment that extends unendingly into the extremities of eternity. In Mark 9:43–48 (see treatment below), Jesus quotes imagery from this verse twice, or possibly even three times.[29] In the Hebrew text, "abhorrence" is the same word as is translated "contempt" in Daniel 12:2 (discussed above). These are the only two occurrences of this word in the Bible. Although nothing is explicitly said here (as in Daniel) about eternity, the use of this same Hebrew term, in similar contexts, provides a double Old Testament witness of the eternal misery of the lost.

Mark 9:43–44: "If your hand causes you to sin, cut it off. It is better for you to enter into life maimed, rather than having two hands, to go to hell, into the fire that shall never be quenched—where 'Their worm does not die and the fire is not quenched.'"

Here, the word "hell" translates the Greek word *Gehenna*. The phrase "Their worm does not die and the fire is not quenched" is placed in quotation marks in the text because Jesus is citing it from Isaiah 66, which we just considered. This clearly ties Isaiah 66:24 directly to Gehenna in a way that the Isaianic passage alone does not. We read here of fire that can never be "quenched" and must burn forever. By implication, those who are cast into such a fire must

---

29. Twice in the *Alexandrian Text* and three times in the *Textus Receptus*.

burn forever as well. Robert Yarbrough believes that "it requires a studied effort not to see eternal conscious punishment implied in the words 'where the fire never goes out.'"[30]

> **Matthew 25:41:** "Then He will also say to those on the left hand, 'Depart from Me, you cursed, into the everlasting fire prepared for the devil and his angels.'"

This parable of the sheep and the goats contains the clearest references to eternal duration of hell to be found anywhere in Jesus's teachings. The fire into which the lost are sent at the judgment is said to be "everlasting." This indicates a punishment that is also eternal, since there would hardly be cause for the fire to burn longer than the punishment was to endure.

According to Jesus, sinners are sent to the identical punishment as has been "prepared for the devil and his angels." On the matter of the devil's fate, we have additional information provided in Revelation 20:10 (see treatment below), which depicts the devil as being cast into the lake of fire (clearly the same fire as that mentioned here). In that passage, we are told that he is to be "tormented day and night forever and ever." This confirms that the torment of hell is eternal. Peterson argues the logical necessity of humans suffering eternally as follows: "The Devil's being cast into eternal fire means that he will be perpetually tormented. When Jesus, therefore, says that wicked human beings will share the Devil's fate, he means that they too will suffer eternal torment."[31]

> **Matthew 25:46:** "And these will go away into everlasting punishment, but the righteous into eternal life."

---

30. Robert W. Yarbrough, in Christopher W. Morgan and Robert A. Peterson, eds., *Hell Under Fire* (Grand Rapids: Zondervan, 2004), 74 (quoting from the NIV).

31. Robert A. Peterson, *Hell on Trial* (Phillipsburg, NJ: Presbyterian and Reformed Publishing, 1995), 46.

These words are found at the close of the same parable that contained the previous passage. Here, again, we find confirmation that the fate of the lost is *everlasting punishment.* If the persons in hell were unconscious, or had ceased to exist, they would not forever be experiencing punishment.

Adversaries of traditionalism might argue that we should not take the word "everlasting" (Gr. *aionios*) to mean "endless," since the Greek word does not always bear this meaning. How, then, can we take the same word "eternal" (Gr. *aionios*) to mean "endless" when, in the same verse, it describes the future life of the saints? To eliminate the endlessness of punishment would prove too much, because it would also seem to eliminate the endlessness of salvation ("life") in Christ. This point was originally observed by Augustine, in *The City of God*: "Christ, in the very same passage, included both punishment and life in one and the same sentence. . . . If both are 'eternal', it follows necessarily that either both are to be taken as long-lasting,[32] but finite, or both as endless and perpetual. . . . Hence, because the eternal life of the saints will be endless, the eternal punishment also, for those condemned to it, will assuredly have no end."[33]

This logic of Augustine in this matter has been followed by most traditional scholars ever since his day.

Luke 16:24–26: "Then he cried and said, 'Father Abraham, have mercy on me, and send Lazarus that he may dip the tip of his finger in water and cool my tongue; for I am tormented in this flame.' But Abraham said, 'Son . . . between us and you there is a great gulf fixed, so that those who want to pass from here to you cannot, nor can those from there pass to us.'"

32. It is clear from Augustine's statement that he considers "long-lasting" to be a possible alternative meaning of *aionios*, but he argues that it cannot mean that *here* because of its juxtaposition with the phrase "*aionios* life" in the passage.
33. Augustine, *The City of God*, ed. David Knowles (Toronto: Penguin Books, 1972), 1001f. (21.23).

Though this passage does not directly address the final fate of
the lost, but the intermediate state (as we have previously observed,
in chapter 4), it speaks of the nature of damnation as an unalterable
and conscious condition. Randy Alcorn wrote: "In his story of the
rich man and Lazarus, Jesus taught that in Hell, the wicked suffer
terribly, are fully conscious, retain their desires and memories and
reasoning, long for relief, cannot be comforted, cannot leave their
torment, and are bereft of hope."[34]

Against the hope of the universalist, this story denies that any
can cross over from the place of the damned to the place of the saved.
This point was made by Douglas Moo: "Since escape from the consequences of sin is possible only in this life, people who die in their
sin will never leave hell."[35]

Traditionalists and conditionalists agree on this point. Robert
A. Peterson and Edward William Fudge, collaborating on a book
contrasting conditionalism (Fudge) and traditionalism (Peterson),
wrote in their introduction: "We believe Scripture points to death as
an end to the opportunity for salvation. The testimony of Hebrews
9:27 seems conclusive: 'Just as man is destined to die once, and after
that to face judgment, so Christ was sacrificed once to take away the
sins of many people.'"[36]

2 Thessalonians 1:9 (NIV): "They will be punished with everlasting destruction and shut out from the presence of the Lord and
from the glory of his might."

In the apostolic writings, we do not find a great emphasis upon
the subject of hell. This may be accounted for by the fact that the
apostles wrote their epistles to Christians, not to unbelievers.

---

34. Randy Alcorn, *Heaven* (Carol Stream, IL: Tyndale House, 2004), 25–26.

35. Douglas J. Moo, in Christopher W. Morgan and Robert A. Peterson, eds., *Hell
Under Fire* (Grand Rapids: Zondervan, 2004), 102.

36. Edward William Fudge and Robert A. Peterson, *Two Views of Hell: A Biblical and
Theological Dialogue* (Downers Grove, IL: InterVarsity Press, 2000), 14.

Nonetheless, there are occasions wherein this subject comes up. This verse is a rare instance of Paul's addressing the ultimate fate of the wicked. As Douglas Moo has pointed out: "Since Paul never uses the Greek words normally translated 'hell,' we will have to depend on the various ways in which Paul depicts the fate of the wicked to determine what he teaches on this matter."[37]

Paul, in this passage, described the punishment of the wicked, at the coming of Christ, as "everlasting destruction," which confirms that hell's destruction (Gr. *olethros*) continues forever. Calvin wrote: "The phrase which [Paul] adds in apposition explains the nature of the punishment which he had mentioned—it is eternal punishment and death which has no end. . . . This is eternal and has no end. Hence the violent nature of that death will never cease."[38]

While the word "destruction" (*olethros*) may sound to us like *extinction*, it may also convey the idea of *ruin*, not *annihilation*. The use of this word in 1 Timothy 6:9–10, for example, suggests the ruination (not annihilation) that comes upon one who inordinately loves money.

The force of the present verse seems to rule out extinction, when one considers that the nature of this destruction is said to be that the sinner is "shut out from the presence of the Lord." Presumably, one must continue to exist in order to experience ongoing exclusion. Thus we read from Gregory Boyd and Paul Eddy: "This destruction cannot be annihilation, for the punishment includes being 'separated from the presence of the Lord and from the glory of his might' (2 Thess. 1:8–9). One can be separated from someone else only if one continues to exist."[39]

37. Douglas J. Moo, in Christopher W. Morgan and Robert A. Peterson, eds., *Hell Under Fire* (Grand Rapids: Zondervan, 2004), 92.

38. John Calvin, in D. W. Torrance and T. F. Torrance, eds., *Calvin's New Testament Commentaries: The Epistles of Paul to the Romans and Thessalonians* (Grand Rapids: Wm. B. Eerdmans, 1959), 392.

39. Gregory A. Boyd and Paul R. Eddy, *Across the Spectrum: Understanding Issues in Evangelical Theology* (Grand Rapids: Baker Book House, 2002), 257. Others argue similarly: "Paul's next words rule out annihilation: '. . . and [they will be] shut out from the presence

Revelation 14:10–11: "He himself shall also drink of the wine of the wrath of God, which is poured out full strength into the cup of His indignation. He shall be tormented with fire and brimstone in the presence of the holy angels and in the presence of the Lamb. And the smoke of their torment ascends forever and ever; and they have no rest day or night, who worship the beast and his image, and whoever receives the mark of his name."

This stands, as almost all commentators agree, as one of the most cogent proofs of the doctrine of eternal torment. Even Clark Pinnock, a staunch critic of this view, admitted: "This text comes closest in my mind to confirming the traditional view."[40] Walvoord wrote: "Though neither *hades* nor *gehenna* is found in Revelation 14, the statement clearly defines hell as eternal punishment."[41]

Those who worship the beast, like all other unsaved people, will experience eternal, restless torment *in the presence of Christ* and His angels. This may sound as if it contradicts the definition of hell as a separation from God, but this is not necessarily the case, as Peterson has explained: "We need to reconsider the common notion that God is absent from hell. In one sense, he is absent from hell. . . . However, since God is everywhere present, he is present in hell. Although he is not there in grace and blessing, he is there in holiness and wrath."[42]

The passage specifically mentions "torment," as does the passage we considered in Luke 16. Gregory Beale noted that "the word

of the Lord and from the majesty of his power' (v. 9). Unbelievers will be excluded from the gracious presence of the Lord. This cannot be annihilation, for their separation *presupposes* their existence" (Robert A. Peterson, *Hell on Trial* [Phillipsburg, NJ: Presbyterian and Reformed Publishing, 1995], 81).

40. Clark Pinnock, in William Crockett, ed., *Four Views on Hell* (Grand Rapids: Zondervan, 1992), 157.

41. John F. Walvoord, in William Crockett, ed., *Four Views on Hell* (Grand Rapids: Zondervan, 1992), 22.

42. Robert A. Peterson, *Hell on Trial* (Phillipsburg, NJ: Presbyterian and Reformed Publishing, 1995), 187.

'torment' (*basanismos*) in 14:10–11 is used nowhere in Revelation or biblical literature in the sense of annihilation of one's existence."[43]

The endlessness of this torment is underscored in two ways in the passage. First, *the smoke of their torment ascends forever and ever.* Second, *they have no rest day or night*—meaning they remain conscious the whole time. This passage appears, *prima facie*, to be a slam-dunk for the doctrine of eternal torment.

> **Revelation 20:10:** "The devil, who deceived them, was cast into the lake of fire and brimstone where the beast and the false prophet are. And they will be tormented day and night forever and ever."

In Revelation 19 and 20, many individuals are said to be thrown into *the lake of fire*—a picture of hell. First, the Beast and the False Prophet are cast in (19:20); second (in this verse), Satan is cast in; third, Death and Hades (20:14); and, finally, "anyone not found written in the Book of Life" (20:15). Only this verse specifically mentions perpetual suffering in the lake of fire, but what is said to take place there in this verse may safely be assumed to be implied in the others.

> **Revelation 20:14–15:** "Then Death and Hades were cast into the lake of fire. This is the second death. And anyone not found written in the Book of Life was cast into the lake of fire."

Here we find the final groups added to the fiery ordeal into which Satan and his two confederates had earlier been consigned (v. 10). The same fate is shared by all who reject God. Walvoord wrote, "The lake of fire . . . serves as a synonym for the eternal place of torment."[44]

---

43. Gregory K. Beale, in Christopher W. Morgan and Robert A. Peterson, eds., *Hell Under Fire* (Grand Rapids: Zondervan, 2004), 116.
44. John F. Walvoord, in William Crockett, ed., *Four Views on Hell*, 23.

THE PHILOSOPHICAL CASE

There are a number of philosophical issues that we must consider in coming to grips with the truth about ultimate judgment. Most of them have to do with the definition of love and the necessity of justice.

1. Eternal Torment and the Love of God

One great objection to the view that God will punish sinners forever is that this seems inconsistent with the biblical affirmations of the love of God for mankind. How does eternal punishment square with such a characteristic in God's nature?

Those who raise this objection are often viewing God as a one-dimensional Being, having a single characteristic—omnibenevolence. However, God's love is not His only attribute.

John Piper wrote, "The statement 'God is love' does not imply that God relates to individuals only in terms of love."[45] Arthur Pink has complained that there is a common tendency among critics to invoke "the love of God" against the traditional doctrine of hell: "The Divine love is commonly regarded as a species of amiable weakness, a sort of good-natured indulgence; it is reduced to a mere sticky sentiment, patterned after human emotion."[46]

Love and wrath can coexist, as separate aspects of justice. Both are attributes of God described in Scripture. There are two alternative explanations by which God's love and His wrath have been harmonized: the Calvinistic and the Arminian.

Calvinism teaches that God maximally loves some people, but not all. God's redeeming love is restricted to the elect, as Calvin, commenting on 1 John 4:8 ("God is love"), wrote: "Here then he does not speak of the essence of God, but only shows what he is

---

45. John Piper, "How Does a Sovereign God Love?" *Reformed Journal* 33, no. 4 (April 1983), 11.
46. A. W. Pink, *The Attributes of God* (Grand Rapids: Baker Book House, 1975), 90.

found to be by us [i.e., by the elect]."[47] Since God really only loves the elect, in the sense of willing to save them, it is not inconsistent for Him to punish others, whom He does not love similarly.

The Arminian explanation affirms that God really does love, and desires to save, every human being, but that mankind is endowed with the capacity and privilege of free will. This means that people have the power, if they choose, to reject God's love, and to choose His wrath and punishment instead. Robin Parry and Christopher Partridge, explaining (though not affirming) such a view, noted: "If humans keep on rejecting God's offer of salvation, God could only save them by disregarding their freedom, and thereby treating them not as persons but as objects."[48]

On this view, God makes every effort to persuade, to convict, to thwart the sinners' headlong dash to damnation—but His love can only do so much. The sinner, on this view, may end up in hell against God's wishes, but does so only by overcoming every obstacle God places in his way *en route*. One might say that whoever ends up in hell must get there by sheer determination!

Both of these explanations (though they cannot both be correct) provide alternative ways by which the fact of hell and the love of God may be harmonized.

2. The Demands of Justice
A. *It Would Be Unjust for Sinners to Go Unpunished*
The judgment of sinners is not a matter concerning which God can remain indifferent. It is the responsibility of the Creator to restore order to His own creation, or else to concede victory to the evil one. God is committed to the vindication of those who suffer

---

47. John Calvin, *The John Calvin Bible Commentaries: The Catholic Epistles*, trans. John King (Altenmünster, Germany: Jazzybee Verlag, 2012), 157.

48. Robin Parry and Christopher Partridge, eds. *Universal Salvation? The Current Debate* (Grand Rapids: Wm. B. Eerdmans, 2003), xxii.

innocently, and cannot leave wrongs done against them in this world forever unredressed.

In addition to this concern, so long as God's insulted glory remains unavenged, the order of the creation cannot be restored. Evil is a cosmic cancer that continues to endanger the universe so long as God is denied the ultimate place of honor. Since the repairing of the effects of the fall depends upon God receiving His proper recognition in His creation, God's perpetual neglect of avenging His honor would leave the central problem of history uncorrected. J. I. Packer wrote: "Far from seeing endless retribution creating a moral problem, as if it were really divine cruelty on those persons who do not deserve it, the New Testament sees it as resolving a moral problem, namely, the problem created by the way in which rebellious evil and human cruelty have constantly been allowed to run loose and unchecked in God's world."[49]

Harry Blamires, by the use of a series of rhetorical questions, drives the same point home: "Is it not healthy to feel outraged when brutal savageries, such as the Holocaust, fail to bring punishment to the perpetrators? If such offenses were never to be punished, would they not cry out that there must be something untrustworthy, something indeed perverse, at the heart of creation? And by something perverse I mean something that is irreconcilable with justice, truth, and even love."[50]

Indeed, Martin Luther argued that hell is among the most *laudable* manifestations of God's perfect character: "Since God is a just Judge, we must love and laud His justice and thus rejoice in God even when He miserably destroys the soul; for in all this His high and inexpressible justice shines forth. And so even hell, no less than heaven, is full of God and the highest Good. For the justice of God is God Himself; and God is the highest Good."[51]

---

49. J. I. Packer, in Christopher W. Morgan and Robert A. Peterson, eds., *Hell Under Fire* (Grand Rapids: Zondervan, 2004), 185.

50. Harry Blamires, *Knowing the Truth about Heaven and Hell* (Ann Arbor, MI: Servant Books, 1988), 4f.

51. Martin Luther, cited in Ewald M. Plass, *What Luther Says*, 3 vols. (St. Louis: Concordia, 1959), 2:628.

B. To Be Just, Punishment Must Not Be Less Than Deserved

Justice demands not only that judgment must fall upon perpetrators, but also that the judgment be fitting and suited to the offense. If all sin truly deserves an infinite penalty (as will be argued presently), then God, who must be just, is not at liberty to reduce the sentence by one iota. The magistrate who allows an arch criminal to get off with the proverbial "slap on the wrist" demonstrates himself to be a corrupt judge, and a danger to society as well. If the judge's nephew were given a lighter sentence than his crimes warranted, simply because the judge had sympathy toward him, one could charge that this soft-heartedness disqualifies him to serve the public good. David Wells argued: "If God is as good as the Bible says he is, if his character is as pure, if his life is as infinite, then sin is infinitely unpardonable and not merely momentarily mischievous. To be commensurate with the offense, God's response must be correspondingly infinite."[52]

Therefore, annihilation would fall short as an adequate punishment for sin, since it has a point at which the punishment ends, whereas the deserved punishment for sinners is endless. Gerstner was offended by the suggestion that punishment may be finite and eventually come to an end: "Even the very expression, 'the annihilation of the wicked,' is an outrage against justice, because sin requires punishment, not non-punishment which non-existence certainly is."[53]

C. The Length of Time It Takes to Commit a Crime Is Not Related to the Magnitude of the Punishment Deserved

The seeming injustice of sentencing one who commits finite crimes committed in a brief lifetime to the fate of infinite misery

---

52. Christopher W. Morgan, "Annihilationism: Will the Unsaved Be Punished Forever?" in Christopher W. Morgan and Robert A. Peterson, eds., *Hell Under Fire* (Grand Rapids: Zondervan, 2004), 212.

53. John Gerstner, *Repent or Perish* (Morgan, PA: Soli Deo Gloria Publications, 1990), 62. But Gerstner, four pages later, represents Fudge's view as *including* punishment: "The impenitent sinner at death is punished in hell according to his degree of guilt and then annihilated." Either Gerstner's criticism on page 62 is wrong, or else his representation of Fudge's views on page 66 is wrong. The latter is not wrong.

stems from a misunderstanding of the true nature of guilt and punishment. It just *seems* so disproportionate when we consider that the sinner's rebellion in this lifetime could barely fill a hundred years, while his penalty must extend billions of years—and that is only its beginning! When we think more clearly, however, we realize that the magnitude of any offense, and its deserved punishment, are never determined by the actual time spent committing the unlawful act. As Shedd put it: "Murder is committed in an instant, and theft sometimes requires hours. But the former is the greater crime, and receives the greater punishment."[54]

Augustine (and, later, Aquinas[55]) made this point long ago: "The duration of a punishment does not match the duration of the act of sin but of its stain; as long as this lasts a debt of punishment remains. The severity of the punishment matches the seriousness of the sin."[56]

D. All Sin Is against an Infinite Being, and Is Thus Infinitely Offensive

The justification for eternal punishment as the fitting penalty for any rebellion against God depends, to a large extent, on the recognition of the status of the eternal God as the offended party. Albert Mohler has made this case: "Some theologians have questioned the moral integrity of eternal punishment by arguing that an infinite punishment is an unjust penalty for finite sins.... The traditional doctrine of hell argues that an infinite penalty is just punishment for sin against the infinite holiness of God."[57]

Shedd wrote: "If therefore the gravity of the act is to be measured

54. William G. T. Shedd, *The Doctrine of Endless Punishment* (1885; repr., Carlisle, PA: Banner of Truth, 1986), 741.

55. Thomas Aquinas, *Summa Theologiae*, Ia2ae, vol. 27, Blackfriars (New York: McGraw-Hill, 1974), 34.

56. Augustine, *The City of God*, ed. David Knowles (Toronto: Penguin Books, 1972), 987–988 (21.11).

57. R. Albert Mohler, "Modern Theology: The Disappearance of Hell," in Christopher W. Morgan and Robert A. Peterson, eds., *Hell Under Fire* (Grand Rapids: Zondervan, 2004), 39.

solely by the nature of the person committing it, and not by that of the thing against whom it is committed, killing a dog is as heinous as killing a man."[58]

This is the same argument made long ago by Thomas Aquinas: "Now a sin that is against God is infinite; the higher the person against whom it is committed, the graver the sin—it is more criminal to strike a head of state than a private citizen—and God is of infinite greatness. Therefore an infinite punishment is deserved for a sin committed against him."[59]

E. Not All Punishment Will Be Equal

Of course, true justice does not prescribe a one-size-fits-all sentence to persons whose crimes are unequal. Some people spend their whole lives hating God and brutally victimizing other people. Others live quiet lives, are respectful of others, and even have an interest in religion, but never come to Christ. It seems an injustice if all of these people are punished equally, without distinction.

The traditional view of hell does not suggest that punishment is equal for all. There are Scriptures that deny such a thing outright. The punishment of all the damned may be equal in duration, but it will not be equal in intensity. Peterson put it succinctly: "Scripture teaches that although hell is everlasting for all its inhabitants, some suffer worse than others."[60]

New Testament scholar Craig Blomberg, in commenting on Jesus's story in Luke 12:42–48 about the unfaithful servants and their variant punishments, wrote: "These verses rank among the clearest in all the Bible in support of degrees of punishment in hell."[61]

58. Shedd, *The Doctrine of Endless Punishment*, 714.
59. Thomas Aquinas, *Summa Theologiae*, Ia2ae, vol. 25, Blackfriars (New York: McGraw-Hill, 1974), 34.
60. Robert A. Peterson, *Hell on Trial* (Phillipsburg, NJ: Presbyterian and Reformed Publishing, 1995), 198.
61. Craig L. Blomberg, *Interpreting the Parables* (Downers Grove, IL: InterVarsity Press, 1990), 192.

F. Sinners Will Keep On Sinning in Hell, and Thus Keep Deserving More Punishment

The objection that sees eternal suffering as a disproportionate penalty for a finite lifetime of sinning fails to take another important factor into consideration: It may not be the case that the sinner's sinning is restricted to his finite lifetime in this world. Sinners may continue in their rebellion for eternity, cursing and resenting God. Perpetual sinning would justly bring upon itself perpetual guilt and punishment. D. A. Carson wrote: "What is hard to prove, but seems to me probable, is that one reason why the conscious punishment of hell is ongoing is because sin is ongoing."[62]

Christopher Morgan similarly opined: "It also seems likely that those in hell remain in their sinful state, at least in the sense of their privation of love for God (see Rev. 16:11; 22:11). If they indeed remain unregenerate, they would likely be continuing in sin and therefore stockpiling more and more guilt and its consequent punishment."[63]

THE PRACTICAL CASE

Our final consideration must be the practical impact of understanding that eternal torment is the sinner's ultimate fate. Lesser views of the sinner's destiny, which anticipate only a temporary hell, followed by extinction or restoration, do not sufficiently alarm and awaken our sensitivities, nor those of sinners. As Greg Boyd and Paul Eddy put it: "Many nonbelievers do not expect to live on after death. The threat of annihilation is thus no incentive to trust God for salvation."[64]

---

62. D. A. Carson, *The Gagging of God: Christianity Confronts Pluralism* (Grand Rapids: Zondervan, 1996), 533.

63. Christopher W. Morgan, "Annihilationism: Will the Unsaved Be Punished Forever?" in Christopher W. Morgan and Robert A. Peterson, eds., *Hell Under Fire* (Grand Rapids: Zondervan, 2004), 212.

64. Gregory A. Boyd and Paul R. Eddy, *Across the Spectrum: Understanding Issues in Evangelical Theology* (Grand Rapids: Baker Book House, 2002), 258.

Robert A. Peterson argues that the prospect of extinction "leads unrepentant sinners to underestimate their fate . . . it is simply not that bad to cease to exist."[65]

The Christian also needs to contemplate hell in its worst conceivable form in order to find motivation to get out and persuade others to turn to Christ. Paul wrote: "Knowing, therefore, the terror of the Lord, we persuade men" (2 Cor. 5:11). As John Walvoord put it: "Eternal punishment is an unrelenting doctrine that faces every human being as the alternative to grace and salvation in Jesus Christ. As such, it is a spur to preaching the gospel, to witnessing for Christ, to praying for the unsaved, and to showing compassion on those who need to be snatched as brands from the burning."[66]

Without such a doctrine to motivate them, it seems unlikely that those who have been missionaries would have been as eager to go to the lost world. Would so many Christians have forsaken their homes, fortunes, and personal safety in order to take the gospel to sinners, had they not regarded them to be on the road to a Christless eternity of unrelenting agony and torment? Can the church sustain its historic missionary zeal without its historical doctrine of the fate of the lost? Many think this doubtful.

---

65. Robert A. Peterson, *Hell on Trial* (Phillipsburg, NJ: Presbyterian and Reformed Publishing, 1995), 178–179.
66. John F. Walvoord, in William Crockett, ed., *Four Views on Hell* (Grand Rapids: Zondervan, 1992), 28.

CHAPTER 8

CROSS-EXAMINATION OF THE CASE FOR TRADITIONALISM

Despite the appeal to certain proof texts, it seems that the eternal torment view derives the majority of its credibility from the momentum it has due to its longstanding acceptance in church history. As Douglas Jacoby wrote: "The traditional view has the strong weight of tradition on its side, but that does not exempt its advocates from the need to prove their position. Too often supporters read the conclusion into the texts instead of properly deriving them."[1]

A number of the points made in favor of the traditional viewpoint depend heavily upon traditionalist presuppositions being read into the texts. With very few exceptions, the passages presented as evidence are *assumed* to support the endless duration of conscious punishment, without the passages actually making any direct reference to such a concept.

In many cases, it is assumed that a given text refers to an eschatological, postmortem judgment, when such is not clearly affirmed. John the Baptist's warning that the fruitless "trees" and the "chaff" were about to be burned (Matt. 3:10, 12) would be a case in point. He clearly spoke of an impending danger (*"even now* the ax is laid

---

1. Douglas Jacoby, *What's the Truth about Heaven and Hell?* (Eugene, OR: Harvest House, 2013), 105.

to the root of the trees. . . . His winnowing fan *is in His hand"*), not an eschatological one. The imminent danger was the coming destruction of the Jewish State by the Roman invasion, seen as God's judgment upon the apostate nation.

A similar example would be John Gerstner's application of Luke 13:5 (from which the title of his book *Repent or Perish* is taken). In commenting on the fates of certain Galileans recently slaughtered by Roman soldiers in the temple, and some other Jews killed by a falling tower in Jerusalem, Jesus said to the crowd, "Unless you repent you will all likewise perish." Gerstner legitimately renders the sentence, "You will all perish as they did."[2] He then proceeds to apply the text to the subject of hell.

There is no suggestion in the text that the persons who died in these disasters went to hell. Some of them died while offering their sacrifices in the temple (v. 1), and may have been righteous Jews, for whom hell was not appointed. We are not told. No exegetical reason is provided for thinking Jesus was talking about the afterlife. Gerstner's paraphrase correctly represents Jesus as telling His listeners that they will die *as they did*—i.e., by Romans slaughtering them in the temple, and by falling masonry—which, of course, did occur when the Romans invaded Jerusalem a few years later. There is no contextual hint that Jesus was referring to hell at all. To read postmortem judgments into such texts is unnecessary and gratuitous.

Since the vast majority of biblical references to judgment are not about postmortem fates, one ought to present exegetical reasons for applying any given passage to such a topic. Traditionalists do this far too seldom.

Let's cross-examine the case presented in the previous chapter.

Genesis 2:17: "For in the day that you eat of it you shall surely die."

---

2. John Gerstner, *Repent or Perish* (Morgan, PA: Soli Deo Gloria Publications, 1990), 4.

As Paul wrote: "The wages of sin is *death*" (Rom. 6:23). As we saw, John Gerstner modified "death" in this verse to "eternal death." Yet, though the Bible speaks of "*aionion* life," it never uses the expression "*aionion* death." The biblical phrase nearest to this concept is the reference to the lake of fire as "the second death" (Rev. 20:14; 21:8). Traditionalists define "death," in such passages, as meaning "conscious separation from God."

Redefining death as "conscious separation from God," even if legitimate, does not provide support for traditionalism particularly. Evangelicals of every persuasion agree that the lost experience separation from God—or spiritual "death"—in this present life (e.g., Eph. 2:2; 1 Tim. 5:6), but what happens after physical death (or after the final judgment) would be a separate question to consider, and it is not necessarily brought up in passages like Genesis 2:17 or Romans 6:23. "Consciousness" would have to be shown to be endless, in order to disprove annihilationism. "Separation" would have to be proven to be endless, in order to eliminate restorationism.

It might justly be suggested that, if the true penalty for sin is a deathless suffering for eternity, then God greatly understated the case, in Genesis 2:17, and would seem to have done a disservice to our first parents. To be told that one will die, and to be told that one will live forever in agony (only wishing that he or she could die), are very different threats. The latter would be much more compelling, and, if it is true, the neglect of communicating it would seem a senseless cruelty. As Gerry Beauchemin has argued: "Consider Adam and Eve, Cain, the Antediluvians (those prior to Noah's time), Sodom and Gomorrah, Pharaoh, and the Canaanites for example. Would you not have expected God to have warned them repeatedly of such a horrific judgment as everlasting torment? . . . If death meant infinite punishment, why did not God say so?"[3]

---

3. Gerry Beauchemin, *Hope Beyond Hell* (Olmito, TX: Malista Press, 2007), 141.

It was the serpent, not God, who told the pair that, even if they sinned, they would never die. If the devil was correct about this (as the traditional view, in one sense, seems to affirm), then it is surprising that God would say just the opposite. In any case, there is nothing in Genesis that provides any clear teaching about eternal torment, nor, necessarily, about postmortem fates at all.

> **Daniel 12:2:** "And many of those who sleep in the dust of the earth shall awake, some to everlasting life, some to shame and everlasting contempt."

The word "contempt" in this passage is the same Hebrew word as that translated "abhorrence" in Isaiah 66:24, where it is corpses, not living men, that are the objects of this indignity. "Contempt" is not the attitude or experience of the corpses, but that of others toward them.

Of course, the interpretation of "everlasting contempt" is subject to all the ambiguities involved in translating the word *olam* ("everlasting"), which we discussed in chapter 5. Hebrew scholars point out that *olam* does not necessarily mean "endless." It only means that the end is beyond the horizon, or hidden from view.

Jeremiah 23:40 uses precisely the same imagery when describing the "perpetual shame" upon Israel due to the Babylonian conquest of Judah: "And I will bring an everlasting [Heb. *olam*] reproach [Heb. *cherpah*] upon you, and a perpetual [Heb. *olam*] shame, which shall not be forgotten."

The word "reproach" in this passage is the same Hebrew word as is translated "shame" in Daniel 12:2. In both places, the shame, reproach, and contempt are said to be *olamic*, or "everlasting," yet, in Jeremiah, there is no suggestion of postmortem judgment at all, but only of the Babylonian conquest of Judah, in 586 BC—a disaster from which (as universalists could point out) there was a later restoration—so that it is not actually "everlasting."

While an eschatological resurrection is often assumed to be in view in Daniel 12:2, there are reasons to be cautious about making this identification. This verse speaks only of *"many* of those who sleep in the dust" arising, whereas, in the eschatological resurrection, *"all* who are in the graves will hear His voice and come forth" (John 5:28f.). The use of "many" in Daniel 12, as opposed to "all" in John 5, raises questions as to whether the same event is in view or not.

The language of resurrection is used figuratively in some Old Testament passages (as in Ezekiel 37:1–14). The wording of Daniel 12:2 (especially the reference to "many") seems to be echoed in Simeon's words, in Luke 2:34: "Behold, this Child is destined for the fall and rising [Gr. *anastasis:* "resurrection"] of many in Israel." This is most likely figurative, and not a reference to the eschatological resurrection.

Like Isaiah 66, these words in Daniel—which echo the threat in Jeremiah 23:40—might best be interpreted in terms of the crisis that came upon Jerusalem subsequent to Christ's rejection there, though it is hardly necessary to enter into such a peripheral discussion here. Whether eschatological or not, there is simply no mention of eternal torment in Daniel 12:2.

> **Isaiah 66:24:** "And they shall go forth and look upon the corpses of the men who have transgressed against Me. For their worm does not die, and their fire is not quenched. They shall be an abhorrence to all flesh."

The standard treatment of this text by traditionalists first assumes that it is a description of eschatological judgment, and then that this judgment is suffered eternally by conscious parties. However, the only parties (apart from, perhaps, the worms) that are said to be conscious in the passage are the righteous ones who go out and look upon the corpses of the wicked. The worms may be said to be immortal, but the wicked are described as dead. Fire and worms may consume a corpse, but there is no pain felt in the process by the dead man.

Most traditionalist commentators take both the fire and the worms as non-literal. They then imbue the corpses with consciousness and suffering—features that find no place in the text. A few, indeed, have sought to make the undying "worm" a symbol of the immortal soul of the lost. For this identification no precedent can be found in Scripture. Worms are associated with the consuming of mouldering corpses (e.g., Job 24:20; Isa. 14:11; 51:8), not with eternally conscious victims. Usually, people die first, and then are eaten by worms. In Herod's case, the order was reversed. He was "eaten by worms," but did not live long to suffer it. He soon afterward "died" (Acts 12:23).

Morey's suggestion concerning Daniel 12:2 that the shame imputed to the dead must be felt by them is neither necessary nor likely. The word translated "shame" is *cherpah*, meaning an object of reproach, and the word "abhorrence" (Heb. *deraon*) refers to an object of aversion. Neither word necessarily speaks of the subjective experience of the corpses, but of the reaction of the living persons viewing them. One might similarly say that Adolf Hitler, today, is held in perpetual infamy and abhorrence. This would not be a statement about the man's conscious experience, but about the attitudes of the living toward that dead man.

We will not revisit the debate here, but, as we discussed in chapter 5, there are interpreters who believe that the subject matter of this portion of Isaiah is the transition from the old covenant to the new, and that the corpses here represent those judged in the destruction of Jerusalem, in AD 70. The fact that Jesus identified this very imagery with the Valley of Hinnom (Mark 9:43–48) and that the prophet Jeremiah identified this valley with the place of corpses after the fall of Jerusalem (Jer. 7:31–32; 19:6, 11) might seem to support this identification.

Though himself a traditionalist, Daniel Block has observed:

"It is tempting to interpret this verse as an Isaianic vision of hell. . . . However, we should not do so too hastily, primarily because the sight that greets the worshipers coming out of Jerusalem is not a netherworldly scene. On the contrary, the image is realistic and earthly . . . we must realize that this is a battle scene. The image is also that of a pile of corpses, victims in battle, ignominiously dumped in a heap and torched."[4]

> **Mark 9:43–44:** "If your hand causes you to sin, cut it off. It is better for you to enter into life maimed, rather than having two hands, to go to hell, into the fire that shall never be quenched— where 'Their worm does not die, and the fire is not quenched.'"

Yarbrough believes that "it requires a studied effort not to see eternal conscious punishment implied in the words 'where the fire never goes out.'"[5] However, the phrase, "never goes out," upon which his argument rests, is the NIV's *paraphrase* of Jesus's actual statement. The word "never" is not found in the Greek text. The phrase "never goes out" (NIV), or "shall never be quenched" (NKJV) translates a single word: *asbestos*—meaning "unquenchable" (as in the NASB, ESV, RSV, NLT, Young's Literal, and others).

The meaning of "unquenchable" is not that the fire can never burn out, but that it cannot be quenched, or put out (i.e., by human means). Jeremiah speaks of the wrath of God in destroying Jerusalem as a burning that "no one can quench" (Jer. 4:4). The concept of God's wrath burning like a fire "that shall not be quenched" is a common expression in the Old Testament, when talking about temporal judgments upon nations (not about hell).[6] The picture is of an *irresistible* judgment, not an *unending* one.

---

4. Daniel I. Block, in Christopher W. Morgan and Robert A. Peterson, eds., *Hell Under Fire* (Grand Rapids: Zondervan, 2004), 60f.
5. Robert W. Yarbrough, in Christopher W. Morgan and Robert A. Peterson, eds., *Hell Under Fire* (Grand Rapids: Zondervan, 2004), 74.
6. e.g., Isaiah 1:31; 34:10; 43:17; Jeremiah 4:4; 7:20; 17:27; 21:12; Ezekiel 20:47, 48; Amos 5:6.

The pertinent phrases in this passage, as we have already discussed, are taken directly from Isaiah 66:24. Like this passage in Mark, the referenced prophecy in Isaiah makes no mention of eternal torment. If humans are innately immortal and indestructible (a contested point), then those cast into unquenchable fire might be expected to endure the torments of that fire so long as it burns. But we are not informed about how long these fires burn any more than we are told how long the "unquenchable" fire that destroyed Jerusalem in 586 BC burned (Jer. 4:4). That unquenchable fire (586 BC), in fact, was eventually followed by a national restoration (after 538 BC), so that even the destruction wrought by "unquenchable fire" was not permanent, in that case. This shows that unquenchable fire might torment eternally, or it might consume the wicked into ashes, or it might be followed by the restoration of those punished by it. Thus, if this verse is describing hell, then it leaves open the possibility of any of our three views being correct.

It may not be the case, however, that these verses have anything to do with hell or with postmortem destinies. The word "hell" in the text is *Gehenna*. In chapter 5, we explored the meaning of this word. While the Jews of Jesus's day used this as a term for the ultimate judgment of the wicked in hell, the prophet Jeremiah used it to speak of the judgment of Jerusalem, in 586 BC. Depending on the general context of the statement in Isaiah, his use of the imagery might refer to the similar destruction of Jerusalem, in AD 70.

As mentioned previously, there is no place for certainty that Jesus intended to support any of the rabbinical views of Gehenna. There were many concepts, like that of "the Messiah," "the kingdom of God," and "the Son of Man," which were found both in rabbinic (Pharisaic) teachings and in the teaching of Jesus. In such cases, Jesus did not slavishly follow Pharisaic interpretations, but often had an entirely different concept in mind from that of His contemporaries. Jesus explicitly warned His disciples to beware of the doctrine of the Pharisees (Matt. 16:6, 12). Does it seem likely that He would then expect His disciples to follow Pharisaic traditions about Gehenna, despite the very different meaning of the word found in the canonical prophets?

> **Matthew 25:41:** "Then He will also say to those on the left hand, 'Depart from Me, you cursed, into the everlasting fire prepared for the devil and his angels.'"

Technically, eternal (*aionios*) suffering is not mentioned in this passage. We are told that the fire is *aionios*, but not that all things thrown into it are equally *aionios*. Jesus says that the fires of hell were not intended, originally, for humans at all, but for Satan and his angels. A common argument of traditionalists from this passage is that offered by Robert Peterson: "The Devil's being cast into eternal fire means that he will be perpetually tormented. When Jesus, therefore, says that wicked human beings will share the Devil's fate, he means that they too will suffer eternal torment."[7]

If we knew that everything cast into the same fire would endure alive and conscious for an equal length of time, then this argument would carry some weight. However, this is begging the very question under dispute. If we should throw three objects—a stone, a newspaper, and a contaminated tin cup—into the same fire, we should not be surprised to find, later, that the stone's condition had remained unchanged, the newspaper had been burned up completely, and the tin cup had been sterilized. The fire, in each case, is the same, but the results of having been thrown into it vary depending upon the item. The devil and his angels may indeed be capable of being eternally burned without losing consciousness, but knowing this would tell us nothing as to whether the same is true of human beings. The passage does not affirm (as Peterson represents it to affirm) that "wicked human beings will share the Devil's fate." Jesus only affirms that the

---

7. Robert A. Peterson, *Hell on Trial* (Phillipsburg, NJ: Presbyterian and Reformed Publishing, 1995), 46.

wicked are cast into the same fire as is the devil. What their "fate" may be beyond that point is unspecified.

To those who already assume the correctness of the traditional view, the eternal suffering of the lost can be read into this verse—a process called *eisegesis*. But then, if the correct starting point for theological inquiry is the assumption that tradition is infallible, there is no need for the presentation of evidence for or against it. If we think such an examination to be legitimate, then we cannot be bringing our conclusions ready-made with us into the discussion of a text.

Matthew 25:46: "And these will go away into everlasting punishment, but the righteous into eternal life."

Outside the book of Revelation, this is the strongest text in apparent support of the traditional view of hell. It is the only text that uses the expression "everlasting (*aionios*) punishment." It thus stands in a different class from passages that merely tell us that fires are eternal or worms are immortal. "Punishment," here, actually seems to address, as most other texts do not, the *sensed experience* of the condemned sinner. Here, it is not only the fires, but the punishment itself, that is said to be *aionios*.

The meaning of *aionios* in various contexts will remain controversial, and this is one passage where this controversy exists. In chapter 5, we considered the various ways in which conservative scholars have understood the meaning of *aionios* (eternal). Though, in certain contexts, it can refer to something endless, its more general meaning seems to be "enduring" or "long-lasting."

Conditionalism and restorationism alike can accommodate the idea that punishment of the lost may be "long-lasting." The possibility of a later annihilation or restoration of the punished party is not ruled out by this expression. Only by insisting that *aionios*, in this specific passage, means "endless" can the traditional view use this text as support.

Augustine argued that the juxtaposition of *"aionion* life" with *"aionion* punishment" requires that the duration of the two be equivalent. He argued that, if we deny the endlessness of the punishment of the condemned, we must also forfeit the endlessness of the *aionion* life of the redeemed as well. But is this the case?

If two things are both said, in the same sentence, to be "long-lasting," it is not necessary that they both be *equally* long-lasting. One may be much more so than the other. If I were to tell you that I have enjoyed long-lasting friendships with two separate friends, you would be very unjustified in assuming that my friendships with them had existed for the exact amount of time. So also, if we were to read that one man was going to jail "for a long time," but another man was going to live as a free man "for a long time," we would be in no position to postulate some equality in the respective lengths of time mentioned.

Alternatively, there is the legitimate possibility of taking *aionios* as meaning "pertaining to the future age." As F. F. Bruce has noted: "When it is used (as here) in an eschatological sense, [*aionios*] means 'pertaining to the coming age.' Thus 'eternal life' is not 'a period of life' but the life of the age to come, which (incidentally) endures for ever."[8]

Wenham has confirmed this thought: "It would be proper to translate 'punishment of the age to come' and 'life of the age to come' which would leave open the question of duration."[9]

The life that pertains to a future age might be endless, while the punishment pertaining to that age might be instantaneous. The feature that the life and the punishment would share in common would not be their equal duration, but only that they were both appropriate to the purposes of that age.

An observation often made by conditionalists is that it is not

---

8. F. F. Bruce, *Answers to Questions* (Grand Rapids: Zondervan, 1973), 62.
9. John Wenham, *Facing Hell: The Story of a Nobody* (Carlisle, Cumbria: Paternoster Press, 1998), 244.

the "punishing" but the "punishment" that is said to be *aionios*. The former would refer to the *process* of inflicting punishment, whereas the latter would refer to its *effects*. If a person's punishment is to be annihilation, and he is never going to be restored to existence, then that punishment is *forever*. It is permanent, irreversible, never-ending. This need not mean that the annihilated party is experiencing the continuing infliction of the punishing process. The results are everlasting, thus it is an everlasting punishment.

The advocate of universal reconciliation has yet another point to make from this statement of Jesus. The word "punishment" is *kolasis* in Greek. Restorationists sometimes point to the fact that this word originally referred to the pruning of a tree, and later came to mean "correction" or "chastisement." Thus, they claim, *kolasin aionion* does not speak of irrevocable condemnation at all. They say it refers to an *enduring correction*, or else *correction pertaining to the age*, which eventually leads to repentance and restoration. Against this claim, many scholars, while acknowledging that *kolasis* bore this meaning in the period prior to the writing of the New Testament, argue that it did not necessarily carry the nuance of correction in the New Testament period, but meant only "punishment." Of course, even the word "punishment" does not necessarily rule out such instances as may be inflicted with correction as its intended result.

> **2 Thessalonians 1:9 (NIV):** "They will be punished with everlast-ing destruction and shut out from the presence of the Lord and from the glory of his might."

Here Paul is evidently describing the judgment to come at the second coming of Christ. It seems reasonable to equate Paul's picture of judgment with the effects of being cast into the lake of fire, or hell, in Revelation 20:10–15—and this identification will not be objected to by most traditionalists, conditionalists, or restorationists.

What does Paul consider, then, to be the ultimate fate of the wicked at the last judgment? His phrase "everlasting destruction" is capable of more than one possible meaning. The most immediate impression given by the words would be that of permanent annihilation, as say the conditionalists. Therefore, the conditionalist sees this passage in the same way as he sees Matthew's reference to "*aionios* punishment" (25:46). The punishment is annihilation from which there is no recovery (it is thus "eternal").

The traditionalist response is that "destruction" can also mean "ruination," as well as "annihilation," and that the words "shut out from the presence of the Lord" suggest a continuing existence in isolation. Peterson is only one of very many who argue thus: "Paul's next words rule out annihilation: '. . . and [they will be] shut out from the presence of the Lord and from the majesty of his power' (v. 9). Unbelievers will be excluded from the gracious presence of the Lord. This cannot be annihilation, for their separation *presupposes* their existence."[10]

It is true that the wording of the NIV here does give the impression of an existence separated from God (though, depending upon the meaning of *aionios*, this separation might not be "everlasting"). The larger problem with this argument is that it depends upon the addition of words to the text that Paul did not include. The Greek text simply reads "destruction from the presence of the Lord."[11] Between the words "destruction" and "from," many translators have supplied their own words, not found in the text, such as "shut out from" (NIV), "away from" (NASB, ESV), and "separated from" (NRSV). This is not the work of translation, but of interpretation. It would seem a disservice to the reader for translators to misrepresent the text in the interest of their own theological preference.

Paul does not actually say that the destruction is "away from" or "shut out from" the presence of the Lord. His words say that

---

10. Robert A. Peterson, *Hell on Trial* (Phillipsburg, NJ: Presbyterian and Reformed Publishing, 1995), 81.

11. e.g., KJV, NKJV, HCSB, Young's Literal.

the destruction *comes from* the presence of the Lord. The phrase "from the presence of the Lord" occurs in only one other place in the New Testament. In Acts 3:19, Peter tells his hearers that, if they will now repent, they will experience "times of refreshing . . . *from the presence of the Lord.*" How bizarre it would be to represent Peter as promising that repentance will bring "times of refreshing *shut out from* the presence of the Lord"!

Though the phrase is identical in its two occurrences, no translator has ever inserted "shut out," "away," or "separated" into the phrase in Acts 3. If Paul had wished to convey the idea that the NIV imports into 2 Thessalonians 1:9, he certainly was capable of saying this himself. It would have been as easy for him to insert the word "away" (if that had been his intended meaning) as it was for the modern translators to do so. Perhaps Paul omitted such words because their inclusion does not reflect his meaning.

While the traditionalist and the conditionalist tend to accept *aionios* as meaning "everlasting" in this passage, the universalist does not see the "destruction" as eternal or permanent, but as a means toward an end. Destruction may refer to the experience of ruination in a disciplinary hell, followed by repentance and restoration.

Often, restorationists[12] speak of the destruction as being the future eradication of the flesh, or of the sinful nature, rather than of the person himself. Paul used the same word for "destruction" (*olethros*) in 1 Corinthians 5:5, where the "destruction of the flesh" is seen as a means to the "spirit [being] saved," ultimately. In any case, the universalist thinks it presumptuous for alternative views to assume that *aionios* here must mean everlasting. As Christian philosopher and universalist Thomas Talbott said, when debating conditionalist Glenn Peoples: "But may I suggest as gently as possible that, given the millions of words written on the correct translation of

---

12. e.g., Thomas Talbott, *The Inescapable Love of God* (Boca Raton, FL: Universal Publishers, 1999), 95.

'aionios,' you need something more at this point than a brief allusion to II Thessalonians 1:9?"[13]

> **Revelation 14:10–11:** "He himself shall also drink of the wine of the wrath of God, which is poured out full strength into the cup of His indignation. He shall be tormented with fire and brimstone in the presence of the holy angels and in the presence of the Lamb. And the smoke of their torment ascends forever and ever; and they have no rest day or night, who worship the beast and his image, and whoever receives the mark of his name."

This is the second (after Matthew 25:46) of the three most cogent proof texts for eternal torment. It combines the element of "torment" in close proximity to the words "forever and ever." In addition, there is reference to "no rest day or night" for the condemned.

This, and the other proofs from the book of Revelation, would provide a stronger case for traditionalism if it were not for the apocalyptic nature of that book. While traditionalist scholars are certainly aware that the Revelation is written in the apocalyptic genre, they seem to ignore that fact when appealing to its descriptions of judgment. As Douglas Jacoby pointed out: "Expositors of infinite torment commonly fail to interpret the genre of apocalypse."[14]

First, the passage makes no claims that it is about hell. There is no specific mention of the "lake of fire," nor "the second death"—Revelation's terminology for hell. It may well be that hell is in view here, since the reference to "fire and brimstone" (v. 10) is found here as well as in descriptions of the lake of fire (Rev. 19:20; 20:10; 21:8). However, "fire and brimstone" were previously seen in Revelation in connection with temporal judgments that are not associated with the

---

13. Thomas Talbott, in online dialogue with Glenn Peoples, http://evangelicaluniversalist.com/forum/viewtopic.php?f=55&t=434.

14. Douglas Jacoby, *What's the Truth about Heaven and Hell?* (Eugene, OR: Harvest House, 2013), 106.

lake of fire (Rev. 9:17–18). As Fudge has correctly observed: "It is not at all clear that Revelation 14:9–11 is even speaking about final punishment, yet advocates of everlasting conscious torment sometimes speak as if this were the Bible's principal passage on the subject."[15]

The imagery of this passage is unmistakably drawn from two Old Testament cases of temporal (not postmortem) judgments upon earthly kingdoms.

SODOM AND GOMORRAH

The elements of "fire and brimstone" were first found in the historical judgment of Sodom and Gomorrah (Gen. 19:24). The obliteration of these cities became a paradigm for a number of later writers to symbolically describe the destruction of wicked societies generally. When Moses warned the Israelites not to violate God's covenant, he warned that disobedience would bring judgment upon them. He likened that judgment to that of Sodom and Gomorrah, and mentioned that the land of Israel would be "brimstone, salt, and burning" (Deut. 29:23). This was not literally how judgment eventually came upon Israel, of course, but Moses made the connection *in principle*. In Psalm 11:6, David used the fire and brimstone imagery from Sodom's destruction in describing God's judgment on the wicked of his own day. Isaiah likewise employed that imagery in describing the Valley of Hinnom at the time of Assyria's defeat in (probably) 701 BC (30:33), and used it again in predicting the destruction of Edom (34:9). Ezekiel adopted the same imagery in his prophecy of the destruction of Gog, the chief prince of Magog (Ezek. 38:22). None of these prophets made reference to hell in their writings. In Revelation, John repeatedly uses the same imagery—but is he always

---

15. William Fudge, in Edward Fudge and Robert A. Peterson, *Two Views of Hell: A Biblical and Theological Dialogue* (Downers Grove, IL: InterVarsity Press, 2000), 74.

using it to describe hell, or does he mean it more like Moses, David, Isaiah (see below), and Ezekiel did?

A growing number of scholars are thinking in terms of this passage as having been fulfilled in AD 70, when Jerusalem fell (Moses had used this very language to describe judgments on Israel). Whether this identification is correct or not, the passage gives no clear indicators that it is discussing hell. In fact, whereas traditionalists are continually reminding us that hell is "separation from the presence of God," this passage specifically describes a torment experienced "in the presence of the holy angels and in the presence of the Lamb" (v. 10). The identification with hell is thus tenuous.

THE DESTRUCTION OF EDOM

In Isaiah 34:8–10, we read not only of burning and brimstone (v. 9) but also of fire that is not "quenched" and smoke that "shall ascend forever" (v. 10). The important thing to note is that Isaiah was not describing hell, but the destruction of Edom, which occurred more than three centuries before Christ.[16] This, too, suggests that, in our present passage, we are not reading of eschatological hell, but of earthly judgment. The imagery of smoke ascending "forever and ever" occurs not only in connection with the destruction of Edom, in Isaiah 34, but also with the fall of Babylon, in Revelation 19:3, which does not appear to be identical with hell.

Having said all of that, however, if we allow that Revelation 14:10–11 *could be* a description of hell, what are we told about it? It is a place of torment and restlessness "day and night" (this would have to be taken symbolically, since "day" and "night" will not exist in hell). Such restlessness would be agreeable with any of the three

---

16. The Edomite nation fell to the Nabataeans between the sixth and fourth centuries BC, and never recovered.

views of hell under our consideration, unless we were to be informed that this restless state continues for eternity—which we are not.

Perhaps the one line that seems, especially, to favor the traditionalist view is the phrase "the smoke of their torment ascends forever and ever" (v. 11). To this it may be answered that it is not the torment itself that continues forever, but only the smoke associated with the torment. John Stott wrote that "it is the smoke (evidence that the fire has done its work) which 'rises for ever and ever.'"[17]

In considering the imagery of Sodom and Gomorrah, which Revelation here adopts, we might recall that the morning after the cities were burned up, Abraham looked in their direction and saw the smoke still ascending as a memorial to the destruction that occurred the day before (Gen. 19:27–28). While it is not likely that anyone in Sodom was still suffering the torment of the previous day's fires, the smoke continued to rise as a testimony, to Abraham, that the cities had been burned up. The smoke bore witness to the suffering of the previous day.

Could the ascending smoke in this passage also refer to a memorial of a destruction earlier completed? When we are later told in Revelation that the smoke of Babylon "rises up forever and ever" (19:3), this does not necessarily allude to the continuing agony of the inhabitants, nor even of the city's continuing to burn. It seems more to be an image of eternal smoldering—with smoke symbolizing a lasting memorial of Babylon's judgment.

So, as we have seen, Revelation 14:10–11 may not even be relevant to our discussion of hell (any more than are the descriptions of the destruction of Israel, Edom, or Babylon in the passages that use the same imagery). Even if it is depicting hell, it does not specifically say that the torment or the restlessness of the condemned continues eternally—only that their smoke does so—and such a description could be as much a hyperbole here as it is in Revelation 19:3.[18]

---

17. John R. W. Stott in David L. Evans and John Stott, *Evangelical Essentials: A Liberal-Evangelical Dialogue* (Downers Grove, IL: InterVarsity Press, 1988), 316.

18. The forever-rising smoke of Babylon, in Revelation 19:3, must necessarily be taken

Revelation 20:10: "The devil, who deceived them, was cast into the lake of fire and brimstone where the beast and the false prophet are. And they will be tormented day and night forever and ever."

This is the third of the three strongest texts supporting eternal torment[19] and the only verse in Scripture that mentions "torment" that continues "forever and ever." But this is not the general experience of all those thrown into the lake of fire. These are very special cases, as Fudge has explained: "According to many Bible scholars these are not actual people but represent governments which persecute believers and false religions which support those governments. Neither institution will be perpetuated forever, nor could either suffer conscious, sensible pain. Other Bible students think the beast and false prophet are actual persons, but even then they are different from ordinary human sinners."[20]

Shortly after this, "Death" and "Hades," which were introduced, symbolically, as villains in Revelation 6:8, are similarly cast into the lake of fire in 20:14. Since these are not even sentient beings, we begin to see reasons to question the literalness of any of these images. Revelation's story has been told in symbolic imagery throughout. We must be careful not to assume that its final acts have suddenly become literalistic.

Revelation 20:14–15: "Then Death and Hades were cast into the lake of fire. This is the second death. And anyone not found written in the Book of Life was cast into the lake of fire."

---

as a hyperbole, since Babylon is clearly depicted as being on earth (Rev. 18:9–10, 15–19, 23), and eventually the earth is to be renewed (Rev. 21–22). Once the earth is burned up and there is a new heaven and a new earth, it can hardly be suggested that Babylon will be placed on the new earth so that its smoke may continue to ascend eternally.

19. The first two were Matthew 25:46 and Revelation 14:10–11.

20. Edward William Fudge, in Edward William Fudge and Robert A. Peterson, *Two Views of Hell: A Biblical and Theological Dialogue* (Downers Grove, IL: InterVarsity Press, 2000), 78.

So here we have the final scene of judgment. Death, Hades, and every unbeliever (not only the most wicked) are cast into the lake of fire—but what then? This is where Revelation's report ends and where our three views diverge. All are willing to acknowledge that the unsaved must go into the lake of fire, but do they ever return from there? Do they burn up completely? Do they exist forever in a state of conscious torment? Are they eventually brought to repentance? Any answer we give to these questions must come from elsewhere, since this passage provides none.

Traditionalists find support in the fact that this same lake of fire was said to be a place of torment for the devil and his confederates (see above discussion of Revelation 20:10), but conditionalists take comfort from the fact that we are told, twice, that, for humans, the lake of fire is "the second death" (20:14; 21:8). Death, they say, sounds like annihilation. Of course, all views would have something to say as to the meaning of "death" in such passages.

To what does the symbolism of "Death" being cast into the lake of fire actually refer? Clearly, this event is parallel with that of 1 Corinthians 15:26, where Paul wrote: "The last enemy that will be destroyed is death." Unlike the devil himself, when Death and Hades are cast into the inferno, this does not mean eternal torment (for how could "Death" or "Hades" be tormented at all?), but for them the lake of fire means (as Paul put it) their being "destroyed."

THE PHILOSOPHICAL CASE: THE DEMANDS OF JUSTICE

Most of the comments made by traditionalists on the necessity of divine punishment of sinners fall short of relevance to the debate, since neither of the two alternative views denies that justice must ultimately be done, including the punishment of unrepentant law breakers. The dispute has more to do with what form justice ought to take—and to what end? Traditionalists argue from the premise that punishment must not be less severe than justice requires. Gerstner thinks that God would be very disappointed if the sinner does not receive the most severe penalties that can be justified—so much so, that God will proactively keep the sinner alive forever in order to make sure that there may be no mitigation of suffering:

> I have shown that a holy and just God must make the sinner's body and soul immortal in order that he receive his deserved punishment. If the sinner died, God's justice would die with him. Anyone, therefore, who admits that God is holy, just, and omnipotent logically admits that the punishment of evil persons will be everlasting ... sinners in hell will curse God inwardly and outwardly in that eternal stench-hole, whose only excuse for existence must be the glorification of God's holiness, justice, and omnipotent power, Rom. 9:18, 22.[21]

While God has the right to punish sinners according to justice, forgiveness has always been an option open to God. In justice, David should have been executed for his sin concerning Uriah and Bathsheba. Yet God pardoned him. The woman taken in adultery and brought to Jesus for His verdict deserved to be executed. Yet Jesus said to her, "Neither do I condemn you; go and sin no more" (John 8:11). With Jesus (and therefore, with God), it is possible for mercy to triumph over judgment (James 2:13).

No one would wish to live in a society where serious crimes regularly went unpunished, but we would object even more to, and question the Christian civility of, a society in which mercy could never triumph over judgment. Even when the guilt of the accused is established, the range of a judge's options in sentencing often includes penalties of greater or lesser severity. A merciful judge need

---

21. John Gerstner, *Repent or Perish* (Morgan, PA: Soli Deo Gloria Publications, 1990), 72, 75–76.

not impose the most severe of justifiable penalties. Randy Klassen wrote: "While the Bible recognizes God as holy and therefore as requiring justice, it does not see God as being vindictive or wanting to punish."[22]

This is why the traditionalist argument (that eternal torment is the inevitable punishment for unrepentant sinners because God can justify it) is unpersuasive. It proceeds on the assumption that God must, and wants to, inflict the most severe penalties that He can legally justify.

Those who insist upon eternal torment "because sin is against infinite majesty" do not seem to recognize that the most stunning manifestation of God's infinite majesty is in the revelation of His grace toward the most undeserving. Certainly, infinite grace is capable of absorbing an affront to infinite majesty. As evangelical universalist Gregory MacDonald wrote: "What makes us universalists is not that we have unusually weak views of sin but unusually strong views of divine love and grace."[23]

For some reason, many Christians seem to think it quite acceptable for God to overlook their own transgressions, and to avert judgment in their own cases, but they argue that it would be quite unbecoming for God to do the same for others—especially those who have been so unfortunate as to die before hearing or responding favorably to the gospel.

Again we face the question: What kind of God is revealed in Scripture—one predominantly concerned to protect and avenge His own offended honor, or one who humbles Himself, even to the death of the cross, in order to provide for Himself a justification to forgive sinners, who have no inherent claim on His clemency? If we are talking about the latter, then it seems out of place to be asking

---

22. Randy Klassen, *What Does the Bible Really Say about Hell?* (Scottsdale, PA: Pandora, 2001), 84.

23. Gregory MacDonald, *The Evangelical Universalist* (Eugene, OR: Cascade Books, 2006), 165.

whether God can justify inflicting the most severe and horrendous penalties imaginable upon His enemies, and more appropriate to be asking whether He has, through Christ, afforded Himself sufficient justification to recover those who have been lost to Him—or at least to mitigate the penalties for their crimes to the most tolerable possible justice. The Bible repeatedly emphasizes that God's anger endures only for a moment, but His love endures forever (Ps. 30:5; e.g., 2 Chron. 5:13; 7:3, 6; 20:21; Pss. 100:5; 103:9; 106:1; 107:1; 118:1–4, 29; 136:10–26). These frequent assurances of God's benevolent nature should raise suspicions about any doctrine that says that God's goodness to sinners lasts only for the "moment" of this lifetime (e.g., Matt. 5:45; Luke 6:35), but that His wrath endures forever!

It is not always clear whether traditionalists believe that an infinite offense really *demands* infinite punishment, or that it simply *justifies* it. The law of an eye for an eye means that, if someone strikes me on the right cheek, I would be justified in striking my offender in the same manner. However, Jesus indicates that such a response is not required, and that I am free to respond in the spirit of Christ instead. Does God reserve the same liberty to Himself? If not, then what has He gained by sending Christ to earth?

While it has been the favorite mantra of traditionalism for centuries, the assertion that sin against infinite majesty requires (or even justifies) infinite torment falls short of persuasiveness on at least three counts:

1. It is not taught in Scripture. As Jacoby wrote: "Advocates of the traditional view, discussing human sin, speak of 'the infinity of the evil.' This concept seems to be an import from theology or philosophy rather than an explicit teaching in the relevant texts themselves."[24]

---

24. Douglas Jacoby, *What's the Truth about Heaven and Hell?* (Eugene, OR: Harvest House, 2013), 106.

This favorite concept is wholly a human invention created to defend a teaching that could not easily be squared with our intuitions of justice without some such explanation.[25] The Bible nowhere teaches that the just penalty for sin is eternal torment, but always identifies the penalty as *death*.

Apparently the death of the sinner alone would satisfy the demands of justice, if God so willed.

2. The concept contradicts the related scriptural point (also affirmed by traditionalists) that not all sin receives the same penalty. If traditionalist W. G. T. Shedd is correct in saying, "Sin is an infinite evil . . . not because committed by an infinite being, but against one,"[26] then traditionalist Anthony Hoekema must surely be wrong in affirming, "Not every lost person will undergo the sufferings of a Judas! God will be perfectly just, and each person will suffer precisely what he deserves."[27] The Bible seems to favor Hoekema's assertion, in that it teaches that every person will be rewarded (judged) "according to his works"[28]—not "according to the status of the offended Party." If the magnitude of the evil is determined by the status of the one sinned against, then all sin is to be punished equally, because every sin is against the same infinite God, and would thus incur infinite (not proportionate) culpability. All things infinite in magnitude are equal in magnitude to each other, so there could be no difference between the guilt of the small (infinite) sin and that of the great (infinite) sin.

---

25. The additional argument, that sinners will continue sinning forever in hell, and thus will perpetually deserve ongoing punishment, is likewise a human invention. Not one line of Scripture can be adduced in defense of the assertion that sinners continue sinning eternally in hell.

26. W. G. T. Shedd, *The Doctrine of Endless Punishment* (1885; repr., Carlisle, PA: Banner of Truth, 1986), 152.

27. Anthony A. Hoekema, *The Bible and the Future* (Grand Rapids: Wm. B. Eerdmans, 1979), 273.

28. Matthew 16:27; Romans 2:6; 1 Peter 1:17; Revelation 20:13.

3. If all sin (or *any* sin) deserves infinite, endless punishment, then at no time in the future will sin have received a "just" degree of punishment, since an infinite penalty deserved can never be completely meted out. There must always be more punishment owed. The books can never be closed. This translates into the impossibility of God ever giving anyone the full and proper degree of punishment that they deserve. In a universe in which the vast majority of rational beings have never received their full penalty for their crimes, justice can never be complete. There is never "closure." Yet the Bible anticipates a time in the future when God will be "all in all" (1 Cor. 15:28). and when "all things" will be reconciled to Himself.[29] This outcome would be possible after the annihilation of the impenitent, or, alternatively, after the repentance and restoration of all rebels. It is not possible, however, if the traditional concept of hell is true.

THE PRACTICAL CASE:
TAKING SIN AND DESTINY LIGHTLY

The assertion that the traditional view alone is sufficient to prevent people from taking sin and eternal judgment lightly is simply incorrect. A penalty does not have to be infinite in order to be feared. No penalties in any earthly criminal justice system are infinite, yet many a would-be felon has abstained from committing crimes for fear of the temporal penalties of our prison system, or has ceased from criminal behavior after having served a finite sentence in prison. Very few hardened criminals (and zero ordinary citizens) would commit a criminal act knowing assuredly that it would result inevitably in a thirty-year prison sentence. Even fewer would do

---

29. Ephesians 1:10; Colossians 1:20.

so knowing that they would certainly face execution. To make the argument that nothing short of eternal torment provides any incentive for the unbeliever to repent of his rebellion, or motivation for the Christian to evangelize him, is to speak like a theological partisan, not like a person living in the real world of human motivations and choices, of crime and punishment.

Many people, who are not repenting today, have heard from their youth about a hell of unending torment. For them, this provides insufficient motivation to repent, primarily because they do not take the threat seriously. It is, no doubt, harder to take seriously a threat that sounds surreal or nonsensical than one that sounds reasonable. Probably the majority of unbelievers don't even believe in hell, regardless of its description, and they are not moved by threats of eternal torment any more than they would be by a hell of annihilation or of prolonged, severe chastisement. In some cases, the alternatives to the traditional view might even carry more conviction, because of their *prima facie* consistency with real justice in the known world, as well as with the character of the God of the Bible. Greg Boyd and Paul Eddy wrote: "It is questionable that the traditional teaching on hell generally installs fear in the hearts of unbelievers. It rather seems that this teaching often has the opposite effect. The notion of unending punishment is so out of sync with people's ordinary sense of justice that it is easily rejected as preposterous."[30]

Conditionalism and restorationism both leave room for penalties as severe as justice may require. People in these camps sometimes speak of the possibility of centuries-long punishments (if that is what is necessary or appropriate). The difference between them and the traditional view is that they see no necessity of torments extending over trillions of years, reaching no end or resolution.

---

30. Gregory A. Boyd and Paul R. Eddy, *Across the Spectrum: Understanding Issues in Evangelical Theology* (Grand Rapids: Baker Book House, 2002), 264.

In any case, the best motivation for the unbeliever to repent, and for Christians to persuade others to do so, does not arise from making God out to be the most implacable judge imaginable, but from appreciation of His gracious and benevolent character. John says that we love Him "because He first loved us" (1 John 4:19), not because He first threatened us. God may actually be more attractive to the lost than traditionalism would suggest (Jesus certainly was!). Perhaps God can actually be loved for who He is, and not merely out of fear of how He might retaliate.

John Wenham, one of the most notable British evangelical leaders of the twentieth century, wrote: "It seems to me to be a complete fallacy to think that the worse you paint the picture of hell the more effective your evangelism will be. I felt a growing distaste as I read through Shedd and a worse distaste as I read through Gerstner. This is not the God that I am trying to present to unbelievers."[31]

---

31. John Wenham, *Facing Hell: The Story of a Nobody* (Carlisle, Cumbria: Paternoster Press, 1998), 249.

PART 3

THE BAD NEWS
IS NOT AS BAD AS
YOU THOUGHT

CHAPTER 9

THE CASE FOR CONDITIONALISM

Summary of the Basic Position

The wages of sin is *death*[1]—not endless *life in misery*. In Scripture, as well as in language generally, death is the condition opposite to being alive—not another kind of ongoing life. It seems unnatural to speak of eternal "death" as if it were an interminable "life of torment."

Conditional immortality is the term for the view that all who fail to obtain the gift of eternal life will eventually cease to exist. Additional labels for this view (or some variety of it) are *conditionalism*, *annihilationism*, *extinctionism*, and *terminalism*. Though some make nuanced distinctions between these different terms, in this chapter we will treat them as essentially interchangeable.

Most evangelicals who advocate this view consider that hell is indeed to be a place of punishment and suffering, but also believe that the punishment will be proportionate to what is deserved by the individual,[2] and that all suffering will be finite. After the final judgment, the unrepentant sinner will be sentenced to the proper degree of punishment in hell, and eventually will be put out of his or her misery by annihilation.

1. Romans 6:23.
2. Luke 12:47–48.

CONDITIONAL IMMORTALITY

As the label indicates, advocates assert that immortality is not the default condition of human beings. Our first parents were created *potentially* immortal. Their eternal life was contingent upon their access to the tree of life in the midst of the garden.[3] God told them that the consequence for disobedience would be their death. This was no idle threat. When they sinned, they were consequently banished from the tree of life and consigned to eventual death. All of their progeny after them also sinned and have incurred the same penalty of death as a consequence.

As Adam and Eve's eternal life depended upon their eating of the tree of life, so the eternal life of every human being depends upon the eating of the true "tree of life"—Christ.[4] This means believing on Him.[5] Immortality is thus "conditioned" upon faith in Christ— hence the term *conditional immortality.*

This arrangement is stated (among other places in Scripture) in the most well-known and oft-quoted verse in the Bible: "For God so loved the world that He gave His only begotten Son, that whoever believes in Him should not perish but have everlasting life" (John 3:16).

The two primary affirmations of conditionalism are stated clearly in this verse:

1. Eternal life is available to people on the condition of faith in Christ.
2. The alternative to receiving this conditional immortality is to "perish."

---

3. Genesis 2:9; 3:22–24. Judging from the fact that the tree of life produces fruit every month (Rev. 22:2), it may be that their eating of its fruit was intended to be repeated or continual—i.e., they would continue living indefinitely, so long as they could continue to eat from the tree.

4. John 6:51–58.

5. Compare John 6:40 with v. 54.

The Greek word translated as "perish" (*apollumi*), in different contexts, means to be "lost"[6] or to be "destroyed" (or ruined).[7] In the majority of its New Testament occurrences, it is an unambiguous reference to death (with the implication of the end of life).[8] In a few cases, the word means to "disappear" or to "pass from existence."[9] In the context of John 3:16 (where the contrast is between perishing and having eternal life), the most likely meaning of *apollumi* would be eventual death, or the cessation of existence.

Jesus warned His disciples that they should fear no man, but to fear only "Him who is able to destroy both soul and body in *Gehenna*" (Matt. 10:28). The soul, then, can be destroyed, just as the body can be killed. Neither the soul nor the body are naturally immortal. As Greg Boyd has explained: "The implication is that God will do to the soul of the wicked what humans do to the body when they kill it. And this implies that the soul of the wicked will not go on existing in a conscious state after it has been destroyed."[10]

CONTRA TRADITION

The traditional belief in eternal torment seems to depend upon the indestructibility of the soul. John Wenham wrote: "The traditional view gains most of its plausibility from a belief that our Lord's teaching about Gehenna has to be wedded to a belief in the immortality of the soul. A fierce fire will destroy any living creature, unless that creature happens to be immortal. If man is made immortal, all our exegesis must change. But is he?"[11]

---

6. Matthew 10:6, 42; 15:24; Luke 15:4, 6, 8, 9; John 6:12; 2 John 8.

7. Matthew 9:17; Romans 14:15; 1 Corinthians 1:19; James 4:12.

8. e.g., Matthew 2:13; 8:25; 12:14; 21:41; 22:7; Luke 6:9; 11:51; 13:33; 17:27; Acts 5:37; Romans 2:12; 1 Corinthians 10:9–10; 2 Peter 3:6; Jude 5, 11.

9. Hebrews 1:11; James 1:11.

10. Gregory Boyd, "The Case for Annihilationism," blog posted January 19, 2008, at http://reknew.org/2008/01/the-case-for-Annihilationism.

11. John Wenham, *Facing Hell: The Story of a Nobody* (Carlisle, Cumbria: Paternoster Press, 1998), 241.

Pinnock opined: "I am convinced that the hellenistic belief in the immortality of the soul has done more than anything else (specifically more than the Bible) to give credibility to the doctrine of everlasting conscious punishment of the wicked."[12]

Pinnock, elsewhere, wrote: "It is this belief in natural immortality rather than biblical texts that drives the traditional view of the nature of hell as everlasting conscious punishment and prevents people from reading the Bible literally."[13]

"SOUL-SLEEP"?

Many conditionalists also hold to a view called *soul-sleep*, though the two views are not necessarily dependent upon one another. Soul-sleep has to do with the state of the dead in the intermediate state (between death and the final resurrection). Traditionalists and universalists generally believe that the soul (or spirit) of the dead lives on after death—either in heaven or in Hades. This would be a natural consequence of possessing innate immortality: you've got to be *somewhere* forever.

By contrast, conditionalists (denying the immortality of the soul) generally believe that, with the death of the body, the consciousness of the deceased is ended—or, more properly, suspended—until the eschatological resurrection. Thus the soul "sleeps" until it awakens in resurrection on the last day.

Any proof of innate immortality would exclude both soul-sleep and annihilation. Annihilationists do not fear that such a scriptural proof of natural human immortality will be forthcoming, since the Bible declares that Christ *"alone* has immortality" (1 Tim. 6:16).

---

12. Clark Pinnock, "The Destruction of the Finally Impenitent," *Criswell Theological Review* 4.2 (1990), 252.

13. Clark Pinnock, "The Conditionalist View," in William Crockett, ed., *Four Views on Hell* (Grand Rapids: Zondervan, 1992), 147.

Humans do not possess immortality by nature, and can only obtain it in Christ.[14] Paul described those who will ultimately be saved as being the ones who "seek for . . . immortality" (Rom. 2:7). If immortality is the default condition of every living person, it seems clear that it would not be necessary for anyone to "seek" to obtain it.

Though often defended together, the doctrines of soul-sleep and annihilationism do not depend upon one another for their mutual validity. The former deals only with the intermediate state of the dead, while the latter has to do with the final fate of the resurrected bodies of the lost after judgment. Of the two doctrines, either may be true without necessarily proving the other to be correct.

Since the interest of our present study is limited to the final destinies of the lost, and not the intermediate state, the defense or disproving of the doctrine of soul-sleep properly lies outside the range of our present concerns.

THE CASE FOR ANNIHILATIONISM

The conditionalists' arguments fall into three broad categories: 1) the biblical vision of eternity; 2) the biblical vocabulary of divine punishment; and 3) the biblical concept of justice.

1. The Biblical Vision of Eternity

The Bible speaks glowingly of the ultimate victory of Christ over all His enemies, resulting in a universe free from all the effects of the curse, including rebellion, sin, death, and suffering.[15] Many would argue that the traditional view of hell—according to which

---

14. e.g. John 3:15–16; 10:28; 17:2; Romans 2:7; 6:23; 1 Corinthians 15:42f.; 50, 54; Galatians 6:8; 1 John 5:11.

15. e.g., John 12:32; Acts 3:21; Romans 8:21; Ephesians 1:10; Colossians 1:20; Philippians 2:10–11; 1 Corinthians 15:28; Revelation 21:5.

the majority of mankind will be endlessly tormented, dwelling in an infernal state of continual rebellion and hatred toward God—does not square with such a vision. It leaves some major business unsettled—or else settled in a very unsatisfactory way. Philip E. Hughes, a convinced conditionalist who lectured at Westminster Theological Seminary and was one of the editors of *Westminster Theological Journal*, wrote:

> The conception of the endlessness of the suffering of torment . . . leaves a part of creation which, unrenewed, everlastingly exists in alienation from the new heaven and the new earth. It means that suffering and death will never be totally removed from the scene. . . . To this must be objected that with the restoration of all things in the new heaven and the new earth, which involves God's reconciliation to Himself of all things, whether on earth or in heaven (Acts 3:21, Col. l:20) there will be no place for a second kingdom of darkness and death.[16]

This is one of the major pillars upon which John R. W. Stott built his case for annihilationism. He wrote:

> The eternal existence of the impenitent in hell would be hard to reconcile with the promises of God's final victory over evil, or with the apparently universalistic texts which speak . . . of God uniting all things under Christ's headship (Ephesians 1:10), reconciling all things to himself through Christ (Colossians 1:20), and bringing every knee to bow to Christ and every tongue to confess his lordship (Philippians 2:10–11), so that in the end God will be "all in all" or "everything to everybody" (1 Corinthians 15:28).[17]

---

16. Philip E. Hughes, *The True Image* (Grand Rapids: Wm. B. Eerdmans, 1989), 405–6.
17. John R. W. Stott in David L. Evans and John Stott, *Evangelical Essentials: A Liberal-Evangelical Dialogue* (Downers Grove, IL: InterVarsity Press, 1988), 319.

Clark Pinnock echoed this same sentiment: "History ends so badly under the old scenario. In what is supposed to be the victory of Christ, evil and rebellion continue in hell under conditions of burning and torturing. . . . The New Testament says that God is going to be 'all in all' (1 Cor. 15:28) and that God is going to be making 'everything new' (Rev. 21:5)."[18]

In the common traditionalist view that sinners remain in a state of rebellion against God forever in hell, the creation is never really free from sin at all. Rebellion has not been conquered. It has only been marginalized and contained in one compartment of the creation. Nor has any final justice been served, since the punishment continues endlessly and is never completed.

According to annihilationists, though, all those who remain impenitent to the end will be removed from existence, leaving only such a remnant as would fit the biblical descriptions of a reconciled world and humanity. Hence, the glorious vision of an undefiled eternity is realized by the complete elimination of the contaminating element.

After surveying various Scriptures about the reconciled creation, Stott remarked: "These texts do not lead me to universalism, because of the many others which speak of the terrible and eternal reality of hell. But they do lead me to ask how God can in any meaningful sense be called 'everything to everybody' while an unspecified number of people still continue in rebellion against him and under his judgement."[19]

2. The Biblical Vocabulary of Divine Punishment

While the biblical vision of the eternal future may equally be claimed as an argument in favor of either restorationism or conditionalism, the scales are tipped toward the latter by appeal to the

---

18. Clark Pinnock, "The Conditionalist View," in William Crockett, ed., *Four Views on Hell* (Grand Rapids: Zondervan, 1992), 154.

19. John R. W. Stott in David L. Evans and John Stott, *Evangelical Essentials: A Liberal-Evangelical Dialogue* (Downers Grove, IL: InterVarsity Press, 1988), 319.

specific language used in Scripture to indicate the terrible end of the wicked under God's judgment.

The Old Testament, with its frequent emphasis on divine judgment of sinners, is replete with picturesque descriptions of the awful fate of those who rebel against God. Typical of the vocabulary and imagery commonly employed in the Old Testament is that found in Isaiah 1:28, 30–31:

> The destruction of transgressors and of sinners shall be
>> together,
> And those who forsake the LORD shall be consumed. . . .
> For you shall be as a [tree] whose leaf fades,
> And as a garden that has no water.
> The strong shall be as tinder,
> And the work of it as a spark;
> Both will burn together,
> And no one shall quench them.

Consumed by Fire

As in the above passage, fire is a very common figure for divine wrath and judgment, in general. Not infrequently, this wrath is seen manifested in the actual burning of wicked societies with literal fire. The most notable case, and the one that often inspires the imagery of later judgment passages,[20] is that of the fate of Sodom and its sister cities of the plain. Gregory Boyd has observed:

> The Old Testament actually has a good deal to say about the ultimate destiny of those who resist God. Peter specifically cites the destruction of Sodom and Gomorrah as a pattern of how God judges the wicked. The Lord turned the inhabitants of these cities "to ashes" and "condemned them to extinction" thus making

---

20. e.g., Deuteronomy 29:23; Psalm 11:6; Isaiah 30:33; 34:9; Ezekiel 38:22; Luke 17:29; 2 Peter 2:6; Jude 7; Revelation 9:17, 18; 14:10–11; 19:20; 20:10.

"them an example of what is coming to the ungodly . . ." (2 Pet. 2:6). Conversely, the Lord's rescue of Lot sets a pattern for how the Lord will "rescue the godly from trial" (2 Pet. 2:9). We thus have a precedent set in the New Testament for learning about the fate of the wicked in the Old Testament. And what we learn is that they are "condemned . . . to extinction."[21]

As the imagery of fire in the Old Testament speaks of things being devoured or consumed (not tormented), so also the New Testament confirms the same picture of the judgment—e.g., "every tree which does not bear good fruit is cut down and thrown into the fire" (Matt. 3:10; cf. 7:19); the Messiah "will thoroughly clean out His threshing floor, and gather His wheat into the barn; but He will burn up the chaff with unquenchable fire" (Matt. 3:12) the wicked will be like "tares" (weeds) that are "burned in the fire" (Matt. 13:40); or like discarded vine branches, which are gathered and thrown "into the fire, and they are burned" (John 15:6).

None of these passages represent fire as a medium of torment, but rather of complete annihilation from a God who "is a *consuming fire*" (Heb. 12:29). As Stott has observed: "It is doubtless because we have all had experience of the acute pain of being burned, that fire is associated in our minds with 'conscious torment.' But the main function of fire is not to cause pain, but to secure destruction, as all the world's incinerators bear witness."[22]

Fire That "No One Shall Quench"

What are we to make of those passages employing images of "eternal" and "unquenchable" fire? Doesn't the perpetuity of the burning suggest unending existence of those who are cast into it?

---

21. Gregory Boyd, "The Case for Annihilationism," blog posted January 19, 2008 at http://reknew.org/2008/01/the-case-for-Annihilationism.

22. John R. W. Stott in David L. Evans and John Stott, *Evangelical Essentials: A Liberal-Evangelical Dialogue* (Downers Grove, IL: InterVarsity Press, 1988), 316.

First of all, why should it? John Stott does not make this assumption, and challenges its validity: "The fire itself is termed 'eternal' and 'unquenchable,' but it would be very odd if what is thrown into it proves indestructible."[23]

John the Baptist used the term "unquenchable fire" to refer to the furnace into which the "chaff" would be thrown (Matt. 3:12; Luke 3:17). There is no suggestion in the imagery that the chaff had the qualities of asbestos, and could not be burned up by any fire, regardless how unquenchable. The mention of unquenchable fire does not impart to the fuel cast into it an indestructible quality. Jesus similarly referred to the prospect of persons also being cast into Gehenna's "unquenchable fire"[24] (Mark 9:43, 45), but elsewhere said the soul is "destroy[ed]" there (Matt. 10:28).

Edward William Fudge, the author of *The Fire That Consumes*, wrote: "Because this fire is 'not quenched' or extinguished, it completely consumes what is put in it. The figure of unquenchable fire is frequent in Scripture and signifies a fire that consumes (Ezek. 20:47, 48), reduces to nothing (Amos 5:5, 6) or burns up something (Matt. 3:12)."[25]

The case is the same with the similar wording of Christ's warning about Gehenna, "where their worm does not die, and the fire is *not quenched*" (Mark 9:48). There is no mention here of the continuing consciousness of the victims in the fire, nor of the endlessness of the burning. The words, as we have seen elsewhere, are taken directly from the closing scene of Isaiah (66:24) that describes the righteous observing with disgust the dead bodies of the rebels being burned and eaten by maggots. This is the original setting of the phrase Jesus used. John Stott pointed out: "Jesus' use of Isaiah 66:24 does not mention everlasting pain. What he says is that the worm will not die

23. Ibid., 316.
24. Though Jesus used the same term that John used (Greek: *asbestos*, unquenchable) some translations, misleadingly, render this word by the phrase "shall never be quenched," which illegitimately adds not only words, but meaning, to the statement.
25. Edward William Fudge, *The Fire That Consumes* (Lincoln, NE: iUniverse.com, Inc., 1982, 2001), 112.

and the fire will not be quenched. Nor will they—until presumably their work of destruction is done."[26]

Fudge wrote: "Both worms and fire speak of a total and final destruction. Both terms also make this a "loathsome" scene. The righteous view it with disgust but not pity. The *final* picture is one of shame, not pain."[27]

In chapter 5, we saw that the term *aionios* (often translated "eternal" or "everlasting") does not always describe phenomena that literally last forever. In fact, various meanings (in different contexts) can be effectively defended, including "long-lasting," "age-enduring," "pertaining to an [or *the*] age," and "of divine origin and character."

The New Testament makes reference to *"aionios* fire" three times. In Matthew 18:8, Jesus described the fires of Gehenna by this term, and He later spoke of *aionios* fire that was "prepared for the devil and his angels" (Matt. 25:41). If it be conceded that both passages speak of the final judgment of the lost in hell, this nonetheless tells us nothing of eternal torment there. In fact, the only other occurrence of the term *"aionios* fire" is in Jude 7, which uses the term to describe the fire that came from heaven and destroyed Sodom and Gomorrah. In that case, such a description neither conveys the notion of unendingness (since that fire is not still burning in Sodom), nor of lasting torment—since there is no reason to assume that the fires of Sodom did not quickly kill the inhabitants, ending their torment.

The expressions "unquenchable" and "eternal," therefore, when added to the generic image of fire, do not add to our knowledge of the subjective experience of those suffering its violence. For all we know, eternal and unquenchable fires burn up their victims as readily as do any other fires.

---

26. John R. W. Stott in David L. Evans and John Stott, *Evangelical Essentials: A Liberal-Evangelical Dialogue* (Downers Grove, IL: InterVarsity Press, 1988), 317.
27. Edward William Fudge, *The Fire That Consumes* (Lincoln, NE: iUniverse.com, Inc., 1982, 2001), 112.

Death, Destruction, and All That . . .

Edward William Fudge has reported: "The Old Testament utilizes some fifty Hebrew words and seventy-five figures of speech to describe the ultimate end of the wicked—and every one sounds . . . like total extinction."[28]

A very common expression used to depict the doom of the wicked is "death" and its equivalents (e.g., to die, to be slain, etc.). Traditionalists argue that "death" simply means a "separation from God" consciously endured (a definition not given in Scripture, nor in dictionaries). Philip E. Hughes wrote: "It would be hard to imagine a concept more confusing than that of death which means existing endlessly without the power of dying."[29]

Other common words used in Scripture in referring to the doom of the lost include "destruction,"[30] being "consumed,"[31] "withering,"[32] "fading,"[33] "melting away,"[34] "being no more,"[35] and "vanishing like smoke,"[36] among others. John Wenham has helpfully summarized the results of his extensive research into the various terms used in the New Testament in speaking of the judgment of the lost. He wrote: "I found 264 references to the fate of the lost. . . . It is a terrible catalogue, giving most solemn warning, yet in all but one of the 264 references there is not a word about unending torment and very many of them in their natural sense clearly refer to destruction."[37]

It seems clear that the language of the Bible, in describing the

---

28. Edward William Fudge, in *Resurrection* 93 (Fall 1990), p. 4, cited by John Wenham in *Facing Hell*, 235.

29. Philip Hughes, cited by John Wenham, *Facing Hell: The Story of a Nobody* (Carlisle, Cumbria: Paternoster Press, 1998), 223.

30. e.g., Deuteronomy 32:24; Job 21:17; Psalms 37:38; 55:23; 73:18; Proverbs 21:15; Isaiah 13:6; etc.

31. e.g., Deuteronomy 28:31; 32:24; Job 31:12; Psalm 73:19; Isaiah 1:28; Jeremiah 9:16; etc.

32. e.g., Psalms 37:2; 129:6; Isaiah 40:24.

33. e.g., Job 14:2; Isaiah 1:30; 64:6.

34. e.g., Psalms 58:8; 68:2; 112:10.

35. e.g., Psalms 37:10–11; 104:35; Ezekiel 26:21; 27:36.

36. e.g., Job 7:9; Psalm 37:20.

37. John Wenham, *Facing Hell: The Story of a Nobody* (Carlisle, Cumbria: Paternoster Press, 1998), 238, 241.

fate of sinners, is that of destruction and death, rather than of living on in torment. The fires of God's judgment consume to ashes those who are delivered to them (Mal. 4:3).

3. The Biblical Concept of Justice

There are few concerns nearer to the heart of God, as revealed in Scripture, than that of justice. God is a God of justice—both in His own character and dealings, and in the requirements placed upon man, embodied in His laws. The Bible assures us that, though the world is currently filled with injustice committed by man against fellow man, there is one ultimate Judge, and one bar at which all people can expect strict and uncompromising justice. What relationship these considerations bear to the question of hell will be immediately obvious. As Matthew Rose wrote: "Any doctrine of Hell must deal with the question of justice. . . . Ultimately, the penalty for sin will fit the crime. . . . It is important to keep in mind, during this discussion, that justice is not a separate compartment of God's character. God is not schizophrenic. God's justice is an aspect of His love. Love seeks justice."[38]

It is sensitivity to this subject that raises serious objections to traditionalism, on the one hand (which is perceived as unjustly harsh), and to universalism, on the other (which is perceived as unjustly lenient). Particularly with reference to the former, John Stott wrote:

> Fundamental to [the biblical vision of justice] is the belief that God will judge people "according to what they [have] done" (e.g. Revelation 20:12), which implies that the penalty inflicted will be commensurate with the evil done. This principle had been applied in the Jewish law courts, in which penalties were limited to an exact retribution, "life for life, eye for eye, tooth for tooth, hand for hand, foot for foot" (e.g. Exodus 21:23–25). Would there not,

---

38. Matthew Rose, in *Hell: A Fresh Evaluation of the Nature of Hell Using the Wesleyan Quadrilateral as an Epistemological Guide* (unpublished Masters thesis), 56.

then, be a serious disproportion between sins consciously committed in time and torment consciously experienced throughout eternity?[39]

Even if it could be said that man's sinfulness somehow justifies God in taking out the maximum vengeance imaginable, there is the separate question of why God would wish to do so. Since Scripture does not prescribe any generic penalty for sin beyond "death," God would seem justified in limiting any sinner's sentence to that penalty, even if more severe punishments could be justified. To suggest that God actually *wants* to punish people more than justice would absolutely require raises serious questions concerning God's personality and character. As Clark Pinnock observed: "The need to correct the traditional doctrine of hell also rests on considerations of the divine justice. What purpose of God would be served by the unending torture of the wicked except sheer vengeance and vindictiveness? Such a fate would spell endless and totally unredemptive suffering, punishment just for its own sake. But unending torment would be the kind of utterly pointless and wasted suffering which could never lead to anything good beyond it."[40]

These sentiments are shared by John Wenham, who wrote: "Whatever anyone says, unending torment speaks to me of sadism, not justice."[41]

If the conditionalist can object that the eternal torment view is too severe to harmonize with justice, the traditionalist can (and does) retort that annihilation is insufficiently severe to be truly just. Mark Talbot wrote: "Hitler, as the ultimate perpetrator of the Nazi Holocaust, ought not to be able to escape being brought to account

39. John R. W. Stott in David L. Evans and John Stott, *Evangelical Essentials: A Liberal-Evangelical Dialogue* (Downers Grove, IL: InterVarsity Press, 1988), 318.

40. Clark Pinnock, "The Destruction of the Finally Impenitent," *Criswell Theological Review* 4 (Spring 1990), 255.

41. John Wenham, "The Case for Conditional Immortality," in Nigel M. de S. Cameron, ed., *Universalism and the Doctrine of Hell* (1991; repr., Grand Rapids: Baker Book House, 1992), 187.

for his crimes against humanity by just blowing out his brains. . . . Indeed, something would be profoundly wrong with a world where its Hitlers could, when the time of reckoning drew near, just step off into nescience."[42]

What is perplexing is that such writers speak as if annihilationists do not reserve a just degree of punishment for the sinner. The conditionalist view affirms that every person will receive punishment that is precisely just, in proportion to what is actually deserved. To some writers, no amount of punishment is just, unless it is eternal. Take Robert Peterson, for example, who said: "Annihilationism is a most serious error because it leads unrepentant sinners to underestimate their fate. . . . Annihilationists can argue that the obliteration of the wicked is a terrible fate if measured against the bliss of the righteous. But when compared to suffering in hell forever, it is simply not that bad to cease to exist."[43] John Gerstner added, "The issue is really eternal versus non-eternal suffering. The conditionalist notion of temporary suffering prior to annihilation is virtually nothing compared with eternal suffering."[44]

While no one would deny that a *finite* degree of suffering is "virtually nothing" when compared to *infinite* torment, what of that? *Any* degree of penalty—even the most severe imaginable—is like "nothing" compared to *eternal* punishment.

This objection begs the question under dispute, by first assuming eternal punishment to be the norm by which other alternatives are to be evaluated, and then declaring anything less than this to be insufficiently severe.

One thing that conditionalism does provide, which traditionalism lacks, is an adequate explanation of those texts which speak of there being various degrees of punishment for different offenders

---

42. Mark Talbot, "The Morality of Everlasting Punishment," *Reformation and Revival Journal* 5 (Fall 1996), 117–34. Cited by Morgan, in *Hell Under Fire*, 208.

43. Robert A. Peterson, *Hell on Trial* (Phillipsburg, NJ: Presbyterian and Reformed Publishing, 1995), 178, 179.

44. John Gerstner, *Repent or Perish* (Morgan, PA: Soli Deo Gloria Publications, 1990), 67.

(Matt. 10:15; Luke 12:47–48). If, as traditionalists teach, the gravity of sin is determined by the status of the one sinned against, then, clearly, all sin must be treated as equal, since every sin is a slight against the same God. There can be no varying degrees between one sin and another, if all are infinite in their magnitude. All sinners must receive equally eternal punishment.

Conditionalism, on the other hand, proposes finite, proportionate punishments, in agreement with the sayings of Christ on the subject. William Fudge addressed this point from the conditionalist perspective: "There will be degrees of punishment, and the destructive process will allow plenty of opportunity for that."[45]

Boyd and Eddy summed this matter up as follows: "From the annihilationist perspective, God's justice and mercy unite in condemning the wicked to extinction. He justly punishes their sin and forbids them a place within the kingdom. Yet he mercifully annihilates them precisely so they will not endlessly endure what the traditional view says they will endure."[46]

CONCLUSION

Conditionalists, in their rejection of the traditional view of eternal torment, are often accused of taking a sentimental approach, or of being theological liberals, who do not affirm the authority of Scriptures. However, this fails to take into account the growing number of theologians and scholars who have always been recognized as leading evangelical voices, whose commitment to Scripture cannot be doubted, but who have either moved, or shown sympathy toward a move, to annihilationism. That number includes, but is not

---

45. Edward William Fudge, in Edward William Fudge and Robert A. Peterson, *Two Views of Hell: A Biblical & Theological Dialogue* (Downers Grove, IL: InterVarsity Press, 2000), 82.

46. Gregory A. Boyd and Paul R. Eddy, *Across the Spectrum: Understanding Issues in Evangelical Theology* (Grand Rapids: Baker Book House, 2002), 263.

limited to, John R. W. Stott, Clark Pinnock, Philip E. Hughes, John W. Wenham, and F. F. Bruce.

Clark Pinnock wrote: "[Traditionalists] claim that believing in everlasting conscious torment is proof of faith in biblical authority and questioning it is proof of the denial of the Bible. Though this might be true in the case of religious liberals, the reader knows by now that this is irrelevant in the present instance. I share this respect for the authority of the Bible with traditionalists and am only contesting their *interpretation* of an authoritative Bible. This is an issue of biblical hermeneutics, not biblical authority."[47]

It is obvious, from the arguments presented above, that they are entirely based upon Scripture, though emotion is not denied its proper domain. Conditionalists often admit that they find traditionalism repulsive, but this only proves that they, while being committed to faithful exegesis, have the same spark of humanity in them that advocates of all views profess to have. Leading traditionalists have also admitted that they find their own view repugnant. When it comes to making their case, annihilationists use Scripture every bit as much as do traditionalists—and, arguably, with a higher degree of literalness in their exegesis. Hundreds of verses of Scripture are presented that sound as if they support annihilation, as opposed to a handful (if we are generous) that may sound as if they affirm eternal torment.

I leave it to the reader to decide whether the biblical arguments presented are persuasive. Clark Pinnock summarized the case well: "In any case, the objections to the traditional view of the nature of hell are so strong and its supports so weak that it is likely soon to be replaced with something else. The real choice is between universalism and annihilationism, and of these two, annihilation is surely the more biblical, because it retains the realism of some people finally saying No to God without turning the notion of hell into a monstrosity."[48]

---

47. Clark Pinnock, "The Conditionalist View," in William Crockett, ed., *Four Views on Hell* (Grand Rapids: Zondervan, 1992), 158.
48. Ibid., 166.

CHAPTER 10

CROSS-EXAMINATION OF THE CASE FOR CONDITIONALISM

Annihilationism's Undesirable Bedfellows

One concern often raised by traditionalists is over the questionable company that conditional immortality, as a doctrine, keeps. Belief in annihilationism, historically, has been largely restricted to cultic groups (like the Jehovah's Witnesses) and Christian groups many view as marginal (like Seventh-Day Adventists)—which invites the suspicion that, if it were the biblical truth, it would have been recognized by more mainstream denominations and theologians.

Guilt by association is an argument that cuts more than one way. Traditionalism could be criticized for its association with the medieval church, which used its beliefs as a justification for the Inquisitions.

THE REJECTION OF INNATE IMMORTALITY

Conditionalists, by definition, believe that immortality is only conferred on those who meet the condition of faith in Christ, which means that unbelievers are not immortal, and cannot suffer eternally. The most important verse of Scripture cited for this position is 1 Timothy 6:16, where Paul affirms that Christ (or God) *"alone* has immortality." This may mean either that Christ is the only Immortal One, or that He alone has immortality to dispense to others. In any case, on the face of it, this sounds as if humans, other than Christ, do not possess immortality, unless and until they obtain it by association with Him.

In response, it may be argued that God's monopoly on immortality, in 1 Timothy 6:16, only refers to *absolute* immortality. Robert Morey wrote, "Only God has absolute immortality, seeing He has no beginning or end."[1] This leaves open the possibility that another, *derived* sort of immortality might nonetheless inhere in humans, since we were created in God's image.

Some annihilationists devote much of their time refuting what they regard to be the Platonic view of an indestructible human soul that survives eternally beyond the death of the body. They say that the doctrine of eternal torment depends upon this pagan concept, and that, once we discard it, we can see the teaching of Scripture more clearly—namely, that only the believer will live forever, and all other people will be eternally terminated.

From the universalist's side, if such conditionality is conceded, it may still be that none will finally be annihilated because all will eventually come to faith in Christ, meeting the conditions for immortality. Those who do not come to faith in this lifetime may do so eventually after this life has passed. A period of postmortem chastening would be required to bring some of the more rebellious ones around to a willingness to embrace Christ. However, this does not demand that, during the time of postmortem resistance, they must be seen as *immortal.* It would only require that their resurrected bodies be permitted to survive until their repentance has been procured. It is not beyond the range of possibilities that God may extend opportunity beyond the grave (just as He prolongs life prior

---

1. Robert A. Morey, *Death and the Afterlife* (Minneapolis: Bethany House, 1984), 218.

to the grave) without this involving the impartation of immortality. Once sinners in hell have been brought to true faith and repentance, immortality in Christ will be theirs just as it is ours who come to Christ in this lifetime.

Belief in soul-survival need not be traced to pagan sources. Appeal can be made to certain references in the Old Testament that seem to suggest consciousness in Sheol (e.g., 1 Sam. 28:11–19; Isa. 14:15ff.). The belief that the human soul survives beyond death (an almost universal intuition) may well have developed independently in several different cultures—Egyptian, Persian, Greek, and Hebrew. Only the latter would have arisen through divine revelation, and would provide the basis for Christians' belief in the immortal soul.

The doctrine of immortality seems further confirmed in various New Testament references. While conversing with the Sadducees (who denied the existence of the afterlife), Jesus declared that "all [people, including the dead] live to Him" (Luke 20:38). Additionally, Peter made reference to the unjust dead being reserved "under punishment for the day of judgment" (2 Peter 2:9), indicating that the wicked dead are consciously suffering punishment while awaiting the final judgment. In 1 Peter 3:19, Peter also speaks of Christ preaching, seemingly, to disembodied spirits in Hades. Morey wrote: "The phrase 'the spirits now in prison' clearly speaks of disembodied spirits in the netherworld."[2]

Conditionalists, of course, have their responses to these points. First, the fact that man was made *in the image of God* does not tell us whether immortality (one of God's attributes) was a feature of that "image" any more than were omnipresence, omniscience, omnipotence, or invisibility (other attributes of God).

The other points made in support of human immortality can be individually answered, but the one overarching answer to them all is that, at best, they do not demonstrate the doctrine of *immortality* so

---

2. Ibid., 214.

much as the doctrine of postmortem *soul-survival*. Even if each cited passage were taken to mean exactly what the traditionalist wishes for it to mean, each one would address only the phenomenon of human consciousness in the intermediate state (where the dead now are). None of these verses go beyond this to address whether or not people are naturally immortal—that is, capable of living throughout the eternal future.

An alternative traditionalist approach is to acknowledge frankly that the doctrine of innate immortality is a myth, but to affirm that immortality will be granted to all people at the time of the resurrection, so that both the righteous and the wicked will live forever, though in very different conditions. It is not the disembodied souls, but the *resurrected bodies* of the wicked, that will face the lake of fire (whatever may transpire there). Paul speaks of our mortal bodies putting on immortality at the resurrection (1 Cor. 15:53), so that the present nature of the soul (whether mortal or not) prior to that time is not directly relevant. As Christopher Morgan wrote: "The real issue is whether God grants endless existence to unbelievers for the purpose of punishing them. . . . The wicked will be punished consciously forever in hell, not because they exist as immortal souls but because God will sustain them."[3]

The reply of the conditionalist to this point is that, while Paul does indeed speak of *Christians* being raised in immortal bodies, no place in Scripture hints that immortality will be granted to the wicked when they are raised.

It is not difficult to see why a loving God would confer immortality upon those who are to live with Him forever. However, conditionalists complain that it is not obvious what constructive purpose is served by the impartation of immortal consciousness to those whose only end is to be tormented.

3. Christopher Morgan, "Annihilationism: Will the Unsaved Be Punished Forever?" in Christopher W. Morgan and Robert A. Peterson, eds., *Hell Under Fire* (Grand Rapids: Zondervan, 2004), 205.

Christopher Morgan offered the traditionalist answer: "What purpose could an endless hell possibly serve? To glorify God by the execution of divine justice—retributive justice."[4]

That God is glorified in the doom of the wicked (however severe it may prove to be) would be justification enough for hell's existence. All Christians desire that God should be ultimately glorified in His justice and His victory over His foes. To many, this would supply a sufficient rationale for hell's eternal torments.

THE VICTORIOUS VISION OF ETERNITY

Conditionalists argue that the Bible envisages a restored creation devoid of sin and rebellion against God, and that the best scenario to satisfy this vision is one wherein all those who finally oppose God have been removed from existence. They argue that a hell in which innumerable lost souls continue eternally in a state of hostility toward God would mar the otherwise complete perfection of the renewed creation.

The evangelical universalist (or restorationist), while agreeing that such a reconciled creation is anticipated in Scripture, disagrees as to the means by which it will be accomplished. While both conditionalism and restorationism may present a future in which every effect of the fall has been remedied, the evangelical universalist believes that the repentance and recovery of all sinners better harmonizes with Christ's stated determination "to seek and to save that which was lost" (Luke 19:10) than does the simple destruction of the stubborn. Annihilation might be the most merciful solution, if God is somehow restricted to this present lifetime in which to reach sinners. Some simply will not repent in this lifetime. Universalists believe, however, that there is no force or authority above God that

---

4. Ibid., 209.

would prevent Him from extending to sinners the opportunity for repentance beyond the grave, if He wished to do so. Until some scriptural or logical reason can be presented for placing such a limit upon God, the advocates of universal reconciliation believe that their view provides a better program for reclaiming creation than does that of the annihilationist.

On the other hand, some traditionalists do not see any conflict between the ideas of God being finally victorious, on the one hand, and of billions of people perpetually tormented in hell, on the other. In fact, such a hell, they believe, is the very definition of perfection—the perfect manifestation of God's holiness and His wrath toward sin. Isaiah 66:24, which is often seen as a description of hell, seems to portray the redeemed taking some sense of satisfaction at the viewing of the lost in the unquenched flames and the gnawing worms. Tertullian, Aquinas, and others argued that the righteous will take pleasure in the sight of the wicked writhing in agony for eternity. Perhaps our view of what defines a "perfect order" differs from God's.

THE IMAGERY OF UNENDING FIRE

Conditionalists believe that the imagery of "fire" best depicts destruction or annihilation. While this is sometimes true, it is not always so. Fire can be the cause of great, enduring pain. It can also be the agent of purification.

Traditionalists argue that, in key passages associated with hell, the concept of annihilation does not really fit the descriptions given. For example, Morey wrote, concerning Isaiah 66:24: "Since the worms are said to be 'undying' and the fire 'eternal' and 'never extinguished,' something more substantial than annihilation is called for."[5]

---

5. Robert A. Morey, *Death and the Afterlife* (Minneapolis: Bethany House, 1984), 218.

Hell's fire is said to be "everlasting." If those cast into it are annihilated, and cease to exist, to what purpose is the continuing fire? How would it continue to burn, after its fuel is gone? Since we are told, in one place, that "everlasting fire" is "prepared for the devil and his angels" (Matt. 25:41), and elsewhere, that the devil is tormented forever in the lake of fire (Rev. 20:10), many logically infer that "everlasting fire" means a place of torment forever.

Though many passages have been pointed out in which the words translated as "eternal" or "forever" do not actually describe endlessness, Morey avers that the situation is different when they are applied to eschatological subjects: "When we observe the contexts where *olam, aion,* and *aionios* are used, they do indeed mean eternal in duration when speaking of the final state."[6]

Ron Rhodes emphasized a related point:

> A critical point to make in regard to Matthew 25:46 is that this punishment is said to be eternal. There is no way that annihilationism or an extinction of consciousness can be forced into this passage. Indeed, the adjective *aionion* in this verse literally means "everlasting, without end." As noted earlier, this same adjective is predicated of God (the "eternal" God) in 1 Timothy 1:7, Romans 16:26, Hebrews 9:14, 13:8, and Revelation 4:9. The punishment of the wicked is just as eternal as our eternal God.[7]

To these things, the annihilationist answers that the adjective *aionios* does not necessarily even speak of duration—whether of life, of fire, of ruin, or of punishment. The word can simply mean that which "pertains to the age." Even the destruction of Sodom is said to have been accomplished by "*aionios* fire" (Jude 7), though that fire, apparently, lasted for a single day.

---

6. Ibid.
7. Ron Rhodes, "Is Annihilationism Biblical?," http://www.bibleprophecyblog.com /2012/10/is-annihilationism-biblical.html#.

THE VOCABULARY OF DEATH
AND DESTRUCTION

It is admitted by all that the wages of sin is "death," but the matter of what is signified by "death" does not enjoy such universal agreement. Though, in the absence of any divine revelation to the contrary, death might be regarded as the absence of life or of consciousness, this cannot be assumed to be the case. Death cannot be asserted, without proof, to mean "nonexistence."

Traditional theologians, in general, believe that "death," in certain cases, is better understood to mean "separation from God." As Peterson contended: "Death signifies separation in Scripture, including the separation of Adam and Eve from God's fellowship on the day that they 'surely die[d]," (Gen 2:17; 3:4)."[8]

There are many passages speaking of the conscious suffering of the damned. There will be "weeping and gnashing of teeth" (Matt. 13:42; 22:13 NASB). Jesus said it would be preferable to have a millstone hung around one's neck and to be cast into the sea,[9] to pluck out an eye,[10] or to cut off a hand or foot,[11] rather than to share in the ultimate judgment of sinners. Boyd and Eddy wrote: "Paul teaches that there will be 'wrath and fury' to all who reject God, adding that this fury will cause 'anguish and distress' (Rom. 2:8–9). The fact that people must be conscious to suffer anguish and distress implies that hell is a conscious state."[12]

The contention of the conditionalist would be that all such miseries may exist for a while without necessarily continuing into eternity. In fact, conditionalists expect such grief to occur at the judgment. However, since it is possible that the sinner's anguish does

---

8. Robert A. Peterson in Edward William Fudge and Robert A. Peterson, *Two Views of Hell: A Biblical and Theological Dialogue* (Downers Grove, IL: InterVarsity Press, 2000), 112.
9. Matthew 18:6; Mark 9:42.
10. Matthew 5:29; Mark 9:47.
11. Matthew 5:30; Mark 9:43, 45.
12. Gregory A. Boyd and Paul R. Eddy, *Across the Spectrum: Understanding Issues in Evangelical Theology* (Grand Rapids: Baker Book House, 2002), 257.

not last forever, one may reasonably postulate an eventual end to the suffering with the annihilation of the sufferer.

Conditionalists see death as *extinction*, and identify a variety of terms employed in the Bible that sound as if they are describing the utter annihilation or termination of the wicked. Such terms as "destroy," "vanish," "be no more," and "melt away" are often pointed to in support of the thesis that hell is a place of complete annihilation. Even traditionalist Robert A. Peterson has conceded that "many passages that contain 'the vocabulary of destruction' could, if taken by themselves, be construed to teach the extermination of the wicked: John 10:28; 17:12; Romans 2:12; 9:22; Philippians 1:28; 3:19; 1 Thessalonians 5:3; Hebrews 10:39; James 4:12; and 2 Peter 3:7, 9."[13]

However, two important observations may caution against seeing such language as teaching ultimate annihilation of the lost at the final judgment:

1. These terms are usually found in poetic passages, which use figurative and impressionistic imagery. These often cannot be pressed as literal descriptions of reality, any more than can the images of a land "flowing with milk and honey" (Ex. 3:8), or trees clapping their "hands" (Isa. 55:12).

2. Almost all of these passages describe temporal judgments of individuals or nations within this present world, not eschatological details of the final judgment. Thus they tell us little or nothing about conditions associated with the lake of fire. Boyd and Eddy make this point: "The majority of passages that speak of the wicked being utterly destroyed are taken from the Old Testament and refer not to the ultimate destiny of the wicked but to the earthly fate of the wicked (e.g., Ps. 37:38; Isa. 1:28, 30–31)."[14]

---

13. Robert A. Peterson, *Hell on Trial* (Phillipsburg, NJ: Presbyterian and Reformed Publishing, 1995), 163.

14. Gregory A. Boyd and Paul R. Eddy, *Across the Spectrum: Understanding Issues in Evangelical Theology* (Grand Rapids: Baker Book House, 2002), 259.

Robert A. Peterson makes the same observation: "The great majority of the Old Testament passages that Fudge cites in support of conditionalism do not speak of the final fate of the wicked at all. Instead, they speak of God visiting the wicked with premature death."[15]

While a few of the passages conditionalists cite concerning "destruction" do, in fact, refer to eschatological judgment (e.g., Matt. 10:28; 2 Thess. 1:9), it does not follow that "destruction," in such places, must mean "annihilation." The Greek verb *apollumi* (destroy) and the noun *olethros* (destruction) can mean "to lose, or be lost" and "to be ruined," with no connotation of annihilation. Douglas Moo explains:

> Definitive conclusions about the meaning of these words in each case are not easy to attain. But this much can be said: The words need not mean "destruction" in the sense of "extinction." . . . None of the key terms usually has this meaning in the Old and New Testaments. Rather, they usually refer to the situation of a person or object that has lost the essence of its nature or function. . . . The key words for "destroy" and "destruction" can also refer to land that has lost its fruitfulness. . . . In none of these cases do the objects cease to exist; they cease to be useful or to exist in their original, intended state.[16]

Even Harold Guillebaud, himself a conditionalist, admitted: "It is not denied that *if* it were clear beyond question from Bible teaching elsewhere that the doom of the lost will be everlasting torment, it would be quite possible to understand 'death,' 'destruction' and the like as meaning a wretched and ruined existence."[17]

The response to this vocabulary of destruction is somewhat

---

15. Robert A. Peterson in Edward William Fudge and Robert A. Peterson, *Two Views of Hell: A Biblical and Theological Dialogue* (Downers Grove, IL: InterVarsity Press, 2000), 91.

16. Douglas Moo, "Paul on Hell," in Christopher W. Morgan and Robert A. Peterson, eds., *Hell Under Fire* (Grand Rapids: Zondervan, 2004), 104f.

17. Harold E. Guillebaud, *The Righteous Judge* (n.p., 1941), 16.

different from the universal reconciliation side of the aisle. As noted in chapter 8, restorationists believe that whatever "destruction" or "ruination" may be alluded to, it may eventually serve to a good end, if it is followed by repentance and restoration. Universalists sometimes[18] take the position that the "destruction" spoken of is redemptive, being that of the flesh, or of the sinful nature, rather than of the person himself. The same word "destruction" (*olethros*), found in 2 Thessalonians 1:9, is used by Paul in 1 Corinthians 5:5, where the "destruction of the flesh" is seen as a means by which a sinner's spirit might ultimately be saved. Thomas Allin wrote: "When sinners, who are immortal, are thrown into [hell], their sins will be destroyed, but they themselves will be saved. See 1 Corinthians 3:12–15 and 5:5."[19]

Thomas Talbott wrote: "From the perspective of those already crucified in Christ, the destruction of the false self is clearly a good thing; it is liberation, salvation itself . . . one way or another, God *will* destroy the false self and will destroy it forever."[20]

The restorationist points out that the word *apollumi* can also be translated as "lost." In some cases, it refers to a condition from which a sheep, a coin, or a prodigal may be recovered (Luke 15). At least in such cases, it clearly does not speak of annihilation, but of a condition from which recovery is possible.

JUSTICE IS COMPROMISED BY ANNIHILATIONISM

Several objections, relevant to God's administration of justice, are raised against conditionalism—most of which come from the traditionalist camp. We will briefly consider each of them.

---

18. e.g., Thomas Talbott, *The Inescapable Love of God* (Boca Raton, FL: Universal Publishers, 1999), 95.
19. Thomas Allin and Mark T. Chamberlain, *Every Knee Shall Bow* (Oxnard, CA: self-published by Mark T. Chamberlain, 2005), 111.
20. Talbott, *The Inescapable Love of God*, 102.

Wrath Is Also a Major Attribute of God

Traditionalists believe that annihilation is too soft on sin and too strong on the love of God. It is argued that God's wrath (identified with eternal torment) is sacrificed to sentimentalism when too much emphasis is placed upon God's love for humanity. J. Gresham Machen reminds us that wrath is also a significant attribute of God: "The New Testament clearly speaks of the wrath of God and the wrath of Jesus Himself; and all the teaching of Jesus presupposes a divine indignation against sin. With what possible right, then, can those who reject this vital element in Jesus' teaching and example regard themselves as true disciples of His?"[21]

D. A. Carson concurs: "The point that cannot be escaped, is that God's wrath is not some minor and easily dismissed peripheral element to the Bible's plot-line. . . . It is not going too far to say that the Bible would not have a plot-line at all if there were no wrath."[22]

To such statements, most annihilationists would reply that their system does not neglect to place proper emphasis upon God's holiness and wrath. There is room for the perfect and complete expression of wrath in the conditionalist system, but they would deny that "holiness" and "wrath" are concepts necessarily equivalent to "eternal torment." In the Old Testament, God's "wrath" was often equivalent to "killing," "devouring," or "consuming" (not eternally tormenting) the wicked.[23] Likewise, in the majority of Old Testament instances God's "wrath" is exhibited in various temporal judgments upon wicked societies,[24] making no allusion to eternal ramifications. Such expressions of God's wrath, by being temporal and finite, do not disqualify as vindications of God's holiness.

---

21. J. G. Machen, *Christianity and Liberalism* (Grand Rapids: Wm. B. Eerdmans, 1923), 12.

22. D. A. Carson, *The Gagging of God* (Grand Rapids: Zondervan, 1996), 223.

23. e.g., Exodus 15:7; 22:24; 32:10, 12; Psalms 21:9; 59:13; Ezekiel 22:31, etc.

24. Deuteronomy 29:23; Joshua 22:20; 2 Kings 22:17; Isaiah 9:19; 60:10; Jeremiah 21:5; 50:13; Ezekiel 21:31; Zechariah 7:12; etc.

Annihilation Is No Punishment

A second complaint against annihilationism is that justice requires appropriate degrees of punishment for criminal behavior. Without suffering, punishment is meaningless, and one ceases to consciously suffer when annihilated. Boyd and Eddy have expressed this thus: "It does not seem as though annihilation is an adequate punishment for the wicked. We instinctively want criminals to pay for their crimes. If criminals simply cease to exist, however, their crimes are not atoned for. Justice is not served. True, they miss out on eternal joy in heaven, but what punishment is this if the wicked are not around to experience their loss?"[25]

Ron Rhodes has added his voice in confirmation: "By no stretch of the imagination can the punishment spoken of in Matthew 25:46 be defined as a nonsuffering extinction of consciousness. Indeed, if actual suffering is lacking, then so is punishment. Let us be clear on this: punishment entails suffering. And suffering necessarily entails consciousness."[26]

The reply of the conditionalist to this point would be similar to that offered to the last argument (considered above): conditionalism does not rule out either conscious suffering or adequate punishment—but conscious punishment (as all criminal justice systems among men demonstrate) does not have to extend into eternity.

Why Raise the Dead Just to Annihilate Them?

If sinners are ultimately going to be annihilated anyway, why would God not simply leave them dead? There seems to be no reason to resurrect the lost if they are simply going to be cast into the lake of fire to burn up into oblivion. Boyd and Eddy are not alone in

---

25. Gregory A. Boyd and Paul R. Eddy, *Across the Spectrum: Understanding Issues in Evangelical Theology* (Grand Rapids: Baker Book House, 2002), 258.

26. Ron Rhodes, "Is Annihilationism Biblical?," http://www.bibleprophecyblog.com /2012/10/is-annihilationism-biblical.html#.

noting that "it seems odd that God would resurrect people from the dead only to annihilate them."[27]

Conditionalists, however, do not generally believe that God raises the wicked only to annihilate them. He raises them in order to judge, sentence, and punish them. Their end will be annihilation, but not necessarily immediately after the resurrection. Only God knows what degree or duration of punishment is truly deserved, and He is committed to judging all people justly. Since not all people deserve the same judgment, and (as conditionalists argue) since no mortal deserves torment throughout eternity, each sinner's suffering will be proportionate to his or her desert, and will end with extinction.

CHRIST'S ATONEMENT IS COMPROMISED BY ANNIHILATIONISM

Since God paid an infinite price, in the death of His eternal Son, to save mankind from penalties, it follows that the penalties from which mankind had to be saved were also infinite. Since conditionalism does not accept that sin's penalties are infinite, it would follow that sin's remedy—Christ's sacrifice—would not be infinite. Conditionalism, thus, is seen as cheapening Christ's atoning work. Larry Pettegrew expressed this concern: "If it were temporary punishment that Christ paid for, His death was certainly less significant than if he took our eternal punishment."[28]

W. G. T. Shedd has similarly argued: "A suffering that in time would cease, surely would not justify such a strange and stupendous sacrifice as that of the only-begotten and well-beloved Son of God.

---

27. Gregory A. Boyd and Paul R. Eddy, *Across the Spectrum: Understanding Issues in Evangelical Theology* (Grand Rapids: Baker Book House, 2002), 256.

28. Larry D. Pettegrew, "A Kinder, Gentler Theology of Hell?," *The Master's Seminary Journal* 9/2 (Fall 1998), 203–217 (online version).

We affirm therefore that the doctrine of Christ's atonement stands or falls with that of endless punishment."[29]

This is, obviously, an abstract argument, and depends upon seeing the value of the atonement in terms of the magnitude of the punishment averted, rather than in terms of the quantity of sins to be remitted. The Bible is far from clear on this matter, and one might be justified in saying that the atoning payment must necessarily have been of infinite value, not because of the magnitude of the punishment, but because of the need, with one sacrifice, to atone for innumerable sins of innumerable sinners. The particular punishment from which each redeemed sinner was thereby rescued—whether an infinite or a finite one—would then be a side issue. According to Scripture, that from which Christ redeemed sinners was their "sins" (Matt. 1:21) and their "every lawless deed" (Titus 2:14)—not simply from some particular kind or quantity of punishment.

Some conditionalists actually appeal to the atonement as an argument *in support of* their own position. Jesus did not endure an eternity in hell for mankind. Everywhere in Scripture, the penalty Christ is said to have paid for sins is "death."[30] This would be appropriate if the wages of sin is, in fact, death, and not eternal torment in hell.

Robert Morey answered this argument by pointing out that the perceived disproportion is "solved by the implications of Christ's divine nature, which is eternal, and the infinite value of Christ's sacrifice."[31] Robert A. Peterson expanded upon this point: "Because of the infinite dignity of Christ's person, his sufferings, though finite in duration, were of infinite weight on the scales of divine justice (much as his righteousness, though displayed during his incarnation over a finite period, is of infinite weight). As God incarnate, Jesus was

---

29. W. G. T. Shedd, *Orthodoxy and Heterodoxy* (New York: Charles Scribner's Sons, 1893), 185.

30. Romans 5:6, 8; 6:3, 5, 10; 1 Corinthians 15:3; 2 Corinthians 5:15; 1 Thessalonians 5:10; Revelation 5:9.

31. Robert A. Morey, *Death and the Afterlife*, 103.

capable of suffering in six hours on the cross what we can suffer only over an infinite period of time."[32]

Like many other arguments used by all sides in the debate, this is a philosophical, not a biblically supported, argument.

MOTIVATION IS COMPROMISED BY ANNIHILATIONISM

Whenever we tamper with the doctrine of hell, we risk incurring unintended consequences. One such consequence is that we may reduce the sinner's—or even the Christian's—motivation to do right. Common sense would dictate that many people will be more inclined to repent or to obey God under the threat of the traditional doctrine than under some lesser threat. Robert A. Peterson worries that "[annihilationism] leads unrepentant sinners to underestimate their fate. Would not the ungodly be more inclined to live selfishly their whole lives, without thought of God, if they expected after death to face ultimate extinction rather than eternal punishment?"[33]

Along the same lines, Boyd and Eddy wrote: "Many nonbelievers do not expect to live on after death. The threat of annihilation is thus no incentive to trust God for salvation."[34] Robert A. Morey thinks that annihilationism leads to hedonism: "If annihilationism is true, then the wicked should practice the gross ethics of hedonism. A lifetime of being a self-conscious ego who experiences the joys of life is intrinsically better than nonexistence. After all, a wicked life is still better than no life at all . . . annihilationists have never been able to

32. Robert A. Peterson in Edward William Fudge and Robert A. Peterson, *Two Views of Hell: A Biblical and Theological Dialogue* (Downers Grove, IL: InterVarsity Press, 2000), 175.

33. Robert A. Peterson, *Hell on Trial* (Phillipsburg, NJ: Presbyterian and Reformed Publishing, 1995), 178.

34. Gregory A. Boyd and Paul R. Eddy, *Across the Spectrum: Understanding Issues in Evangelical Theology* (Grand Rapids: Baker Book House, 2002), 258.

explain why hedonism is not the most obvious and logical way of life if their position is true."[35]

This is, no doubt, a good example of careless speech uttered in the heat of debate, since we would not expect a Reformed scholar, like Morey, to affirm as a conviction that, were hell *not* to be eternal, "the wicked should practice the gross ethics of hedonism." The word "should" is an expression of ethical or moral propriety. We may be certain that Morey does not wish to imply that conditionalists like John R. W. Stott, Clark Pinnock, John Wenham, Philip Hughes, Gregory Boyd, et al., along with Seventh-Day Adventists, have lived hedonistic lives, or, at least, could not find in their theology any compelling motivations not to do so.

However, such arguments as these are often raised in traditionalist attacks against conditionalism. In reading them, one cannot help but wonder:

1. What is it about the hedonistic life that these traditionalists think to be so desirable?
2. Do they believe that those who have followed such a course are truly the happiest class of people?
3. Is their own abstinence from such behavior motivated only by their fear of hell?

They certainly cannot believe what their words suggest—namely, that the only legitimate motive for following God's ways would be the selfish consideration of personal consequences. It is no wonder that many non-Christians view Christianity as a fear-based religion.

The pros and cons of exploiting the fear of hell as an evangelistic tactic may be debated. In any case, conviction over a life of having fallen short of God's glory (Rom. 3:23), a proper reflection on the goodness of God (Rom. 2:4), and a consequent love for the God

---

35. Robert A. Morey, *Death and the Afterlife* (Minneapolis: Bethany House, 1984), 156f.

who first loved us (1 John 4:19) should at least be acknowledged as legitimate alternative motivations for abandoning a life of hedonism.

Many traditionalist writers also think that the cause of world missions would suffer if conditionalism were to replace the traditional understanding of hell. Robert A. Peterson is among them: "I fear that if annihilationism is widely accepted by Christians, that will hinder the missionary enterprise. Many people have devoted their lives to bringing the gospel to the unsaved around the globe. Would they continue to do so if they really thought that the worst fate awaiting those who reject Jesus is final extinction? I seriously doubt it."[36]

Yet, some missionaries have valued winning the lost *for the glory of God*, rather than for their own sakes. There is a famous story about young Moravian missionaries, who sold themselves into actual slavery in order to gain access to unconverted slaves who had been forcibly kept isolated from the gospel in the West Indies. The last words of the young missionaries to their families, which they called out across the breakers as their ship pulled away from their homeland, are reported to have been, "May the Lamb that was slain receive the reward of His suffering!"

This illustrates that at least *some* missionaries make huge sacrifices, motivated by a love for God and for Christ. This is God-centered, rather than man-centered, motivation—little understood in modern times. It is doubtful that faithful, properly motivated servants of God would do anything differently were they to alter their opinions about hell. Those who are not sufficiently motivated to serve God by their love for Him might best serve the interest of missions by staying at home.

---

36. Robert A. Peterson, *Hell on Trial* (Phillipsburg, NJ: Presbyterian and Reformed Publishing, 1995), 179.

PART 4

THE GOOD NEWS IS BETTER THAN YOU THOUGHT

CHAPTER 11

THE CASE FOR RESTORATIONISM

Am I not destroying my enemies when I make friends
of them?
    —*Abraham Lincoln*

If you are going through hell, keep going.
    —*Winston Churchill*

SUMMARY OF THE BASIC POSITION

From beginning to end, the Bible tells the story of the one purpose of God throughout history—namely, the recovery of the creation from the effects of the fall. We find the creation fallen in the beginning of Genesis, and we see it recovered at the end of Revelation. The material between unfolds God's program by which He sets about to reach this final goal. It is to be accomplished through Jesus Christ. Jesus's self-announced mission was "to seek and to save that which was lost" (Luke 19:10). In Colossians 1:16 Christ is said to have been the agent through whom "all things" were created; four verses later He is identified as the agent through whom the same "all things" are to be reconciled.

Evangelical universalism, which is also called "universal reconciliation" or "restorationism," is the view that God intends to save every person, whom He originally made in His image and for His glory, and that no opposing power can prevent God from fulfilling His sovereign purpose. Notwithstanding the denials from some of its critics, restorationism was a respectable theological option in the early church. While both annihilationism and universalism were eventually marginalized (and even anathematized by the Roman Catholic Church), all three of the current views were held and taught by Christian leaders of the first rank until at least the fifth century. We saw this documented in chapter 6.

Most evangelical universalists today would agree with the basic contours of Origen's views on this subject, while disagreeing with him on a number of peripheral theological positions. What was Origen's view? William Barclay wrote: "Origen believed that after death there were many who would need prolonged instruction, the sternest discipline, even the severest punishment before they were fit for the presence of God."[1]

Unlike the Catholic doctrine of purgatory, which proposes a third state between heaven and hell, where those not yet fit for heaven may experience postmortem purging, Origen assigned this disciplinary role to hell itself. Also, unlike pluralistic universalists (of whom John Hick is a notable modern example), the evangelical restorationist believes that salvation is through faith in Christ alone. There is no suggestion that other religions, or general good works, can provide the necessary atonement for sins. The blood of Jesus is necessary for that, as surely in this system as in any other evangelical alternative. The outstanding distinctive of the restorationist doctrine is that God may continue to draw sinners to Himself, not only in this lifetime, but also after they have died and are in hell.

Evangelical universalism does not deny that a great deal of suffering may be experienced in hell. That suffering, however, is neither infinite, meaningless, nor merely destructive, but tends to a

---

1. *William Barclay: A Spiritual Autobiography* (Grand Rapids: Wm. B. Eerdmans, 1977), 65–67.

positive end—the repentance and restoration of every lost sheep that has strayed from the Good Shepherd. William Barclay continued: "Origen did not eliminate hell; he believed that some people would have to go to heaven via hell. . . . And so the choice is whether we accept God's offer and invitation willingly, or take the long and terrible way round through ages of purification."[2]

Why would brilliant, orthodox theologians, like Origen and Gregory of Nyssa, advocate such a doctrine, which seems so marginal to modern evangelicals? This chapter will explore that question, by examining the writings of modern advocates of the view. With reference to the ancient Christians' acceptance of the doctrine, Barclay explained:

> Gregory of Nyssa offered three reasons why he believed in Universalism. First, he believed in it because of the character of God. "Being good, God entertains pity for fallen man; being wise, he is not ignorant of the means for his recovery." Second, he believed in it because of the nature of evil. . . . Evil is essentially negative and doomed to non-existence. Third, he believed in it because of the purpose of punishment. The purpose of punishment is always remedial. . . . Punishment will hurt, but it is like the fire which separates the alloy from the gold; it is like the surgery which removes the diseased thing.[3]

In the following pages, we will examine the main arguments found in the modern literature of evangelical universalism. They will be found to fall under a few broad headings, namely:

1. Restorationism is logical.
2. God is love, which has ramifications.

---

2. Ibid.
3. Ibid.

3. There is nothing preventing God from extending the opportunities for reconciliation beyond the point of death.
4. God is determined to restore all that was lost.
5. Christ is Victor!

RESTORATIONISM IS LOGICAL

Talbott's Template

Evangelical philosopher Thomas Talbott has attempted to make the case for restorationism accessible by presenting a series of three theological statements—all of which are affirmed by one or another mainstream group, but at least one of which must logically be rejected, if the other two are valid. Here are the three propositions:

1. It is God's redemptive purpose for the world (and therefore His will) to reconcile all sinners to Himself.
2. It is within God's power to achieve His redemptive purpose for the world.
3. Some sinners will never be reconciled to God, and God will therefore either consign them to a place of eternal punishment, from which there will be no hope of escape, or put them out of existence altogether.[4]

That these three propositions cannot all be true is self-evident and is acknowledged by all. No theological system attempts to harmonize them, but every system must jettison one or the other, retaining the other two, in order to maintain its own internal coherence.

The first proposition is rejected by the Augustinian/Calvinist, or Reformed, theology. Affirming that God sovereignly fulfills His ultimate purposes (#2) and that some will ultimately not be saved (#3),

---

4. Thomas Talbott, *The Inescapable Love of God* (Boca Raton, FL: Universal Publishers, 1999), 43.

it becomes necessary to refute #1, and to affirm that God redemptively loves only a subgroup within humanity, a group labeled "the elect." Thus God is able to save all that He really chooses to save, while others will remain unsaved.

The second proposition is rejected by the Wesleyan/Arminian theology, which affirms that God desires to save all (#1) and also that not all will be saved (#3). If these two are correct, then #2 cannot be accepted, which states that God saves all that He truly wishes to save. Thus the Arminian theology asserts that human free will is the wrench in the works, which prevents some from ultimately believing in Christ, though God intensely desires that they would do so.

Both of these major theological camps accept proposition #3, that some will be finally damned—but at what expense do they do so? In order to affirm their view of hell (a subject seldom mentioned in Scripture), each camp is compelled to deny some other significant, oft-repeated proposition about God. Given the large number of scriptural affirmations supporting the first two propositions, one would imagine that any view to which evangelicals seem willing to sacrifice either of them must itself enjoy enormous exegetical support. But this is hardly the case! We would be lucky to find half a dozen verses of Scripture that seemingly affirm the specific idea that some will be *eternally* lost to God, either by eternal torment or by annihilation,[5] whereas the verses asserting the first two propositions number in the scores, if not the hundreds.[6]

We will consider, in this chapter, an array of scriptural passages defending the first two propositions, which, if true, must lead to the rejection of the third. Thus, Talbott argues, even if there were no

---

5. This statement is justified by the fact that, even though traditionalism and conditionalism each present a large number of texts in their arguments, very few of them can be said to contain actual wording establishing the finality of damnation.

6. This can be demonstrated by the published polemics for the two major systems: Standard published defenses of Calvinism, typically, employ approximately fifty biblical passages; and those defending Arminianism draw upon at least as many, if not more (since every command and every divine complaint in Scripture implicitly argues for human free will).

verses affirming Christian universalism directly (but, he believes, there *are*), the doctrine could be established logically by proving God's universal love and His undefeatable sovereignty. Thus, the evangelical universalist accepts the first two of Talbott's propositions, and rejects the third.

> Every reflective Christian who takes a stand with respect to our three propositions must reject a proposition for which there is at least some *prima facie* biblical support. . . . If one rejects proposition (1), then one . . . must concede . . . that God's love has definite limits and does not extend to all created persons. . . .
>
> Those who reject proposition (2) can no longer regard God as being sovereign or undefeated with respect to his own redemptive purposes; he simply does his best to cut his losses, to minimize the defeat, and to produce the most favorable balance of good over evil that he can.
>
> Those who reject proposition (3), however, can continue to believe *both* that God's love is unlimited *and* that his redemptive purposes are unthwarted.[7]

The Wrong Premise Can Mislead

Restorationists believe that traditionalists and conditionalists have placed the emphasis in theology where the Bible does not place it. Advocates of all three views acknowledge that some biblical texts sound somewhat (or very) universalistic, while others sound as if hell is the ultimate, irreversible destiny awaiting those who reject Christ in this lifetime.

All can see that these two sets of texts exist, and that some tension exists between them, requiring harmonization. The traditionalist and the conditionalist take the damnation texts to be determinative,

---

7. Thomas Talbott, *The Inescapable Love of God* (Boca Raton, FL: Universal Publishers, 1999), 47f.

and seek to interpret the universalistic texts in harmony with each one's respective take on that theme.

The universalist does just the opposite, arguing that the sovereignty and benevolence of God are the primary themes revealed in Scripture and in Christ, in harmony with which the relatively few texts about damnation ought to be required to conform. This can be done more readily than most non-universalists think, simply by entertaining the possibility of repentance after death. One can then affirm both the reality of hell and the eventual salvation of all for whom Christ died. It's a win-win, for God and for the theologians seeking the uniting principle in theology! As Mercy Aiken wrote in "If Hell Is Real":

> Traditional doctrines teach us to interpret the "victorious" scriptures in the light of the "judgment" scriptures. But what if God wants us to see it the other way around? . . . Is not Christ's victory the greatest revelation in the Bible? Standing on this highest peak—that is, the finished work of the cross, causes us to see a much larger and far more beautiful panoramic view of God's plan throughout the ages. We do not throw out one set of Scriptures in favor of another. Rather, we seek to harmonize them. . . . It is time to stop ignoring the parts of the Bible that do not fit in with our theology.[8]

The gospel is the "good news," the proclamation that God has acted to fulfill His gracious purpose, which He planned from eternity past to work out through eternity future. We should expect that a story authored by God would be the very best story imaginable—or even unimaginable! Can we not imagine that God would recover all that was lost to Him? Do we think He is not wise or competent enough to acquire what He sets out to retrieve for Himself?

---

8. Mercy Aiken, "If Hell Is Real," www.tentmaker.org/articles/ifhellisrealprintable.htm.

Scripture affirms that God "is able to do exceedingly abundantly above all that we ask or think" (Eph. 3:20). Why shouldn't the good news of Jesus Christ be expected to be a great story? As Rob Bell argued: "It's important that we be honest about the fact that some stories are better than others. Telling a story in which billions of people spend forever somewhere in the universe trapped in a black hole of endless torment and misery with no way out isn't a very good story. Telling a story about a God who inflicts unrelenting punishment on people because they didn't do or say or believe the correct things in a brief window of time called life isn't a very good story."[9]

Too Good to Be True?

Our first impression may be that the evangelical universalist story is "too good to be true." However, given the infinite wisdom of God, who contrived and carried out the plan, and who declared that His gospel is "good tidings of great joy . . . to *all people*" (Luke 2:10), one might reply that this view is actually "too good *not* to be true." Why would a God of infinite goodness and infinite wisdom fail to come up with the best of all plans? Is He less imaginative than we are—or less compassionate? We should give God credit for having had a perfect plan on the drawing board before He ever laid the first brick of the created order.

The logic of this position also provides the only fully satisfying answer to the age-old conundrum: How can suffering coexist in a universe with a perfectly good and all-powerful God? We can blame human free will, if we wish, but that does not remove the difficulty as to why God, knowing that men would use their free will thus, did not either refrain from creating them in the first place, or else ordain the most optimal outcome that He could engineer.

If all of God's judgments are remedial, and are employed to bring "many sons to glory" (Heb. 2:10) then there is no mystery

---

9. Rob Bell, *Love Wins* (New York: HarperCollins, 2011), 110.

why He would allow a finite season of suffering (in this life, and possibly in the next) to prepare His children for infinite and eternal delight—both to themselves and to Him.

Talbott wrote:

> I assume that God permits no evil, however horrendous it may appear to us in the present, that he cannot eventually turn to good; and he permits no harm to befall his loved ones that he cannot in the end repair. I also assume that, given a long enough stretch of time, the Hound of Heaven can overcome all of the obstacles that our wrong choices present and can thus achieve *all* of his redemptive purposes; in that respect, he is like the grand chessmaster who, though exercising no direct causal control over the moves of a novice, is nonetheless able to checkmate the novice in the end.[10]

GOD IS LOVE, WHICH HAS RAMIFICATIONS

God's Love Is Universal

If we begin with the biblical affirmation that "God is love" (1 John 4:8), we are compelled to believe that love is not simply one of His characteristics, which may be counterbalanced or cancelled out by other traits, at times. Rather, the verse affirms something about God's unchangeable nature—love is the essence of His nature. The form of the biblical declaration is identical to two others, both in John's writings: "God is Spirit" (John 4:24), and "God is light" (1 John 1:5). To say, as some do, that "God is love toward the elect, but not toward all people" would make as much sense as saying that "God is Spirit to some, but He is material to others." The similar

---

10. Thomas Talbott, *The Inescapable Love of God* (Boca Raton, FL: Universal Publishers, 1999), 183.

statement, "God is light," means that "in Him is no darkness at all" (1 John 1:5). If God is light, then He is light to all—in fact, elsewhere, John tells us of Christ that He is "the true Light which gives light to every man coming into the world" (John 1:9). If God is, in the same sense and degree, "love," then that love must be universal, embracing all that He has made. Whatever God does, He does because He is love. This includes His dealings with every human being. Thomas Allin wrote: "God is not anger though He can be angry, God is not vengeance though He does avenge. These are attributes, love is essence. Therefore, God is unchangeably love. In judgment He is love, in wrath He is love, in vengeance He is love—'love first, and last, and without end.'"[11]

Since God is unchangingly love, this fact is manifested and celebrated throughout the Old Testament as well as in the New. Consider how often God's Word tries to get this across to Israel:

> The LORD is merciful and gracious,
> Slow to anger, and abounding in mercy. (Ps. 103:8)

> He is good!
> For His mercy endures forever. (Ps. 136:1)
>   (Repeated twenty-six times)

> The LORD is gracious and full of compassion,
> Slow to anger and great in mercy. (Ps. 145:8)

> His anger is but for a moment,
> His favor is for life;
> Weeping may endure for a night,
> But joy comes in the morning. (Ps. 30:5)

---

11. Thomas Allin, *Christ Triumphant*, 1878, repr. 9th ed. (Canyon Country, CA: Concordant, n.d.), 76f.

I know that You are a gracious and merciful God, slow to anger
and abundant in lovingkindness, One who relents from doing harm.
(Jonah 4:2)

> He delights in mercy . . .
> will again have compassion on us,
> and will subdue our iniquities. (Mic. 7:18–19)

Love suffers long and is kind . . . endures all . . . never fails. (1 Cor.
13:4–8)

> The LORD is good to all,
> And His tender mercies are over all His works. (Ps. 145:9)

He is kind to the unthankful and evil. Therefore be merciful, just
as your Father also is merciful. (Luke 6:35–36)

God so loved *the world*. (John 3:16)

Even human fathers, though evil, know to do good to their
children. Jesus asked, "How much more" is this the case with the
perfect Father (Matt. 7:9–11; Luke 11:11–13)? One misleading notion
among many evangelicals is that God is not the Father of all people,
and that His special love is only for "the elect," who are His *real*
children. This is based upon a misunderstanding of biblical phrases
like "children of God" (when applied distinctly to Christians—John
1:12; 1 John 3:2), and "children of the devil" (applied to those who
hate and murder—John 8:44; 1 John 3:10, 12). These expressions
describe the loyalties and affinities of different people in their present course of life. They do not mean that Satan is anything like a
literal father, having begotten and brought these people into the
world. One of Cain's descendants was said to be the "father" of all
who live in tents and have livestock, and another the "father" of all

musicians (Gen. 4:20–21). This clearly does not mean that every migrant rancher or every guitarist was born from these family lines. It means that those in such vocations are following the precedents of the men who first pioneered those activities. Likewise the idea that some are "children" of Satan means that they are people who follow his rebellious vocation. Satan is neither their creator nor their literal father—as God is. In that sense, God is the Father of all. As Thomas Allin clarified: "We are told God is not the Father of all men; He is only their Creator! What a total misapprehension these words imply. What do we mean by paternity and the obligations it brings? The idea rests essentially on the communication of life to the child by the parent . . . assuming all the responsibility involved in the very act of creating a reasonable immortal spirit."[12]

If the prodigal son story teaches us anything about God, it is that He is the Father even of those who are in rebellion against Him. The son in the far country was not enjoying any of the benefits associated with that relationship (he was "dead" and "lost" to his father), but even in that state, he was, in reality and in his father's heart, declared to be his father's "son" (Luke 15:24). Allin, again, wrote: "If our sin and rebellion has caused our Father to disown us, how could He have said, 'Return, you backsliding children, and I will heal your backslidings' (Jer. 3:22)? Or what was Jesus saying in His parable of the prodigal son in Lu. 15:11–32? Does the prodigal son not represent all the Father's wayward children? Though he had fallen into sin in all its degradation, he never ceased being a son. . . . [God declares], 'Behold, all souls are mine' (Ez. 18:4)."[13]

While earthly fathers often exhibit the sinful tendency to show partiality to one child over another, ultimately, God loves all of those whom He has brought into existence. His universal and impartial fatherhood of all humanity is declared in both the Old and the New Testaments:

---

12. Ibid., 173.
13. Ibid.

Have we not all one Father? Has not one God created us? (Mal. 2:10)

Men of Athens . . . "We also are His children." Being then the children of God. . . . (Acts 17:22, 28–29 NASB)

I bow my knees to the Father . . . from whom the whole family in . . . earth is named. (Eph. 3:14–15)

The Father . . . without partiality judges. (1 Peter 1:17)

There is no partiality with God. (Rom. 2:11; see also Acts 10:34; Gal. 2:6; Eph. 6:9; Col. 3:25)

Universal Love Seeks Universal Salvation of Mankind

God's universal love for His creation translates into His unwillingness to lose any of it to His enemy. A father cannot resign himself to the loss of any child who could otherwise have been saved through his efforts. Nor is God willing that any person made in His image be permanently lost. William Barclay reminds us:

If God was no more than a King or Judge, then it would be possible to speak of his triumph if his enemies were agonizing in hell or were totally and completely obliterated and wiped out. But God is not only King and Judge, God is Father—he is indeed Father more than anything else. No father could be happy while there were members of his family for ever in agony. No father would count it a triumph to obliterate the disobedient members of his family. The only triumph a father can know is to have all his family back home.[14]

Is this Barclay's private opinion? Is it not declared repeatedly in Scripture? Let the reader judge:

---

14. Excerpted from *William Barclay: A Spiritual Autobiography* (Grand Rapids: Wm. B. Eerdmans, 1977), 65–67.

> Look to Me, and be saved,
> All you ends of the earth! (Isa. 45:22)

[I came] to save *the world*. (John 12:47)

God was in Christ reconciling *the world* to Himself. (2 Cor. 5:19)

The grace of God has appeared, bringing salvation to *all men*. (Titus 2:11 NASB)

He Himself is the propitiation for our sins, and not for ours only but also for the *whole world*. (1 John 2:2)

God our Savior, who desires *all men* to be saved and to come to the knowledge of the truth. For there is one God and one Mediator between God and men, the Man Christ Jesus, who gave Himself a ransom *for all*. (1 Tim. 2:3–6)

For to this end we both labor and suffer reproach, because we trust in the living God, who is the Savior of *all men*, especially of those who believe. (1 Tim. 4:10)

The Lord is not slack concerning His promise, as some count slackness, but is longsuffering toward us, not willing that *any* should perish but that *all* should come to repentance. (2 Peter 3:9)

He purposed in Himself, that in . . . the fullness of the times He might gather together in one *all things* in Christ. (Eph. 1:9–10)

We must die. But that is not what God desires; rather, he devises ways so that a banished person does not remain banished from him. (2 Sam. 14:14 NIV)

Like a Loving Father, God Chastens and
Judges Those Whom He Loves

Many people are living under God's judgment and wrath. As a father hates the cancer that is killing his child, so also God's wrath burns hot toward the cancer of sin, because it destroys His people and His creation. Those who embrace sin as a way of life place themselves on a collision course with this wrath. The Father of spirits is committed to the total correction of those who, having been deceived, have rebelled against Him. The reason behind all of His judgments upon sinners is that He desires their repentance. Owing to the free will of the rebels He must use such inducements to accomplish His one purpose for His creation—the restoration of all things that have been lost or damaged by sin. The "destruction" and "torments" that God inflicts upon His enemies are intended to purge them of sin, whether in this life or the next.

None of God's actions, including His judgments, are without a positive purpose. This is often affirmed in Scripture:

> When Your judgments are in the earth,
> *The inhabitants of the world will learn righteousness.*
> (Isa. 26:9)

And *if by these things you are not reformed by Me*, but walk contrary to Me, then I also will walk contrary to you, and I will punish you yet seven times for your sins. (Lev. 26:23–24)

When the Lord has washed away the filth of the daughters of Zion, *and purged* the blood of Jerusalem from her midst, by the spirit of judgment and by the spirit of burning. (Isa. 4:4)

Deliver such a one to Satan for the destruction of the flesh, *that his spirit may be saved* in the day of the Lord Jesus. (1 Cor. 5:5)

Along the same lines, see also: Job 5:17–18; Jeremiah 9:6–7; Habakkuk 1:12; Zephaniah 3:8–9; 1 Timothy 1:19–20. Jan Bonda pointed out that even those judgments that are figuratively said to be "eternal" are intended to have a good end:

> Thirteen times[15] Jeremiah uses the words "eternal" or "eternity" in the context of divine punishment.[16] . . . We hear this twice: "The anger of the LORD will not turn back until he has executed and accomplished the intents of his heart" (Jer. 23:30; 30:24). . . . Here we are told precisely what "eternal" means when the prophet speaks of fire that will burn in eternity. It does not mean that God's wrath will burn forever, that is, without end. His wrath will burn without ceasing *until* his purpose has been accomplished.[17]

If this is true of the "eternal" judgments of God in Jeremiah's day, why would we doubt that the same is true of the punishments associated with the final judgment? To suggest that God's postmortem judgment of sinners in hell is merely for retribution, when we find that all of His temporal judgments on earth intend to restore fellowship between Himself and His lost children, is to suggest a disconnect, *in principle*, between God's judgments before and after death, which seems unwarranted by Scripture. It suggests that the same Father who desperately sought the recovery of His lost sons prior to their death suddenly experiences a change in heart toward them at the point of their passing away. Why would God have a complete change of attitude toward a person simply because he died?

Restorationists believe that God's judgments, though severe, are an expression of His mercy and love. God cannot be accused

---

15. *Bonda's footnote:* Five times in the context of the judgment on Israel (17:4; 18:16; 20:11; 23:40; 25:9) as well as eight times in connection with the judgment on other nations: on Babel (25:12; 51:26, 39, 57, 62); on Edom (49:13); on Kedar (49:33);—all 'olam; in 50:39 netsach.

16. Jan Bonda, *The One Purpose of God*, English trans. (Grand Rapids: Wm. B. Eerdmans, 1998), 212.

17. Ibid., 214.

of unnecessary harshness in His administration of justice. The inseparable link between God's mercy and His judgment acts is repeatedly affirmed in Scripture:

> To You . . . belongs mercy;
> For You render to each one according to his work.
>   (Ps. 62:12; see also 101:1)

> You were to them God-Who-Forgives,
> Though You took vengeance on their deeds. (Ps. 99:8)

> In wrath remember mercy. (Hab. 3:2)

> The Lord will not cast off forever.
> Though He causes grief,
> Yet He will show compassion
> According to the multitude of His mercies.
> For He does not afflict willingly,
> Nor grieve the children of men. (Lam. 3:31–33)

Since there are many such places that speak of God's judging as a function of His love and mercy—while there are none that tell us that God's judgments are *merely* retributive, having no merciful end in view—it seems inappropriate and gratuitous to interpret the few verses in Scripture about hell as if we did not have ample testimony elsewhere revealing the divine purpose and intention of saving all that were lost.

Though not necessarily known as a theologian, Abraham Lincoln is known for having a generous and, in many respects, "Christlike" disposition. Lincoln was apparently inclined to the view that God will eventually save everyone, as William J. Johnson related in *Abraham Lincoln the Christian*: "[Abraham Lincoln] did not nor could not believe in the endless punishment of anyone of the human race. He understood punishment for sin to be a Bible doctrine; that the punishment was parental in its object, aim, and design, and intended for the good of the offender; hence it must cease when justice is satisfied. He added that all that was lost by the transgression of Adam was made good by the atonement."[18]

Kind-hearted people, in general, tend to see this aspect of God's character rather more clearly than do those of a different temperament. We are all in danger of either seeing God through the lens of our own dispositions, or, alternatively, conforming our dispositions into the likeness of what we perceive God to be like. If I cannot imagine hating my enemies enough to wish for their eternal misery, it is difficult to believe that God, whose love is infinitely greater than mine, would wish to do such things to His enemies. This is not a case of one merely shaping a god in his own image, but seems only consistent with the fact that Jesus commands us to love our enemies, to bless those who curse us, and to do good to those who abuse us— so that we might be like our Father in heaven (Matt. 5:44–45). How strange these instructions would be if God Himself failed to have such a disposition toward those who curse and abuse Him. Allin and Chamberlain wrote:

> One of the worst things about the traditional creed is that it teaches us to forgive our enemies while at the same time God refuses to forgive His. . . . God is truly a God of kindness, compassion, and forgiveness for everyone, and not a cruel sadist who created millions, perhaps billions, knowing that, whether through their own choice or not, they were destined for a torture chamber infinitely worse than anything the Marquis De Sade, Hitler, or Saddam Hussein could ever dream up because it is infinitely longer in duration![19]

18. William J. Johnson, *Abraham Lincoln the Christian* (Milford, MI: Mott Media, 1976), 62f.

19. Thomas Allin and Mark T. Chamberlain, *Every Knee Shall Bow* (Oxnard, CA: self-published by Mark T. Chamberlain, 2005), 12.

Of course, universal reconciliation is not the only alternative to the prospect of eternal torment. There remains the possibility of annihilation, which is infinitely more merciful than is the traditional idea of hell. However, the annihilation of the lost still leaves Christ (who came to save the lost) the loser, and the devil the winner, of most of the chips in the game. The conditionalist rightly sees the judgment of the sinner as "death," but does not prove that there can be nothing improved beyond death. The lake of fire is called the "second death," but is that really the last word? Some restorationists point out that, whatever the "second death" may mean, there are hints that, even after the lost are cast into it (Rev. 20:15), there may remain an invitation from "the Spirit and the bride" offered to "him who thirsts" (Rev. 22:17) to come into the radiant city, whose gates will never be shut (Rev. 21:25). Those who eventually enter that city include "the kings of the earth" (Rev. 21:24), who had previously fornicated with Babylon (Rev. 17:2; 18:9) and had died while making war against the Lamb (Rev. 19:19).

If death, whether the first or the second, is to have the last word in the judgment of sinners, what does the Scripture mean that says, "He will swallow up death forever, and . . . will wipe away tears from all faces" (Isa. 25:8)? In Revelation's final scene, we are told, "There shall be no more death" (Rev. 21:4).

Hell for Any Person Is Hell for God and for Any Who Loved That Person

Many theologians speak about the eternal torment of hell as if this is the means of bringing relief and satisfaction to God because of His love for justice. This would suggest that God's love for *justice* is in conflict with His love for *people*, rather than a function of it. How could God, who says that He has "no pleasure in the death of the wicked, but that the wicked turn from his way and live" (Ezek. 33:11) be thought to find pleasure or satisfaction in even the well-deserved death (or worse, the eternal torture) of sinners, whom He created for Himself, and for whom Christ died?

In Christ, God paid a hefty ransom, but in order to get what? A one percent recovery of that which was lost—or even less? Jesus died for all mankind. Much as this is denied in certain theological systems, the Bible is emphatic:

Behold! The Lamb of God who takes away the sin of the world! (John 1:29)

He Himself is the propitiation for our sins, and not for ours only but also for the whole world. (1 John 2:2)

The LORD has laid on Him the iniquity of us all. (Isa. 53:6)

My flesh, which I shall give for the life of the world. (John 6:51)

Christ died for the ungodly. (Rom. 5:6)

When we were enemies we were reconciled . . . through [His] death. (Rom. 5:10)

Justification . . . to all men. (Rom. 5:18 NASB)

For it pleased the Father . . . by Him to reconcile all things to Himself . . . through the blood of His cross. (Col. 1:19–20)

He . . . taste[d] death for everyone. (Heb. 2:9)

[He] gave Himself a ransom for all. (1 Tim. 2:6)

Can it be thought that Christ, or God, could "see the labor of His soul, and be satisfied" (Isa. 53:11) to have suffered death in the attempt to regain the whole world, only ultimately to lose to His enemy the vast majority of that for which He paid? John A. T.

Robinson wrote: "Christ, in Origen's old words, remains on the Cross so long as one sinner remains in hell. That is not speculation: it is a statement grounded in the very necessity of God's nature. In a universe of love there can be no heaven which tolerates a chamber of horrors, no hell for any which does not at the same time make it hell for God."[20]

If anyone ends up permanently in hell, it will not only be that person but God and anyone else who loved that person who will also suffer. The Christian who has the spirit of Christ cannot be happy to be "saved alone," if he has learned, from Christ, to love his neighbor as himself. If you love somebody as you love yourself, then your happiness is tied to theirs. Thus, Paul could say that, if his beloved kinsmen after the flesh could not be saved, it would be no better to him than for himself to be accursed from Christ (Rom. 9:3). This is the nature of genuine love for one's neighbor. If we can be happily partying upstairs while our neighbors are being tortured in the basement, then we know nothing of love as Jesus taught us to love. As Talbott explained: "If I truly love my daughter *as myself*, then God cannot love (or will the good for) me unless he also loves (or wills the good for) her. For I am not an isolated monad whose interests are distinct from those of my loved ones, and neither is anyone else. If God should do less than his best for my daughter, he would also do less than his best for me; and if he should act contrary to her best interest, he would also act contrary to my own."[21]

Talbott, elsewhere, wrote: "When the mother of Ted Bundy declared, so agonizingly and yet so appropriately, her continuing love for her son who had become a monster, she illustrated how in harming himself her son had also harmed his own mother. She also illustrated this all-important point: that not even God can impart supreme joy to such a mother or vindicate his righteousness in

20. J. A. T. Robinson, *In the End God* (New York: Harper & Row, 1968), 133.
21. Thomas Talbott, *The Inescapable Love of God* (Boca Raton, FL: Universal Publishers, 1999), 138.

permitting her to suffer so, unless his forgiveness can find a way to reclaim her son."[22]

Is Talbott illegitimately placing man-made limits upon God's prerogatives, or is he simply stating the true nature of love? It is God's nature to love, thus restricting His actions to only such as are consistent with love. If God loves me, He must also love my children, as well as all those whom I love. It is God's own stated principle—if you love a parent, you love that parent's children: "Everyone who loves Him who begot also loves him who is begotten of Him" (1 John 5:1).

Whoever desires my eternal happiness must necessarily will the eternal happiness of all those to whom my happiness is inextricably bound. Hell for anyone who is loved by a believer must necessarily also be hell for that believer. Many traditionalists dispute this. For example, John K. La Shell wrote: "How will the gloriously transformed saints respond when they see people they loved on earth cast into hell? They will not look on them as their beloved 'Mother' or 'Aunt Matilda.' They will see human beings stripped of their attractive shell, enemies of God cursing their beloved Savior. Hence their former affection will be turned to utter rejection. We will then rejoice at the destruction of all who have opposed our heavenly husband, the Lord Jesus Christ."[23]

But this explanation is lacking in two important features. The first is in scriptural support. It is entirely speculative, and no biblical writer ever suggested that Christians would ever have such a postmortem change of heart toward their loved ones. The second deficiency is that it is counterintuitive. It suggests that, when we see Jesus and become like Him, we will thereby become less compassionate than we presently are in this life. Gregory MacDonald has protested against this suggestion: "The beatific vision of God's love does not make us *less* aware of the pains of others but *more*. It makes no sense

---

22. Ibid., 165.
23. John K. La Shell, *Christianity Today*, July 8, 2002, 8.

to me to imagine that we shall be so full of God that we will forget others, let alone hate them or even love them less (1 John 4:20)."[24]

THERE IS NOTHING PREVENTING GOD FROM EXTENDING THE OPPORTUNITIES FOR RECONCILIATION BEYOND THE POINT OF DEATH

While there is no verse of Scripture affirming, in clear terms, the specific possibility of persons in hell receiving further opportunities for repentance, neither is there any passage denying this possibility.[25] In fact, there are very few verses saying anything at all about post-mortem conditions. Gregory MacDonald has raised the question:

> What possible reason would God have for drawing a line at death and saying, "Beyond this point I will show no mercy to those who repent and turn to Christ"? There is no obvious reason why God would draw the point of no return at death (or anywhere at all). There is, however, a good reason for thinking that he would not— namely, he is loving, gracious, and merciful and will accept all who turn to him in repentance. This is not to suggest that God some-how owes it to the lost to leave the door open forever, but it is to suggest that his love would seem to motivate him in this direction.[26]

Even Martin Luther expressed openness to this prospect, in a letter he wrote to Hanseu Von Rechenberg, in 1522. Luther wrote:

---

24. Gregory MacDonald, *The Evangelical Universalist* (Eugene, OR: Cascade Books, 2006), 17.

25. Often Hebrews 9:27 and Luke 16:26 are said to exclude opportunities for repentance after death, but the former only looks as far into the future as the judgment, without discussing any subsequent issues, and the latter is irrelevant to eternal destinies because it does not deal with a post-judgment scenario.

26. Gregory MacDonald, *The Evangelical Universalist* (Eugene, OR: Cascade Books, 2006), 32.

"God forbid that I should limit the time of acquiring faith to the present life. In the depth of the Divine mercy there may be opportunity to win it in the future."[27]

To say that there is some power or authority higher than God that forbids His continuing to seek this objective beyond the grave is to insist upon what the Bible does not assert. In fact, it is to deny what the Bible does assert:

> I know that You can do everything,
> And that no purpose of Yours can be withheld from You.
> (Job 42:2)

> According to the purpose of Him who works all things according to the counsel of His will. . . . (Eph. 1:11)

> He is able even to subdue all things to Himself. (Phil. 3:21)

> When His disciples heard it, they were greatly astonished, saying, "Who then can be saved?" But Jesus looked at them and said to them, "With men this is impossible, but with God all things are possible." (Matt. 19:25–26)

Gerry Beauchemin has raised seemingly unanswerable questions: "What mysteriously happens at death making it impossible for God to bring someone to repentance? Has He been stripped of His power? Where does Scripture declare His impotence in the face of death?"[28]

Elsewhere, Beauchemin wrote: "Some even scorn the thought that unbelievers may be able to trust Christ beyond this life. How sad. 'Of course they'll believe then,' they say, 'it will all be

---

27. From Luther's letter to Hanseu Von Rechenberg in 1522. Cited by Gerry Beauchemin, *Hope Beyond Hell* (Olmito, TX: Malista Press, 2007), 69.
28. Gerry Beauchemin, *Hope Beyond Hell* (Olmito, TX: Malista Press, 2007), 65.

too obvious. There will be no merit to that!' Merit? Since when is faith meritorious?"[29]

GOD IS DETERMINED TO RESTORE ALL THAT WAS LOST

There are certainly those who challenge the very premise that God has determined to recover all that has been lost. It is argued that God has only determined to save the elect, or else that God wishes He could save all people, but is rendered impotent in this by the sovereign power of human free will. Those who deny that all will be restored to God must find their own (generally counterintuitive) ways of interpreting Scriptures like the following:

> Your enemies shall submit themselves to You.
> All the earth shall worship You
> And sing praises to You. (Ps. 66:3–4)

> All the families of the nations
> Shall worship before You. . . .
> All those who go down to the dust
> Shall bow before Him. (Ps. 22:27, 29)

> All nations whom You have made
> Shall come and worship before You, O Lord,
> And shall glorify Your name. (Ps. 86:9)

> Look to Me, and be saved,
> All you ends of the earth! . . .
> I have sworn by Myself . . .

---

29. Ibid., 88.

That to Me every knee shall bow,
Every tongue shall take an oath. (Isa. 45:22–23)

That at the name of Jesus every knee should bow, of those in heaven, and of those on earth, and of those under the earth, and that every tongue should confess that Jesus Christ is Lord, to the glory of God the Father. (Phil. 2:10–11)

[Jesus] whom heaven must receive until the times of restoration of all things, which God has spoken by the mouth of all His holy prophets since the world began. (Acts 3:21)

Therefore, as through one man's offense judgment came to all men, resulting in condemnation, even so through one Man's righteous act the free gift came to all men, resulting in justification of life. (Rom. 5:18)

That in the dispensation of the fullness of the times He might gather together in one all things in Christ, both which are in heaven and which are on earth—in Him. (Eph. 1:10)

For it pleased the Father . . . to reconcile all things to Himself, by Him, whether things on earth or things in heaven, having made peace through the blood of His cross. (Col. 1:19–20)

And every creature which is in heaven and on the earth and under the earth and such as are in the sea, and all that are in them, I heard saying: "Blessing and honor and glory and power be to Him who sits on the throne, and to the Lamb, forever and ever!" (Rev. 5:13)

In light of such biblical declarations, what strong scriptural inducements ought to be required, if we are obliged to settle for any theology that does not give God His full due, or acknowledge that

His eternal purpose will ultimately be fulfilled in Christ? Are there similarly clear and strong declarations somewhere telling us that Christ will fail in His search-and-rescue mission for the recovery of all that was lost? Thomas Allin wrote: "We are altogether apt to forget whose the loss is, if any one soul perishes. It is God's loss: it is the Father Who loses His child. The straying sheep of the parable is the Great Shepherd's loss: the missing coin is the Owner's loss. In this very fact lies the pledge that He will seek on and on till He find it."[30]

With reference to the parables alluded to above, Rob Bell observed: "The God that Jesus teaches us about doesn't give up until everything that was lost is found. This God simply doesn't give up. Ever."[31]

CHRIST IS VICTOR!

Those who acknowledge that Jesus died to save the whole world, but believe that many will ultimately be lost, must face yet another important issue. The New Testament consistently describes Jesus as the conqueror of the inferior powers, including Satan.[32] If Satan desires to steal souls from Christ, and ultimately succeeds in bringing about the permanent damnation of the majority, then how is this viewed in any sense as Christ's victory? If a team of Navy SEALs were dispatched to safely recover a thousand people taken hostage by pirates, and they returned from their mission having permanently lost all but ten to the enemy, that mission would be an embarrassment to the team, not a victory to be heralded. Allin and Chamberlain wrote: "As odious and repulsive as the idea of endless suffering is, it is not the main point. The vital question is who will win the battle for men's souls, God or the devil? Which is more

---

30. Thomas Allin, *Christ Triumphant*, 1878, repr. 9th ed. (Canyon Country, CA: Concordant, n.d.), 70.
31. Rob Bell, *Love Wins* (New York: HarperCollins, 2011), 101.
32. e.g., Matthew 12:29; Mark 1:24; Luke 10:18; Colossians 2:15; Hebrews 2:14f.; 1 Corinthians 15:25–27, 55; Revelation 5:5; 11:15.

powerful, righteousness or sin? . . . [We] believe that if the Father sent the Son to save the world, the world is going to be saved! To me, any other view basically means that the Son of God was unable to accomplish what the Father sent Him to do!"[33]

Universalists believe that traditionalism and annihilationism deny Christ His proper satisfaction. They agree with Allin and Chamberlain, who said: "The eternal existence of sin and rebellion against God is sin triumphant. Sin, which God was unable to remove without annihilating the sinner, is sin triumphant and death victorious."[34]

William Barclay wrote: "I believe implicitly in the ultimate and complete triumph of God. . . . If one man remains outside the love of God at the end of time, it means that that one man has defeated the love of God—and that is impossible. . . . Further, there is only one way in which we can think of the triumph of God. . . . The only victory love can enjoy is the day when its offer of love is answered by the return of love. The only possible final triumph is a universe loved by and in love with God."[35]

33. Thomas Allin and Mark T. Chamberlain, *Every Knee Shall Bow* (Oxnard, CA: self-published by Mark T. Chamberlain, 2005), 117, 11.

34. Ibid., 118.

35. Excerpted from *William Barclay: A Spiritual Autobiography* (Grand Rapids: Wm. B. Eerdmans, 1977), 65–67.

CHAPTER 12

CROSS-EXAMINATION
OF THE CASE FOR
RESTORATIONISM

For reasons somewhat inexplicable, restorationism (universal reconciliation) arouses much hostility from its opponents. There are, of course, exegetical criticisms of its case, as we shall see. However, there are also objections raised that are strictly emotional. Origenists seem to be one class of Christians whom their opponents regard as unworthy of honest representation. Consider, for example, the following comments—each made by notable traditionalist writers:

> Modern universalism's basic idea is that no one deserves to be damned.[1]

> Talbott's universalistic paradigm is in essence anthropocentric rather than theocentric.[2]

> Once grace becomes something which God owes to all men, then it loses its "gift" character and takes on a "debt" significance. But

---

1. J. I. Packer, "Good Pagans and God's Kingdom," *Christianity Today*, January 17, 1986, 22–25.
2. Daniel Strange, "A Calvinist Response to Talbott's Universalism," in Robin A. Parry and Christopher H. Partridge, *Universal Salvation? The Current Debate* (Grand Rapids: Wm. B. Eerdmans, 2003), 146.

the Scriptures are clear in their definition of grace that grace must be a free gift and not a debt (Rom. 4:1–5; 11:6).[3]

Of course, not one of these criticisms remotely affects or represents the actual beliefs of evangelical universalists.[4] No evangelical universalist whom I have encountered has ever suggested that men do not deserve hell, nor that grace is "owed" to any man. I have not found any advocate of this viewpoint who presented an argument that was in any point *anthropocentric* ("man-centered"). In fact, the case for restorationism, as near as it can be discerned from its published advocates, is entirely based upon the character, the sovereignty, and the plan of God, as well as the work of Christ. If there has been an anthropomorphic case found in any of my research, it has been that of the traditionalist, who argues his case, very largely, upon the basis of man's great sinfulness, not on the accomplishments of God or of Christ.

SCRIPTURAL OBJECTIONS

"Slender Exegetical Basis"

A charge commonly brought against universal reconciliation is that the view enjoys very little scriptural support. Traditionalist Harry Buis has made this criticism against the restorationist viewpoint: "Its advocates quote sparingly from Scripture. . . . If they are honest they will admit that their position is based on human reasoning, not on divine revelation. As Shedd says, 'Universalism has a slender exegetical basis.'"[5]

---

3. Robert A. Morey, *Death and the Afterlife* (Minneapolis: Bethany House, 1984), 237.

4. This is very disconcerting, since all of the writers quoted have written lengthy critiques of what they represent as "universalism." One would assume that leading evangelical writers would first acquaint themselves with the views of Christian brethren whom they wish to demonize. If they have not done so in this case, then upon what other points might they prove to be equally unreliable (we will refrain from saying "dishonest")?

5. Harry Buis, *The Doctrine of Eternal Punishment* (Grand Rapids: Baker Book House, 1957), 115.

Douglas Jacoby, who seems to favor the conditionalist view, presented the same criticism: "Not many serious Bible students will be won over [to universalism] given the thinness of the scriptural case. . . . Like universalism, conditionalism deserves a better hearing than it has received. Unlike universalism, conditionalism has ample scriptural support."[6]

To anyone who read our previous chapter, such an assessment must evoke perplexity. The case for universal reconciliation is defended by appeal to scores of relevant scriptural declarations concerning God's universal love, His determination to save all mankind, and His competence to accomplish His purposes—the major, much-attested, biblical themes from which universal reconciliation draws its conclusions. That scriptural case may be exegetically critiqued by those holding other theological commitments, but it seems misleading to represent the evangelical universalists as having somehow failed to marshal an abundance of scriptural data to their defense. The *prima facie* scriptural case presented for universal reconciliation seems as strong as that presented for conditionalism, and considerably stronger than that given for traditionalism.[7]

No Scriptural Support for Postmortem Repentance

A plank of the universalist platform for which little or no direct scriptural testimony exists, and upon which the view depends heavily, is the affirmation that sinners will be given postmortem opportunities to repent. Francis Chan (along with many others) has correctly pointed out: "No passage in the Bible says that there will be a second chance after death to turn to Jesus. And that's frightening. It's frightening because the idea of an after-death conversion is the most important ingredient for the Universalist position. It makes

---

6. Douglas Jacoby, *What's the Truth about Heaven and Hell?* (Eugene, OR: Harvest House, 2013), 111.

7. By "*prima facie* scriptural case" I mean the sheer numbers of verses, which, on the surface, appear to confirm the position's primary distinctives.

or breaks this view. But there is no single passage in the Bible that describes, hints at, hopes for, or suggests that someone who dies without following Jesus in this life will have an opportunity to do so after death."[8]

Bringing the same criticism, Howard Marshall wrote: "There is no positive evidence anywhere for the view that there will be a post-mortem opportunity for salvation or for the view that this will inevitably lead to the salvation of all. The burden of proof is on those who assert these two propositions."[9]

Since Marshall's comment regarding the "burden of proof" was directed specifically as a challenge to Thomas Talbott, we might consider how Talbott replies to such a challenge:

> In the presence of Paul's clear statement affirming that justification and life comes to all [Rom. 5:18], the burden of proof, it seems to me, is just the opposite of what Marshall claims it to be. If someone should affirm that, according to Paul, those who fail to repent before their 50th birthday will never be saved, then that person must bear the burden of proof; and similarly, if someone should affirm that, according to Paul, those who fail to repent during their earthly lives will never be saved, then that person must also bear the burden of proof . . . does Paul say anything remotely like this?[10]

While there is no *positive* statement in Scripture promising a second chance after death for those who die unprepared, the absence of *negative* scriptural declarations render it difficult to assume that

8. Francis Chan and Preston Sprinkle, *Erasing Hell* (Colorado Springs: David C. Cook, 2011), 35.

9. I. Howard Marshall, "The New Testament Does *Not* Teach Universal Salvation," in Robin A. Parry and Christopher H. Partridge, *Universal Salvation? The Current Debate* (Grand Rapids: Wm. B. Eerdmans, 2003), 65.

10. Thomas Talbott, "Reply to My Critics," in Robin A. Parry and Christopher H. Partridge, *Universal Salvation? The Current Debate* (Grand Rapids: Wm. B. Eerdmans, 2003), 269n28.

no such opportunities will be given. The Scripture is simply silent on the question. How shall we interpret this silence?

Most interpret the silences as does Carl Henry, who affirms that "a man's fate is finally settled at death."[11] Robert Morey, similarly, wrote: "Throughout Scripture, the issue of salvation is limited to the lifetime of the hearer (Heb. 9:27; 3:15–4:11, etc.)."[12]

In the last comment cited, reference is made to two passages as proof that there is no postmortem salvation. However, these passages work better for this purpose if we approach them with the preconceived idea that this is what we will find them affirming. Hebrews 9:27 tells us only that the judgment comes after death. It does not mention what may occur after the judgment. When an accused criminal is brought to trial, he faces judgment. What happens then? That will depend on the court's verdict and the judge's sentencing. Hebrews 9:27 mentions the judgment, but not the verdict, nor sentence. Talbott wrote: "There is no suggestion anywhere in Scripture . . . that God's forgiveness has a built-in time limit or that the judgement associated with the parousia eliminates every possibility of repentance in the future. It is precisely evidence for this kind of *final judgement* that is lacking."[13]

Hebrews 3–4 may be somewhat better for the point, in that it has a tone of urgency, encouraging the reader to take action "while it is called 'Today.'" However, this warning not to neglect present opportunity is not based upon the assumption that opportunities end at death but rather a danger that exists of hardening the heart in this life, through delay. Since death and postmortem circumstances are not mentioned, this passage's relevance to opportunities in the next life is uncertain.

---

11. Carl Henry, *Christian Personal Ethics* (Grand Rapids: Baker Book House, 1957), 556.
12. Robert A. Morey, *Death and the Afterlife* (Minneapolis: Bethany House, 1984), 234.
13. Thomas Talbott, "Reply to My Critics," in Robin A. Parry and Christopher H. Partridge, *Universal Salvation? The Current Debate* (Grand Rapids: Wm. B. Eerdmans, 2003), 255.

Though many passages describe an eschatological judgment, at the coming of Christ, there is no actual declaration that the judgment or its penalties are final or irremediable. They may indeed be, and it is common enough to assume it. To read of people being cast into the lake of fire, and to be told that this is the "second death" probably conveys the impression of a final end to our minds. But does death (whether the first or the second) really have the final victory? Talbott doubts it: "If death should achieve a final victory in the life of a single person, then that would provide a clear answer to Paul's rhetorical question: 'Where, O Death, is your victory?' (1 Cor. 15:55). But the question is not supposed to have an answer."[14]

Responding to Talbott's view, Howard Marshall wrote: "There will be a final judgement, the outcome of which will be justification for some and condemnation for others, and . . . there is no indication that these outcomes are anything other than final. The intensity of the New Testament appeals to people to repent and believe lest they suffer final separation from God is such that it is difficult to believe that this separation is purely temporary and will come to an end."[15]

Universalist Passages?

The primary scriptural texts universalists use to base their arguments on are those that speak of God's intention of saving all people,[16] of restoring or reconciling all things to Himself,[17] and of the final result of universal worship of God.[18] In such passages, it is the use of such terms as "all" and "every" and "the world" that give the impression of universal salvation. We will consider and cross-examine a few examples.

---

14. Ibid., 254.

15. I. Howard Marshall, "The New Testament Does *Not* Teach Universal Salvation," in Robin A. Parry and Christopher H. Partridge, *Universal Salvation? The Current Debate* (Grand Rapids: Wm. B. Eerdmans, 2003), 56.

16. e.g., John 1:29; Romans 5:18; 1 Corinthians 15:22, 28; 1 Timothy 2:4; 4:10; Hebrews 2:9; 2 Peter 3:9.

17. e.g., John 12:32; Acts 3:21; 2 Corinthians 5:19; Ephesians 1:9–10; Colossians 1:19–20.

18. e.g., Isaiah 45:22–23; Philippians 2:9–11; Revelation 5:13.

Ephesians 1:9–10; Colossians 1:19–20; 2 Corinthians 5:19; Acts 3:21

In Ephesians 1:9–10 and Colossians 1:19–20, Paul expresses God's purpose to be the ultimate reconciliation of "all things" to Himself "through the blood of His cross" (Col. 1:20). The mention of the blood of His cross as the agency of reconciliation seemingly identifies this reconciliation with individual salvation—a reconciliation with God, in Christ, which is also mentioned in 2 Corinthians 5:19, where God, in Christ, is said to have been "reconciling the world to Himself." In Acts 3:21, Peter also anticipated the "restoration of all things." These, and other similar texts, at first blush, seem to support universalism. However, as Morey has argued: "What the universalists fail to observe is that biblical words should be interpreted in terms of how they are used. Once it is admitted that the words 'all' and 'world' are used in passages where they cannot mean all of humanity, the simplistic assumption of the universalist must be rejected."[19]

Francis Chan has made the same point: "You've got to figure out from the context what 'all' means. For instance, when Mark said that '*all* the country of Judea' and '*all* the people of Jerusalem' were going out to be baptized by John (Mark 1:5 NASB), he certainly didn't mean every single individual in Judea—man, woman, and child. 'All' here simply denotes a large number of people."[20]

It is true that the word *all* is often used as hyperbole in Scripture, meaning not "literally all" but only "most," or even "many." The problem is, of course, that the word used is also the best word available, if Paul had wished to speak of "every one, without exception." How can we know whether he is using "all" literally or hyperbolically? In some contexts, this may be impossible to decide. However, in both Ephesians and Colossians, he modifies "all things" with the phrase "both which are in heaven and which are on earth"—expressions that

---

19. Robert A. Morey, *Death and the Afterlife* (Minneapolis: Bethany House, 1984), 243.
20. Francis Chan and Preston Sprinkle, *Erasing Hell* (Colorado Springs: David C. Cook, 2011), 29.

seem to convey all-inclusiveness.[21] Additionally, in Colossians 1:20, the term "all things" which are to be reconciled mirrors the same expression "all things" in verse 16, describing the things that were created through Christ. Paul's thought, in context, seems to be: "By [Jesus] *all things* were created. . . . It pleased the Father . . . by Him to reconcile *all things* to Himself" (vv. 16, 19, 20). The things Christ reconciled seem coextensive with the things He created.

In the restoration of all things, mentioned in Acts 3:21, "all things" seems to require some limitation by the explanatory "which God has spoken by the mouth of all His holy prophets since the world began." Unless universal reconciliation was predicted by all the prophets, it must not be what Peter had in mind (unless, of course, "all" is here being used as a hyperbole!). Also, two verses later, there is the cryptic reference to those who will be "utterly destroyed from among the people"—usually considered to discourage any hope of universal salvation. Of course, the universalists also believe in the "destruction" of many people. The question is whether there may be any restoration on the other side of that destruction.

These texts have not convinced most scholars that Peter and Paul taught restorationism. J. I. Packer disposes of all such universalist texts with a sweeping dismissal: "All these texts are juxtaposed with texts in the documents from which they are drawn which refer specifically to the prospect of some perishing through unbelief. And *unless we assume that the writers did not know their own minds, we have to conclude that they cannot in the texts quoted, really have meant to affirm universal final salvation*"[22] (italics added).

Universalist Thomas Talbott, who seldom allows such careless criticisms to go unanswered, responded to Packer's dismissal: "But isn't this an obvious non sequitur? Suppose we replace Packer's second sentence above [the one italicized] with the following: 'So unless

---

21. Philippians 2:10 adds "those under the earth" to the list of categories.

22. J. I. Packer, "The Problem of Universalism Today," in J. I. Packer, *Celebrating the Saving Work of God* (Carlisle: Paternoster Press, 1998), 176.

we assume that the writers did not know their own minds, we cannot suppose that by "perishing" they had in mind an everlasting separation from God.'"[23]

Philippians 2:9–11

The prospect of the ultimate, universal acknowledgment of Christ ("every knee should bow . . . and that every tongue should confess that Jesus Christ is Lord, to the glory of God the Father") is an inspiration to all Christians, regardless of their eschatology. The universalist assumes this refers to adoring worshippers, but this is disputed. There is disagreement over whether all these knees and tongues will be acknowledging Christ *happily*, or whether some will do so grudgingly. Robert Morey has suggested: "They could be bowing in defeat as they acknowledge Christ's lordship as they go off into eternal perdition."[24] Howard Marshall agrees with this suggestion: "Universalists argue that the confession in Philippians 2:11 is not 'forced' but voluntary and salvific, but who could possibly come to this conclusion in the light of 1:28 and 3:19? Further, the language used here is paralleled in Romans 14:10–12 where the context is one of judgement on the disobedient."[25]

Marshall's appeal to Philippians 1:28 and 3:19 is not as cogent as his statement implies. These two passages speak of certain unbelievers who are facing the prospect of "perdition" or "destruction." Both English words translate the Greek word *apoleia*, which also means "ruin" or "loss." Universalists have no qualms about admitting that a life of sin incurs ruin and loss to the sinner. These verses are not necessarily referring to postmortem (nor clearly permanent)

---

23. Thomas Talbott, "Reply to My Critics," in Robin A. Parry and Christopher H. Partridge, *Universal Salvation? The Current Debate* (Grand Rapids: Wm. B. Eerdmans, 2003), 251.

24. Robert A. Morey, *Death and the Afterlife* (Minneapolis: Bethany House, 1984), 245.

25. I. Howard Marshall, "The New Testament Does *Not* Teach Universal Salvation," in Robin A. Parry and Christopher H. Partridge, *Universal Salvation? The Current Debate* (Grand Rapids: Wm. B. Eerdmans, 2003), 69.

conditions, and are therefore not particularly relevant to the point under consideration.

That Romans 14:10–12 is in a context of "judgement on the disobedient" is a perplexing claim. Like Philippians 2, Romans 14 quotes from Isaiah 45:23. But neither passage does so in the context of negative judgment. Philippians 2 quotes it in the context of Christ's exaltation to glory, and Romans 14 does so in the context of every Christian ("brother" in verse 10, and "us" in verse 12) having to answer directly to God—not to man—for our behavior. There is no discussion of the judgment of the disobedient (certainly not of the "lost") in this entire chapter.

Paul's term "confess" is used eleven times in the New Testament, and never refers to a begrudged or coerced confession. There is no hint that the word ever refers to the forced confession of a rebel. To confess Christ to be "Lord," according to Paul, is that which saves a person (Rom. 10:9) and can only be done by the Holy Spirit's prompting (1 Cor. 12:3).

Besides all of this, Paul says that every tongue will confess Christ, "to the glory of God the Father." God would not be glorified by a grudging confession made under threats of torture or annihilation. If a man were to ask a woman, "Do you find me witty and attractive?" and she replied, "Yes, I do!" he would rightly be flattered. But imagine if he were to ask the same question, and the woman were to say, "Not particularly." If he were then to place a gun to her head and to say, "How about *now*?" she might answer more agreeably, but can we suppose that any sane man would feel honored by the woman's praise under such conditions? Restorationists argue that God is glorified only in the worship of sincere believers, not coerced confessions, and that this passage cannot reasonably be said to describe any other.

An important and easily overlooked point is that, in the Greek, all this bowing and confessing is not said to occur "*at* the name of Jesus," but "*in* the name of Jesus." Paul seems to be saying that all people will eventually worship God *in the name of Jesus.* That which is truly done "in the name of Jesus" is only done by believers (Col. 3:17).

Robert Morey, though an unflinching traditionalist, apparently acknowledges that Philippians 2 refers to true and sincere worship, but does not think that what Paul describes can be taken as inevitable. He wrote: "Notice that the text does not say 'shall bow' but 'should bow.'"[26] However, since Paul is referring to Isaiah 45:23, where every major translation reads "shall bow" or "will bow," this would seemingly be Paul's intended meaning as well.

Romans 5:18

In Romans 5:12–19, Paul compares and contrasts the actions of two men—Adam and Christ—and their respective impacts upon mankind. Much in the passage is obscure and difficult, and some scholars have regarded it as one of the more perplexing portions of the New Testament. To put it succinctly, Adam involved the race in disaster, and Christ had the opposite effect. Verse 18 is particularly significant to the debate over universalism, because Paul wrote: "Therefore, as through one man's offense judgment came to all men, resulting in condemnation, even so through one Man's righteous act the free gift came to all men, resulting in justification of life."

The reason that this verse becomes the focal point in this controversy is that Paul tells us "the free gift resulting in justification" actually "came to all men" through Christ. This is another case wherein the meaning of "all" is disputed. A common suggestion against the universalist interpretation is mentioned by Douglas Moo: "One possibility is that he is affirming that Christ's work on the cross is of potential benefit to all people. Christ has won for all people 'the sentence of justification' and this justification is offered freely to all."[27]

---

26. Robert A. Morey, *Death and the Afterlife* (Minneapolis: Bethany House, 1984), 244.
27. Douglas J. Moo, "Paul on Hell," in Christopher W. Morgan and Robert A. Peterson, eds., *Hell Under Fire* (Grand Rapids: Zondervan, 2004), 99.

This view is also presented in Godet's *Commentary on Romans*.[28] Moo, however, admits the weakness of this suggestion, observing that "Paul usually uses 'justification' language to refer to the actual transfer from the realm of sin and death to the realm of righteousness and life."[29] He therefore concludes (in agreement with Herman Ridderbos[30]): "Probably, therefore, as in 1 Corinthians 15:22, the 'all' in the second half of verse 18 refers to 'all who are in Christ.'"[31]

Peterson takes a different approach (following N. T. Wright), suggesting that the "all men" who are justified in Christ are not "all men individually," but "Jews and Gentiles alike."[32] Wright sees Romans 5:18 as confirming "the point Paul has been making all along since 1:5 (see particularly 1:16–17; 2:9–11; 3:21–4:25) . . . that all men, Jew and Gentile alike, stand on a level before God."[33]

To this the restorationist replies that, in this verse, Paul sets up a precise dichotomy between Adam's effect on "all men" and Christ's effect upon "all men." It is difficult, without doing violence to the natural structure of the verse, to render the "all men" in one case as a subset of the "all men" in the other. The verse that follows (Rom. 5:19) refers to the same two groups as "the many." By Adam's disobedience "the many" were made sinners, so also by Christ's obedience "the many" will be made righteous. It seems hard to deny that "the many" are the same group in both parts of the verse. What's more, in verses 15 and 20, Christ is given credit for accomplishing for good "much more" than Adam accomplished for evil. Anything short of universal salvation make's Christ's impact "much less" than that of Adam, whose influence for harm was indeed universal.

---

28. F. Godet, *Commentary on Romans*, repr. (Grand Rapids: Kregel, 1977), 224–25.

29. Douglas J. Moo, "Paul on Hell," in Christopher W. Morgan and Robert A. Peterson, eds., *Hell Under Fire* (Grand Rapids: Zondervan, 2004), 99.

30. Herman Ridderbos, *Paul: An Outline of His Theology* (Grand Rapids: Wm. B. Eerdmans, 1974), 340–41.

31. Douglas J. Moo, "Paul on Hell," in Christopher W. Morgan and Robert A. Peterson, eds., *Hell Under Fire* (Grand Rapids: Zondervan, 2004), 99.

32. Robert A. Peterson, *Hell on Trial* (Phillipsburg, NJ: Presbyterian and Reformed Publishing, 1995), 154.

33. N. T. Wright, "Towards a Biblical View of Universalism," in *Themelios* 4, (1978), 56.

The Old Testament Passages

A number of passages from the Psalms and the Prophets were cited in the previous chapter, in which God's everlasting loving-kindness and the brevity of His anger are extolled by the inspired writers. One serious objection to the use of these texts to describe God's universal policies is that virtually every one of them is talking specifically about God's behavior toward *Israel,* His chosen people—not mankind in general. The extrapolation of God's policies with Israel to the ultimate destinies of the whole world might seem an inappropriate stretch.

The universalist's response is that Israel was indeed God's "chosen people"—but chosen for what? God chose Abraham and his Seed—not to be saved alone and to leave the heathen to become fuel for hell's fires—but so that *through them* His salvation would reach the rest of the population of the world. Upon initially calling Abraham, God told him, "In you all the families of the earth shall be blessed" (Gen. 12:3).

Israel, ultimately epitomized in Christ, was God's chosen "Servant." Like all servants, Israel had an assignment—to bring God's salvation to the rest of the world:

> Behold! My Servant whom I uphold,
> My Elect One in whom My soul delights!
> I have put My Spirit upon Him;
> He will bring forth justice to the Gentiles. (Isa. 42:1)

> Indeed He says,
> "It is too small a thing that You should be My Servant
> To raise up the tribes of Jacob,
> And to restore the preserved ones of Israel;
> I will also give You as a light to the Gentiles,
> That You should be My salvation to the ends of the earth."
> (Isa. 49:6)

Israel was the first nation to whom God would reveal things that would ultimately belong to the rest of God's creation as well. Israel was God's microcosm of the world, in which He would reveal His character, and make known His power, His faithfulness, and His mercy, through His saving acts. As it is written:

> Declare His glory among the nations,
> His wonders among all peoples. (Ps. 96:3)

> Men shall speak of the might of Your awesome acts,
> And I will declare Your greatness. (Ps. 145:6)

> All men shall fear,
> And shall declare the work of God;
> For they shall wisely consider His doing. (Ps. 64:9)

I will set a sign among them; and those among them who escape I will send to the nations . . . who have not heard My fame nor seen My glory. And they shall declare My glory among the Gentiles. (Isa. 66:19)

Though many of the Old Testament verses about God's mercy and reluctance to retain His anger pertain to Israel, this is not true of all of them. It was concerning God's compassion on the pagan Ninevites that Jonah said, "I know that You are a gracious and merciful God, slow to anger and abundant in lovingkindness, One who relents from doing harm" (Jonah 4:2). Likewise, Jeremiah was musing over God's mercy toward not only Israel but also all *the children of men*, when he wrote:

> For the Lord will not cast off forever.
> Though He causes grief,
> Yet He will show compassion

According to the multitude of His mercies.

For He does not afflict willingly,

Nor grieve the children of men. (Lam. 3:31–33)

God is not one kind of God to Israel and another kind of God to the rest of the world. He is the one God of all creation, as Paul wrote: "Is He the God of the Jews only? Is He not also the God of the Gentiles? Yes, of the Gentiles also" (Rom. 3:29). God's character, as revealed to Israel, is His character universally. His policies of mercy and of wrath are "to the Jew first and also to the Greek" (Rom. 2:9–10). There is no difference (Rom. 3:22) and no partiality (Rom. 2:11).

This inclusion of all the Gentiles with Israel was, as Paul called it, "the mystery" hidden from previous ages, but revealed to the apostles through the Holy Spirit (Eph. 3:1–7). Perhaps this was primarily what Jesus meant when He told the disciples that He had more to tell them than they could then endure, but that the Holy Spirit would reveal those things to them (John 16:12–13). There may still be those among His disciples today who "cannot bear" this. God's universal love has always scandalized those who regard themselves alone as "the elect."

Passages That Don't Fit

In addition to passages that seem to affirm universalism (which were cross-examined above) there are a number of biblical texts that seem to be directly at odds with the idea that all will be ultimately reconciled to God. A few will be considered here.

Matthew 12:32: "Anyone who speaks a word against the Son of Man, it will be forgiven him; but whoever speaks against the Holy Spirit, it will not be forgiven him, either in this age or in the age to come."

Howard Marshall brings this up in his rebuttal of universal reconciliation: "[Jesus] spoke about the one sin which could never be forgiven, the sin against the Holy Spirit, which is to be understood as the sin of refusing to see and acknowledge the work of God in Jesus himself."[34]

If Jesus is affirming that there is some sin that is never going to be pardoned, then some people—i.e., those guilty of committing that sin—can never be saved. Jesus thus seems to refute universalism.

One thing that must be acknowledged is that the passage before us is difficult to explain from a universalistic point of view—but then all theologians, if honest, will confess that they find certain things about this particular statement of Jesus to be difficult. It might be pointed out that, when Marshall speaks of a "sin which could never be forgiven," he is not using language found in the passage. The word "never" is not there. True, the parallel passage, in Mark 3:29, reads, "He who blasphemes against the Holy Spirit never has forgiveness," but the word "never" is likewise not found here in the Greek text. Rather, it reads, "Has not forgiveness unto the age." Thus, Matthew and Mark, though citing the statement in different terms from each other, both emphasize the lack of forgiveness as pertaining to an age or ages—not necessarily eternity.

Though this is difficult to decipher, some universalists argue that Jesus is saying this particular blasphemy will not be forgiven within a certain range of time "*in this age or in the age to come.*" Since Paul speaks of multiple ages to come (Eph. 2:7; 3:21), we might conclude that those blaspheming the Holy Spirit would not find forgiveness in Jesus's current age (the Mosaic age) nor in the coming church age (post-Pentecost). If they are to be forgiven at all, it must be in some later age than these. Andrew Jukes wrote: "[According to Matthew 12:31–32] some sins, those, namely, against the Son of Man, can be forgiven, apparently in this age . . . other sins, against the Holy Ghost cannot be forgiven either here or in the coming age; which last

34. I. Howard Marshall, "The New Testament Does *Not* Teach Universal Salvation," in Robin A. Parry and Christopher H. Partridge, *Universal Salvation? The Current Debate* (Grand Rapids: Wm. B. Eerdmans, 2003), 57.

words surely imply that some sins not here forgiven may be forgiven in the coming age, the sin or blasphemy against the Holy Ghost not being of this number."[35]

> **Matthew 26:24:** "The Son of Man indeed goes just as it is written of Him, but woe to that man by whom the Son of Man is betrayed! It would have been good for that man if he had not been born."

This is a classic and severe challenge to the universalist position. Jesus is apparently saying that Judas would have been better off never having been born. Even if we postulate a very severe period of punishment in hell for Judas, yet if he is ultimately to be saved for eternity, then how could that not be an improvement over never having been born?

This is not easily answered. It could be suggested that Jesus is here using hyperbole. It is also possible, as some suggest, that He is saying not that it would have been better for Judas, but for Christ, if Judas had never been born. The Greek reads slightly differently, as if this could be the meaning: "Woe to that man by whom the Son of Man is betrayed; good were it for Him [that is, for the Son of Man] if that man [Judas] was not born." This does not remove all problems, and might still require the recognition of hyperbole in the statement. Gregory MacDonald made the following observation: "It is worth adding at this point that if some texts remain that perplex the universalist, this need not pose a serious obstacle to the acceptance of universalism. Virtually all the key Christian beliefs have some texts that seem to run against them. We may well maintain that, properly interpreted, they do not actually contradict what we take to be the clear teachings of other texts. Nevertheless, we are content to hold firm our faith in the central Christian claims *in spite of some awkward texts*."[36]

35. Andrew Jukes, *The Restitution of All Things*, 1867 (put into electronic format by Kenneth W. Eckerty), http://tgulcm.tripod.com/cu/jukes2.html, 121.

36. Gregory MacDonald, *The Evangelical Universalist* (Eugene, OR: Cascade Books, 2006), 37.

"Point of No Return" Passages

Douglas A. Jacoby has written a book comparing various views of heaven and hell, in which he seems to lean toward conditionalism. In his critique of universalism, he wrote that those advocating this view "ignore the 'point of no return' often found in Scripture. . . . The Bible speaks of a line people can cross, after which there is no repentance or even a desire for repentance."[37]

The verses he lists in this category are the following: Proverbs 29:1; Hebrews 6:4–6; 10:26–31; 2 Peter 2:20–22. These verses speak of a high degree of obstinacy to which one, by continually hardening one's heart against truth, may sink in this life. This condition is described in terms of being "without remedy," "impossible . . . to renew them again to repentance," facing "a certain fearful expectation of judgment, and fiery indignation which will devour the adversaries," and wherein "the latter end is worse for them than the beginning."

Universalists might respond that, while these are clear warnings of judgment and destruction, they are not necessarily commenting on *postmortem* conditions. Proverbs 29:1 speaks of a destruction that is without remedy, and Hebrews 10:26–31 warns of a fiery judgment—but it can be argued that both passages speak of earthly consequences of sin, without addressing longer-range conditions after the judgment. Both Hebrews 6:4–6 and 2 Peter 2:20–22 speak of persons rejecting truth they had earlier embraced, and becoming more hardened than they previously had been, and more resistant to future repentance. It may even be literally impossible to bring about their repentance before they die. Whether things may change for them after being subjected to the chastening conditions of hell is another matter, arguably beyond the purview of the passages in question.

---

37. Douglas A. Jacoby, *What's the Truth about Heaven and Hell?* (Eugene, OR: Harvest House, 2013), 109.

PHILOSOPHICAL AND THEOLOGICAL OBJECTIONS

Universalism Gives Up God's Justice

One of the most common and intuitive objections to the suggestion that all sinners will ultimately be reconciled to God is that this would mean their escape from the demands of justice. Justice is a prominent characteristic in God, which, many feel, would be compromised if He allowed His love for mankind to result in the forgiveness of all. Daniel Strange wrote, "Retributive righteousness cannot be seen to be discretionary as if God has the choice not to punish sin."[38] Paul Helm added, "He [God] cannot but exercise justice. . . . If God has to exercise mercy as he has to exercise justice then such 'mercy' would not be mercy."[39]

God must certainly exercise justice. Yet, if justice necessarily means that every sinner must pay the full penalty for his own sins, then how can *any* be saved? All are sinners, and by this rule, *all must be condemned*. Any logic that suggests God's justice would be compromised by His forgiving *all* sinners would, on the same basis, require that God's justice is compromised by His saving of *any* sinners. If God, through Christ, should save *all* men, how would this violate His justice any more than if, through Christ, He should save only *some* men? One feature of the gospel is its claim that God, without sacrificing His justness, is able to forgive and justify the utterly unworthy (Rom. 3:24–26). Eric Reitan explained this succinctly: "Christians believe that God has met the demands of justice on the cross. Christ has paid the penalty for human sin. If the penalty for human sin has already been paid by Christ, how can justice be an impediment to his mercy and His love?"[40]

---

38. Daniel Strange, "A Calvinist Response to Talbott's Universalism," in Robin A. Parry and Christopher H. Partridge, *Universal Salvation? The Current Debate* (Grand Rapids: Wm. B. Eerdmans, 2003), 151.

39. P. Helm, "The Logic of Limited Atonement," *Scottish Bulletin of Evangelical Theology* 3, no. 2. (1985), 50.

40. Eric Reitan, "Human Freedom and the Impossibility of Eternal Damnation," in

Robert Morey argues, against universal reconciliation, that "the God of Scripture is infinite and since His salvation is eternal, even so His wrath is eternal."[41]

This argument seems to assume that God's own infinitude translates into the infinitude of all of His traits—particularly His wrath. Yet, if this argument is sound, then one might also argue that other traits of His, like love and forgiveness, would also, of necessity, be infinite.[42] There is reason to believe, from the Bible's own declarations, that God's wrath is not infinite,[43] but even if it were, what would prevent one from arguing that this infinite wrath was poured out on Christ on behalf of mankind? While there is no Scripture affirming that God's wrath is infinite, there seem to be many that tell us that His love and grace in Christ are universal.[44]

As Talbott points out, Jesus's teachings rejected and denounced the idea of retaliatory justice (Matt. 5:38–42), which prevailed in His day (and among traditionalists today), along with the prevailing notions of limited forgiveness (Matt. 18:21–22) and limited love (Matt. 5:43–48). The reason Jesus gave for our obligation to forgive everyone who offends us, and to love and bless those who wrong us, is that we might "be perfect, just as [our] Father in heaven is perfect" (Matt. 5:48).[45]

When Jesus prayed, "Father, forgive them, for they do not know what they do" (Luke 23:34), He was praying not for "the elect," nor for the repentant, but for the very sinners who were even then crucifying Him. His benevolence toward those offenders, on that

---

Robin A. Parry and Christopher H. Partridge, *Universal Salvation? The Current Debate* (Grand Rapids: Wm. B. Eerdmans, 2003), 126f.

41. Robert A. Morey, *Death and the Afterlife* (Minneapolis: Bethany House, 1984), 242.

42. Psalms 103:8; 135:1ff.; 145:8f.; Micah 7:18f.; 1 Corinthians 13:4–8; Luke 6:35f.; John 3:16; 1 John 4:8.

43. e.g., Psalm 30:5; Jeremiah 23:20; 30:24; Lamentations 3:31–33; Jonah 4:2; etc.

44. e.g., 2 Samuel 14:14; John 12:47; 2 Corinthians 5:19; 1 John 2:2; 1 Timothy 2:3–6; 2 Peter 3:9; etc.

45. Thomas Talbott, "Reply to My Critics," in Robin A. Parry and Christopher H. Partridge, *Universal Salvation? The Current Debate* (Grand Rapids: Wm. B. Eerdmans, 2003), 257f.

occasion, renders it difficult to imagine any degree of sinfulness that would be beyond the boundaries of His merciful disposition.

Free Will Prevents Universal Salvation

Even if God were willing to save all sinners, there remains the problem of human free will. Some people just don't love God and do not want Him. No amount of coercion or chastisement in hell will necessarily change some people. To guarantee the salvation of all, God would have to override the free choices of some. David Powys put this argument quite succinctly: "Without coercion universal reconciliation would not be achievable."[46]

Richard Bauckham stated the same concern: "Logically it might seem that Origen's conviction of the inalienable freedom of the soul ought to prevent him from teaching both universalism (for any soul is free to remain obstinate for ever) and the final secure happiness of the saved (who remain free to fall again at any time)."[47]

It is philosophically sound, at one level, to say that a person possessing complete freedom of choice might, theoretically, continue eternally to make a choice that only does himself harm. However, finding one who could never be persuaded to do otherwise might begin to raise doubts in our minds as to whether our subject was really intelligent enough to be entrusted with choices about his own destiny. While the concept of free will can be demonstrated from Scripture, it is nowhere stated that human autonomy is absolute. In fact, it is not. Whenever it may serve God's purpose, He reserves the right to manipulate human decisions, so that He hardens Pharaoh's heart to prevent premature repentance (Ex. 4:21), or He puts it in the hearts of ten kings to give their authority to the Beast (Rev. 17:17). He can direct the hearts of kings like He directs the rivers of water

---

46. David J. Powys, *"Hell": A Hard Look at a Hard Question—The Fate of the Unrighteous in New Testament Thought* (Carlisle: Paternoster, 1997), 337.

47. Richard Bauckham, "Universalism: A Historical Survey," *Themelios* 4.2 (Sept. 1978), 48.

(Prov. 21:1). God has no obligation to give a man unlimited free choices. Man is given enough freedom to be held responsible for his rebellion, but not necessarily enough to thwart God's eternal purposes. As Gregory MacDonald pointed out: "When you see that a person you love has irrationally chosen to do irreparable harm to himself or herself (in the case of the traditional doctrine of hell such harm amounts to suffering unbearable torment forever and ever), is freedom so sacrosanct that you are not justified in interfering with it?"[48]

Universalists argue that the possession of true, responsible freedom of choice requires certain preconditions. Christian philosopher Thomas Talbott has explained free moral agency as follows:

> For freedom surely requires, among other things, a minimal degree of *rationality*, including an ability to learn from experience, an ability to discern reasons for acting, and a capacity for moral improvement.
>
> With good reason, therefore, do we exclude small children, the severely brain damaged, paranoid schizophrenics, and even dogs from the class of free moral agents: They all lack the required rationality.[49]

Universalism Makes Atonement Unnecessary

Daniel Strange, finding agreement with Shedd, raises the point that universalism undermines the atoning work of Christ: "W. G. T. Shedd shows profound insight when he comments: 'The doctrine of Christ's vicarious atonement logically stands and falls with that of eternal punishment.' Let us be quite clear. If we lost hell, we will

---

48. Gregory MacDonald, *The Evangelical Universalist* (Eugene, OR: Cascade Books, 2006), 23.

49. Thomas Talbott, "Reply to My Critics," in Robin A. Parry and Christopher H. Partridge, *Universal Salvation? The Current Debate* (Grand Rapids: Wm. B. Eerdmans, 2003), 263.

eventually lose the cross, for if there is no hell, there is no real point in the cross."[50]

It is not clear why the condition, "If there is no hell . . . ," is mentioned, since there is no participant in the debate who would deny the existence of hell. Of course, even if there were no hell, the value of the atonement would remain the same. The atonement has to do with restoring sinners to God *for His own sake*, and not with the identification of any specific punishment from which the redeemed have been rescued. If all were to be saved, their salvation would be as dependent upon the atonement as would that of any lesser number who were saved.

Hell Cannot Reform Hearts, Where Grace, in This Life, Has Failed to Do So

What confidence can we have that the sinner's experience in hell would bring about true heartfelt repentance, when one has managed to resist, unto death, the persuasive drawing of God's grace? Can extended torment produce genuine love for the tormentor? There is no evidence that hell can accomplish in the next life what grace has failed to achieve in the present world. It is difficult to believe that torture would produce genuine penitence in the heart, or that God would value highly a love for Him elicited only under such duress.

In fairness, it should be pointed out that defenders of universal reconciliation do not necessarily claim that repentance will be brought about in hell *through torture*. It is not necessary to assume that what one experiences in hell will be the direct imposition of torture from the hand of God. Traditionalists themselves often make the same point, in defending their view from the charge of cruelty.

Hell may be seen merely as deprivation of the presence of God, and of all those blessings and consolations from His hand that sinners

---

50. Daniel Strange, "A Calvinist Response to Talbott's Universalism," in *Universal Salvation? The Current Debate* (Grand Rapids: Wm. B. Eerdmans, 2003), 154.

in this life foolishly take for granted. The removal of all God's blessings is not the same thing as torture, though it would certainly be torment. One may learn to love another person after he or she is no longer available, when a sense of delayed appreciation has set in. No doubt many a man or woman has gained a newfound appreciation for his or her parents only after they had died and were no longer around. The removal of God's presence (formerly taken for granted) may well inspire a belated appreciation for the wonderful God who so freely had conferred so many previously unappreciated blessings.

In order for restorationism to be true, all that needs to be affirmed is that, given enough time and incentives, people in hell will experience a change of heart toward God. This could be due to His total absence (never previously experienced), or a response to severe discipline, or simply the result of having seen Him as He really is for the first time, and being disabused of previously held, slanderous ideas about Him. If conversion in hell is a possibility at all, there is no compelling reason to rule out that grace plays as major a part in it as it does in this life, where it is not uncommon for people, under great suffering or stress, to turn genuinely to God, surrendering to His grace.

Still, there is no proof from history that everyone is capable of being won over, regardless what inducements may be offered. As Douglas Jacoby wrote: "If the devil and his angels have for ages past chosen to resist God, despite the overwhelming evidence that they are on the losing side (James 2:19; Rev. 12:12), then there is no strong reason for believing that even with eons of time to consider one's fate, any would actually change sides."[51]

Universalism Makes Evangelism and Mission Unnecessary

Many traditionalists ask, if all are to be ultimately saved, what is the point in evangelizing sinners? As Erwin Lutzer wrote in his

---

51. Douglas Jacoby, *What's the Truth about Heaven and Hell?* (Eugene, OR: Harvest House, 2013), 108.

book *One Minute After You Die*: "Obviously, if this teaching were true there would be no pressing reason to fulfill the great commission or to urge unbelievers to accept Christ in this life."[52]

J. I. Packer wrote: "It follows that the decisiveness of decisions made in this life, and the urgency of evangelism here in this life, immediately, are undermined. . . . You can see what the missionary implications of this are going to be."[53]

The proper motivation for evangelism and missions was discussed in chapter 10, when answering the identical accusation made against conditionalism. There we pointed out that the desire to glorify God, and to see His kingdom advance in the earth, is the proper Christian motivation for evangelism, as for every other activity in life (Matt. 6:33; 1 Cor. 10:31). Those who know such motivations are the ones who should be sharing the love of Jesus with the lost—not those who know of nothing but threats to motivate themselves and others.

Having Our Friends in Hell Will Not Spoil Our Heaven

In the previous chapter, universalism charged that the traditional view of hell would make our heaven (and God's) a hell also, since our sympathies would naturally be with people cherished (or even *liked*) by us in this life, but whom we would know to be tormented endlessly in hell. Traditionalists have answered this with various suggestions—from God hiding hell from the eyes and minds of the saved to our being totally transformed in our sentiments, so that our present sympathies toward suffering people will be superseded by our agreement with God concerning the sufferings of our former friends, neighbors, and family members. Howard Marshall wrote: "A traditional standard reply to this point is that the redeemed will be sufficiently sanctified that they share the attitude of God towards

---

52. Erwin W. Lutzer, *One Minute After You Die* (Chicago, IL: Moody Press, 1977), 101.
53. J. I. Packer, "The Problem of Universalism Today," in Packer, *Celebrating the Saving Work of God* (Carlisle: Paternoster, 1998), 171.

the lost in that they are being justly punished for their rejection of goodness and therefore their lot is not to be regretted."[54]

Calvinist Daniel Strange takes this traditional view: "However, far from believing the existence of hell was a cause of distress for the redeemed, Calvinists of the stature of Jonathan Edwards and Murray McCheyne wrote that believers will rejoice in the existence of hell. The basis for their argument is not a feeling of superiority or a perverse sadism but can be summed by McCheyne himself: 'The redeemed will have no mind but God's. They will have no joy but what the Lord has.'"[55]

Many, including some traditionalists, would object to such a strange concept of heaven. Apparently, people who agree with this concept of heaven believe that our present sympathies for the misery of others is actually a defect of our fallen nature, from which we will be delivered when we are glorified in the resurrection.

This means that Christ's commandment that we love our neighbor as He loved us will expire and be replaced with the obligation to hate and exult in the misery of sinners, as He then will. Our obligation to love our fellow man, far from reflecting an eternal attribute of God, really has a natural shelf-life—despite Paul's declarations that "love never fails. . . . And now [remain] faith, hope, love, these three; but the greatest of these is love" (1 Cor. 13:8, 13).

Conditionalism's answer to this problem is more satisfying existentially than is traditionalism's. If conditionalists are right, then our unsaved loved ones will not be suffering the whole time that we are in the eternal presence of God. Eventually, they will be nonexistent. As much as we may miss them, we will not have to live with the knowledge that, somewhere, they are screaming out in agony from

54. I. Howard Marshall, "The New Testament Does *Not* Teach Universal Salvation," in Robin A. Parry and Christopher H. Partridge, *Universal Salvation? The Current Debate* (Grand Rapids: Wm. B. Eerdmans, 2003), 60.

55. Daniel Strange, "A Calvinist Response to Talbott's Universalism," in Robin A. Parry and Christopher H. Partridge, *Universal Salvation? The Current Debate* (Grand Rapids: Wm. B. Eerdmans, 2003), 164.

which they will never know the slightest relief. Those whom we have loved, but who are taken from us by death, are missed, but not eternally grieved over. Conditionalist John Sanders wrote: "It is possible even now to live with loss. Perhaps we will be given the ability in the new creation to live with loss just as God does. Consequently, I find unpersuasive the argument that my eternal blessedness will be ruined if everyone is not redeemed."[56]

So if our sentiments, as Marshall wrote, "will be sufficiently sanctified that they share the attitude of God towards the lost," do we have any insight from Scripture as to what God's sentiments may actually be toward the lost? Is there no clue given in the parables of the lost sheep, the lost coin, and the prodigal son? The God of the Old Testament declared: "As I live . . . I have no pleasure in the death of the wicked, but that the wicked turn from his way and live. Turn, turn from your evil ways! For why should you die . . . ?" (Ezek. 33:11).

Peter insisted that God is "not willing that any should perish but that all should come to repentance" (2 Peter 3:9). If anyone ultimately perishes, says the restorationist, then God, who was not willing that any would perish, is eternally disappointed with the results of His creation experiment. That all people should be saved is God's stated sentiment. Those in heaven whose sentiments have been wholly sanctified, then, would grieve God's loss of the billions of children He desired to bring to glory, even if most of them were not personally known to them. The tragedy of an eternal hell is not man's loss, but God's.

---

56. John Sanders, "A Freewill Theist's Response to Talbott's Universalism," in Robin A. Parry and Christopher H. Partridge, *Universal Salvation? The Current Debate* (Grand Rapids: Wm. B. Eerdmans, 2003), 172f.

EPILOGUE

> When you speak of heaven let your face light up. . . . When
> you speak of hell—well, then your everyday face will do.
> —*Charles Haddon Spurgeon*[1]

B y any description, hell is a disagreeable subject—or at least, it
should be. Dwight L. Moody said, "When we preach on hell,
we might at least do it with tears in our eyes." In considering the
scriptural, philosophical, and practical arguments in the previous
pages, the reader may have reached some degree of conviction as to
exactly *how disagreeable* we are obliged to see it. Or, possibly, that
conclusion awaits further consideration.

Those who find themselves suddenly undecided upon an issue
they thought they had understood previously may be wanting to
ask, "How, then, am I to answer when unbelievers, or even other
Christians, ask about hell?" To this I can only recommend that one
be very truthful. My own approach is to truthfully say, "The Bible
is not as clear as I once believed concerning the details of God's final
judgment, and various theories exist among Christians. However,
the Bible is clear on the one thing we need to know, namely, that
Jesus Christ is Lord, and that God calls all men to repent and submit
to His authority. Those who do so genuinely will be reconciled to

---

1. Charles Spurgeon, quoted in R. C. Sproul, *Developing Christian Character Study Guide* (Orlando, FL: Ligonier Ministries, 1988), 67.

God, and need not worry about the precise nature of the fate that they have escaped."

Potentially, the happiest or the unhappiest result of a study such as this is the vision of the character of God that necessarily arises from whichever view seems the most persuasive. My own sentiments, I am afraid, have not remained entirely hidden in the presentation—though I remain genuinely undecided, at the time of this writing, as to which view best represents the complete synthesis of the biblical information. I know what I would *prefer* to be true, and probably the reader knows also. In the absence of certain knowledge, I think, it is some comfort in knowing that more than one possibility—not only the worst one—is worthy of consideration.

Several questions have been deliberately left unaddressed, as being peripheral to my primary focus. For example, all views of hell accommodate the imagery of "fire." Is this to be understood as fire such as we know it in this world? Is it the burning of remorse, or of the deprivation of pleasures to which the heart has, in this life, become addicted, but which are not present in hell? I have seen no reason to burden these pages with such speculations.

Is it possible that the truth about hell may lie in some amalgam of more than one of the views? Some, having become persuaded that postmortem repentance cannot scripturally be ruled out, and yet wishing to preserve the free will of the eternally obstinate, have entertained notions of the postmortem conversion of some of the lost, coupled with either the annihilation or eternal torment of the incorrigible. This ends up being essentially identical to the "wider hope" concept, wherein many of the lost, having never heard of Christ in their lifetimes, are thought to receive a second chance to choose Him when they encounter Him beyond the grave.

The one fact, above all others, which I have desired to get across is that our view of hell is inseparably joined to our view of God. I believe that many Christians have simply assumed that they already know what the Bible teaches about hell, and have formed their notions of the character of God to accommodate their theory. My suggestion is that this is doing things backward. The purpose of Scripture, and of Christ Himself, is to put us back in touch with God—to reintroduce alienated children to their Father. Certain inaccurate notions of hell may actually interfere with a correct perception of the Father's nature. We should first discover God's character in Christ, as well as in the Scriptures, and then attempt to harmonize the obscure statements about His ultimate judgment with the vision that we have found to be true by such prior inquiries.

The fact that the Bible actually exhibits sufficient ambiguity on the subject of hell as to allow three very disparate viewpoints to be maintained by Christians of equal intelligence and sincerity raises the question whether God even thinks it important that we reach final conclusions on the matter. It may be that God, in His wisdom, has chosen not to satisfy our curiosity about the fates of others, so that we might redirect our energies to fulfilling our own assigned tasks. When Peter, wondering about John's destiny, asked Jesus, "But Lord, what about this man?" Jesus said to him, "What is that to you? You follow Me" (John 21:21–22).

APPENDIX

Side-by-Side Comparison of Arguments

CHART A: ARGUMENTS FOR TRADITIONALISM

Argument for the View	Cross-Examination of Argument	Further Discussion of the Point
1. Eternal torment has been the orthodox view of hell for two thousand years. How could everyone be so wrong?	This was not true until the sixth century. There were always alternative views held among believers. They were not considered heretical until the Roman Catholic Church condemned them.	But the Reformers also held the traditional view, and they were not controlled by the Roman Catholic Church. *Response:* But they did retain a number of Catholic traditions not supported in Scripture.
2. Jesus warned about hell more than anyone else. How can we call it "unloving"?	Jesus talked about the loving Father more than about hell. Whatever He may have believed about hell (He really didn't say much about it), He must have understood it in light of God's love for all mankind.	On the contrary, Jesus's teaching on love should be interpreted as limited by His teaching on final judgment. *Response:* That would only be true if judgment was His primary teaching, and the love of God a subordinate feature of His ministry.
3. *Gehenna* was seen by rabbis, in Jesus's time, as eternal torment.	By some of the rabbis, yes, but not by all. Among the Jews, all three views existed as in the church today. The school of Hillel believed in annihilation.	But the school of Shammai, who taught eternal torment, was more prominently represented among the Pharisees. *Response:* Precisely! Among the *Pharisees*, with whom Jesus often found Himself at odds.

Argument for the View	Cross-Examination of Argument	Further Discussion of the Point
4. Jesus would use the term as the rabbis did, unless He clarified otherwise.	Why should He, when there was a precedent of the term being used differently in the Old Testament? How often did Jesus really agree with the traditions of the rabbis against the Old Testament Scriptures?	Jesus's hearers would have understood His use of *Gehenna* in the sense of the final judgment of sinners, because they heard the rabbis teach in the synagogues. *Response:* True! This same familiarity with the rabbis' teachings often caused people to misunderstand Jesus.
5. "Death" is not unconsciousness, but means eternal separation from God (Gen. 2:17).	Separation from God is experienced by sinners in this life (Eph. 2:1, 12), but there is no Scripture declaring it to mean a separation that is *everlasting*.	But the separation continues after death, if there is no repentance. *Response:* Even if so, it may not necessarily be endless.
6. Daniel 12:2 describes the wicked as eternally ashamed. That is conscious suffering.	There is no reference to the subjective shame felt by the lost. They are held in contempt by others, whether alive or dead themselves.	But it could be read as if they were conscious. *Response:* Or not.
7. Isaiah 66:24 talks about unquenchable fires and worms, which speaks of eternal torment.	This verse talks about "corpses" being consumed by fire and maggots. There is no hint that the corpses are conscious of their condition.	But they are an "abhorrence." This is the same as "contempt" in Daniel 12:2. *Response:* And it no more speaks of the consciousness of the corpses than does Daniel 12:2.

Argument for the View	Cross-Examination of Argument	Further Discussion of the Point
8. Mark 9:43–44 says it's better to be mutilated than to go to Gehenna. This would not be true if people are annihilated or restored to God from hell.	First, *Gehenna* may not be a reference to hell, but to the Valley of Hinnom. Second, even if it is hell, its torments may be prolonged and excruciating without necessarily being *eternal*.	But it seems that it must be really bad, if it is better to be mutilated. *Response:* No doubt it is! But "really bad" is not a synonym for *everlasting*.
9. There will be weeping and gnashing of teeth—that's conscious suffering, not annihilation.	Agreed. But this does not prove eternal torment, since the duration of this grief is not mentioned. All views anticipate such.	But these emotions are associated with hell. *Response:* Maybe, but neither hell nor these sufferings are declared to be endless for the lost.
10. Hell's fires are "everlasting" (Gr. *aionios*) (Matt. 25:41). This everlasting punishment mirrors eternal (*aionios*) life (Matt. 25:46) in the same verse—if one is endless, then both are.	*Aionios* ("everlasting" or "eternal") is a word that needn't be translated that way. It can often mean "enduring" or "pertaining to the age." Permanent annihilation is "eternal." Burnable things (people) may not last as long as the fire does.	But if it is not "endless" when referring to punishment, it can't mean "endless" referring to life. *Response:* It might not mean "endless." The alternative definitions work for both cases.
11. Sinners will share the devil's fate, which is eternal torment (Matt. 25:41 w/ Rev. 20:10).	They are not said to share the devil's "fate." They are cast into the same fire. What becomes of them there might not resemble what happens to the devil—a nonhuman being.	But the Beast and the False Prophet also are tormented with Satan there. *Response:* These entities are not necessarily human individuals either—nor are "Death" and "Hades," which are also cast into the same place (Rev. 20:14).

Argument for the View	Cross-Examination of Argument	Further Discussion of the Point
12. The rich man was in flames, from which there was no escape (Luke 16:24, 26), contra to what universalists claim.	The story is not about final judgment, but about the intermediate state in Hades, before the resurrection.	But both Hades and hell have the same features: fire and torment. *Response:* Possibly true. However, this is a story about Hades, not hell.
13. The punishment of the wicked is to be everlastingly shut out from the presence of God (2 Thess. 1:9), suggesting conscious existence.	There is no reference to being shut out from God in the Greek of this verse. Translators enhanced the English with their own words. This is simply "destruction from God."	But it could involve being shut out from His presence. *Response:* It could, and Paul could have said that, if that's what he meant to convey.
14. The smoke of their torment ascends forever (Rev. 14:11) — meaning they suffer forever.	The smoke of their torment is not the same thing as their torment itself. It is only the memorial of their suffering that is permanent.	Smoke doesn't keep ascending after the fire is gone. *Response:* But it may ascend long after its victims are dead (Gen. 19:27f.).
15. They have "no rest day or night" (Rev. 14:11) — so they are conscious.	There is neither day nor night in hell. This idiom means "continuously." It does not say how long this lasts.	It is connected with the smoke of their torment arising forever. *Response:* True. We mustn't make more of it than does the text itself.
16. The devil is tormented forever in the lake of fire, thus the lake of fire means eternal torment (Rev. 20:10).	It apparently means that for him — and for the Beast and the False Prophet with him. It is not said to mean that for others (vv. 14–15).	People may suffer there as long as the devil does. *Response:* If they are immortal, they may. We are not told that this is so.

Argument for the View	Cross-Examination of Argument	Further Discussion of the Point
17. God's love is not His only trait; He also has wrath.	The Bible tells us His wrath is brief, but His love is forever. Whatever expression of His wrath there may be must serve the interests of love.	But God only loves the elect. He hates the non-elect. *Response:* Not all are Calvinists. If Calvinism is true, this is correct.
18. For justice to be served, punishment must not be less than deserved.	Christians expect to receive less punishment than they deserve, don't they? Where's the justice in *that?*	Well, those who repent are forgiven. *Universalist response:* Then, if all eventually repent, it's all good.
19. The only reason we recoil at the concept of eternal judgment is that we are ourselves sinners and naturally sympathize with sinners.	God and Jesus are not sinners, and they recoil even at the death of sinners (Ezek. 33:11; Luke 19:41–44). How much more, then, would they object to eternal torment?	God sees sinners as criminals deserving judgment. *Response:* God also sees sinners as lost sheep needing a shepherd (Ezek. 34:11–16; Matt. 9:36).
20. Sins committed in a short space of time may be severe enough to deserve the strictest of punishments.	True, but no sin committed in finite time deserves infinite judgment.	Next . . .
21. Sins committed in finite time nonetheless deserve infinite punishment because they are offenses against an infinite God.	If the Bible said this, it would be worthy of acceptance. As it is, it is neither affirmed by Scripture, nor by common sense.	But the magnitude of sin is determined by the magnitude of the offended party. *Response:* This sounds more like feudal jurisprudence than the Bible.

Argument for the View	Cross-Examination of Argument	Further Discussion of the Point
22. Not all punishments will be equal in intensity. God recognizes degrees of guilt and punishes proportionately.	Then the previous argument must be false. If all sins against infinite Majesty deserve infinite punishment, then there can be no degrees of guilt.	Next . . .
23. Even if finite sins do not deserve infinite punishment, sinners will continue to sin eternally in hell, which justifies their being eternally punished.	If the Scripture affirmed anything like this, we might be obliged to see this as true. As it is, the Scripture's silence on such matters renders this argument 100 percent speculation.	Next . . .
24. For God to annihilate sinners would be immoral. It violates the dignity of their being made in God's image.	This is a questionable philosophical point. If it is an affront to human dignity to execute a criminal, how much worse an affront it must be to consign him to eternal indignity and contempt (as per Dan. 12:2).	But to be put out of existence is worse than being allowed to live under punishment. *Response:* By whose assessment? Why do men commit suicide in prison then?
25. Annihilation is no punishment. One who is annihilated feels no pain.	Annihilationism allows there to be pain enough, as necessary—followed by extinction.	But men will endure pain for a while, if they know it will end, at some point, in death. *Response:* Your point being?
26. There is no opportunity of repentance after death (Heb. 9:27).	This is not stated in Hebrews 9:27 (or anywhere else in Scripture). It is scripturally unjustified speculation.	But after death comes the "judgment." *Response:* Yes. But hell (whatever it may involve) comes after that.

Argument for the View	Cross-Examination of Argument	Further Discussion of the Point
27. Jesus said that those who blaspheme the Holy Spirit will never be forgiven. They must be punished eternally.	*Conditionalist:* Someone who has been annihilated can hardly be said to have been "forgiven" any more than a man executed for a crime can be said to have been "acquitted." *Restorationist:* Those who are punished have not been "forgiven," even if their punishment is finite. A man who serves time in jail has not been "forgiven." Had he been forgiven, he would not have gone to jail.	But someone who has been annihilated, or who has suffered only finite punishment, has gotten off pretty easy, compared to eternal torment. *Response:* On what basis are we justified in using "eternal torment" as the standard against which to measure the severity of finite punishments? Unless the Bible teaches infinite punishment, there is no reason to measure against that standard.
28. Jesus talks about the unforgiving servant being delivered to tormentors until he has paid his whole debt (Matt. 18:34). His debt was millions of dollars. How could he pay that from prison? He is never getting out.	Technically, there is no indication that this parable describes postmortem circumstances. It could refer to the tortured conscience of one who does not forgive others. *Restorationist:* The parable does not say that the man will never pay the debt. Even a huge debt, paid a little at a time, would not require eternity to repay. The wording actually does speak of the possibility of release from that situation.	But we see a judgment made here that is best understood as eschatological, and the man's debt was enormous. The impression given is that it was unpayable. *Response:* This is not stated, nor implied. We don't know what resources or rich friends may have been available to resolve his debts. In fact, the man had claimed that, given some time, he could repay it (v. 26). In fact, the original debt had already been forgiven (v. 27). All that this man now "owed" was to forgive his neighbor (vv. 32–33).

Argument for the View	Cross-Examination of Argument	Further Discussion of the Point
29. If there is no eternal torment, there is no compelling reason to live righteously. Why not eat, drink, and be merry, if tomorrow we are merely annihilated?	True, unless one loves God and wishes to please Him. If one doesn't, chances are, his fear of hell alone will not lead him to live a sincerely good life. The Pharisees believed in an eternal hell.	But some don't love God enough to serve Him without threats. *Response:* The worse for them—and the worse for God, to be stuck with such grudging worshipers!
30. If there is no eternal torment from which to save people, there is no reason to risk our lives going out as missionaries to reach the lost.	There is such a thing as loving God and wishing to spread His kingdom. On the other hand, it is harder to love one who torments His enemies endlessly. Perhaps those who believe in this doctrine will require it to motivate them.	But why give up our lives, if the worst that will come to sinners is annihilation? *Response:* Why indeed? If we are man-centered, rather than God-centered, it is very hard to think of a good answer.

CHART B: ARGUMENTS FOR CONDITIONALISM

Argument for the View	Cross-Examination of Argument	Further Discussion of the Point
1. Man was made only potentially immortal (Gen. 2:17; 3:22).	No, man was made only potentially *mortal*. He was created sinless, and would not die unless he sinned.	The fact that he could sin and die meant that his *immortality* was not guaranteed. His eternal life depended upon his access to the "tree of life." *Response:* You could argue this either way. His death depended upon his eating of the "tree of the knowledge of good and evil."
2. Only God (not man) is immortal (1 Tim. 6:16).	This may refer to God's absolute self-existence from all eternity. If no one else than God has eternal life, then we do not.	Our eternal life is *in Christ* (1 John 5:11–12). Without Him we do not have it. With Him, we share in His immortality. This is conditional. *Response:* Next . . .
3. Man must seek immortality (Rom. 2:7).	This means immortality in heaven. In the passage, it is contrasted with indignation, wrath, tribulation, and anguish (vv. 8–9), which means conscious torment in hell.	These sufferings are not said to continue eternally. *Response:* It is implied, by being contrasted with immortality in the previous verse.
4. Immortality is offered only to those who believe in Christ (John 3:16).	It speaks of "everlasting (*aionios*) life" (not the word "immortality"). Such a term can speak of a quality of life enjoyed by believers, but not given to unbelievers.	When *aionios* is connected to punishment, judgment, and similar terms, traditionalists want it to mean "endless." Why not here? *Response:* Why do conditionalists want it to mean "endless" here, but not when applied to punishments?

Argument for the View	Cross-Examination of Argument	Further Discussion of the Point
5. Those not in Christ "perish" (John 3:16).	This word does not necessarily mean "annihilation," but it can speak of experiencing ruin. A person's life can be ruined without being annihilated.	In the vast majority of its occurrences in Scripture, this word refers to physical death. *Response:* Yes. Physical death. It is not, in those places, talking about ultimate postmortem consequences. For those, we need to consult other passages.
6. God told Adam, "The day that you eat of it you shall surely die" (Gen. 2:17). This is the ultimate penalty for sin, confirmed elsewhere in Scripture.	Adam didn't die physically that day. He "died" spiritually. He was separated from God. This is a conscious condition that can continue into eternity.	Such *eternal* separation is not affirmed in Scripture. It would be strange, if it were true, for God not to warn them of the true penalty. *Response:* It is possible (as in some translations) that 2 Thessalonians 1:9 speaks of such an eternal separation.
7. "The wages of sin is death" (Rom. 6:23). "Death" means not living (e.g., Gen. 42:2; Deut. 33:6; Isa. 38:1; Eze. 18:28).	Physical death is the opposite of physical living, but this does not apply when "death" is used of something other than physical death.	It would be interesting to see this demonstrated. Whether used physically, spiritually, or metaphorically, "death" is always the opposite of "life." *Response:* But the absence of "life" may refer to the absence of *a certain kind or quality of life.*
8. The soul "sleeps" unconscious until resurrection (Matt. 9:24; 1 Thess. 4:13–15).	This is disputable, but not really relevant to the question of post-resurrection immortality.	Next . . .

Argument for the View	Cross-Examination of Argument	Further Discussion of the Point
9. The lake of fire is "the second death" (Rev. 20:14), not perpetual life in torment.	This "death" is the ultimate "wages of sin." It is not physical death, or loss of consciousness, but loss of the life of the kingdom of God. We are told that those in the lake of fire continue to be tormented (Rev. 20:10).	The devil, the Beast, and the False Prophet, yes. Death is also cast in there (20:14), and we specifically know that it is there destroyed (1 Cor. 15:26) and will be "no more" (Rev. 21:4). Ordinary *people* are not said to be eternally tormented there.
10. Jesus said that the soul itself can be "destroyed" in hell, after the body has been killed (Matt. 10:28). This speaks of annihilation, not immortality of the soul.	1. *Gehenna* might (or might not) be intended as a reference to hell (see chapter 5). 2. "Destroy" can mean "ruin." The soul in hell can be ruined, but continue to exist. 3. Even if the soul is annihilated at death, the person is later raised for the judgment. It is not the soul, but the resurrected body, that ends up in the lake of fire.	But the impression given by Jesus's statement seems to speak of the ultimate destruction of body and soul after the judgment. It may be ambiguous on that point, but the impression given is strongly in favor of annihilation. *Response:* Next. . . .
11. Someday all creation will worship God, the wicked being no more. If there is a cosmic torture chamber somewhere being eternally maintained, then there is no resolution and no complete victory of righteousness.	*Traditionalist:* The word "all" often is not to be taken literally in Scripture. It is often a hyperbole. *Restorationist:* The same conditions may be achieved through the conversion of everyone in hell.	Next. . . .

Argument for the View	Cross-Examination of Argument	Further Discussion of the Point
12. "Fire" is primarily for consuming combustibles (e.g., Isa. 9:18; Jer. 21:14; Hos. 8:14; Amos 1:4).	*Traditionalist:* Fire can also be used as an emblem of torture (Luke 16:24; Rev. 20:10). *Restorationist:* It can also be a refining or purifying agent (e.g., Isa. 4:4; 6:6–7; Mal. 3:3; 1 Peter 1:7).	But consuming and burning up are the most frequent scriptural concepts associated with fire. *Response:* Of course, the imagery must be evaluated case-by-case, and harmonized with the whole theme of judgment in Scripture.
13. Twenty-six times in the New Testament the wicked are said to be "burned up."	Most of these passages are figurative, and, in their context, they speak of temporal punishment and physical death. They do not necessarily relate to hell or its effects.	Next . . .
14. "Fire that is not quenched" does not necessarily burn forever. This imagery is often used in the Old Testament to refer to temporal judgments.	This is a good reason to question whether such "unquenchable fire" is a reference to postmortem destinies at all. As it refers to temporal judgments in the Old, so in the New.	In the New Testament, these terms are applied to eschatological punishment (e.g., Matt. 3:12; Mark 9:43). *Response:* These texts may not be speaking of the final judgment, but of Jerusalem's destruction in AD 70.

Argument for the View	Cross-Examination of Argument	Further Discussion of the Point
15. God is a "consuming fire" (Heb. 12:29).	What He consumes is not stated. It may be a reference to His judgment on Jerusalem (context could encourage this). It is also possible that He consumes dross in the purifying of His people. The statement proves little about annihilationism, except as an example of fire having the function of consuming fuel.	Next …
16. The wicked, like chaff, and fruitless trees, are to be burned up (Matt. 3:10, 12).	To make these statements refer to hell is to ignore the context, in which John the Baptist describes imminent judgment on those in his day. "The ax is laid to the root …" speaks of a stroke about to fall. It is not the final judgment that is here in view.	Next …
17. Branches broken off the Vine are burned up (John 15:6).	They are being disposed of. The imagery of discarded "branches" (which represent people) suggests throwing them into fire. In reality, people are not branches. The analogy should not be pressed beyond its intended limits.	Branches thrown into fire are eventually consumed. If the case is otherwise with people thrown into the fire, we are never informed of it. There is no hint that the case is different with people than with branches.

Argument for the View	Cross-Examination of Argument	Further Discussion of the Point
18. The wicked "melt away" (Ps. 58:8), "wither" (Ps. 37:2), "fade" (Job 14:2), and "vanish like smoke" (Ps. 37:20).	Where these images are found, they appear to speak of the vanishing of the wicked from the earthly scene, rather than postmortem fates.	The burden of proof would seem to rest upon those who wish to make the ultimate fate of these people different from the fate described. *Response:* The burden of proof, rather, rests with those who wish to make the passages speak of subjects beyond their intended theme.
19. In fifty-nine New Testament passages, the fate of the wicked is "destruction."	The Greek words for "destroy" and "destruction" can refer to being ruined or damaged beyond repair, which does not require the additional assumption of annihilation.	To be destroyed sounds severe, but not nearly so severe as to be tormented eternally—a fate for which no definite scriptural support exists. *Restorationist response:* True. But eternal torment and annihilation—neither of which are clearly taught as the final state of the lost—are not the only alternatives available.

CHART C: ARGUMENTS FOR RESTORATIONISM

Argument for the View	Cross-Examination of Argument	Further Discussion of the Point
1. The ultimate salvation of all is the only logical corollary to the doctrines of God's omnibenevolence and God's omnipotence.	God's omnibenevolence is not an accepted doctrine by Calvinists, and Arminians do not believe that God's omnipotence cancels human free will with reference to salvation.	But God's omnibenevolence and sovereign power to accomplish His purposes are well-established in Scripture. *Response:* Not all agree upon the interpretations of the relevant texts.
2. It is possible that repentance may occur beyond the grave for those who died unsaved.	There is no Scripture affirming this possibility. The strong urgings of Scripture to repent now, rather than to delay, suggest this life provides the only opportunities for this.	Scripture does not deny that such opportunities may exist. There are good reasons to repent and serve God in this life (justifying the strong appeals) even if there are further opportunities beyond death. *Response:* Still, Scripture promises no such opportunities.
3. Only this view provides adequate explanation for the existence of suffering. If God can turn everything, eventually, to every person's salvation, earthly sufferings may be justified as means to that end.	Such sufferings may also be justified as being merely *potentially* effective in bringing about repentance, whether they actually accomplish this desired effect or not, just as radical surgery may be justified even in cases where it may not necessarily prove effective.	Next . . .

Argument for the View	Cross-Examination of Argument	Further Discussion of the Point
4. God's love is universal, because He is love.	Love is not God's only attribute. He is also a just judge, and has wrath toward sin. Calvinists do not affirm that God loves all people equally, nor is He obligated to do so.	Love is God's very nature. There is no question of God's *obligations*, but only of His nature. Parents love their children irrespective of any obligation laid upon them. *Response:* But God is not everybody's Father. Some are children of the devil (John 8:44).
5. God is Father to all people, by virtue of creation. As a result of bringing people into the world, God has the same reasons to love them as an earthly father has to love those whom he brings into the world (Mal. 2:10; Acts 17:25–29) — and similar responsibility for them too.	God is not responsible for, nor obligated to love, those of His creation who have rebelled against Him to the enemy's side. Those who have rebelled are children of the devil, not of God.	God counts even rebels to be His children (Isa. 1:2; Luke 15:24, 32). Children may join the family of their father's enemy, but this does not change the natural relationship. *Response:* Regardless of having created all people, God loves some and hates others (Rom. 9:13).

Argument for the View	Cross-Examination of Argument	Further Discussion of the Point
6. No father would give up on any of his children who could be saved by his continued pursuit of them.	This is still assuming that God counts all people to be His children. A case can be made against this. There are two families on earth: 1) those in Adam, who are in rebellion, and 2) those in Christ, who are God's children. God has a special, parental commitment only to the latter.	The compassion of God toward even the lost (Matt. 9:36; Luke 6:35) is evidence that He regards all to be His children and proper objects of His love. *Response:* God may love only the elect (Calvinist); or even those who are loved may choose to reject God's loving overtures (Arminian).
7. A father chastens his children, which is what trials in this life, and hell in the next, is for.	God does chasten His true children (Christians) "for our profit" (Heb. 12:10). However, Scripture mentions no such commitment of God to the unsaved.	Those who are converted are definitely ahead of others, chronologically, but God loves all people, and is committed to their eventual inclusion in His fold. *Response:* This statement depends upon disputed interpretations of certain texts.
8. All of God's actions are for a purpose. His purposes are consistent with His loving character and His benevolent will for mankind (Eph. 1:11).	The manifestation of God's wrath against vessels of wrath is also declared to be consistent with His revealed purposes (Rom. 9:17, 21–23).	The judgment of sinners is consistent with His purposes. The question is, what kind of judgment (He is not obligated to settle for one He doesn't like) is consistent with His character—restorative chastening or mere vengeance?

Argument for the View	Cross-Examination of Argument	Further Discussion of the Point
9. All of God's judgments have restoration in view.	This requires extrapolating what God said about certain cases and making them apply to every instance. Most cases mentioned in Scripture apply directly to God's dealing with Israel, His chosen people.	Israel was chosen to bring the same mercy to the nations as that which God showed to them. They were chosen for this task, not to be saved exclusively. God's character and purpose is not one way toward Israel and another way toward Gentiles.
10. Though all people deserve condemnation, God's mercy can override the demands of justice (e.g., Pss. 32:1; 103:10; Luke 18:13–14; John 8:11).	Mercy can triumph over justice, but not automatically. The mercy of God is given to the repentant—not to everybody.	Unless, of course, everybody becomes repentant. There are Scriptures that seem to describe this result (e.g., Isa. 45:22–23; Phil. 2:10–11).
11. Jesus absorbed the wrath of God on our behalf (Isa. 53:6; 2 Cor. 5:21; 1 Peter 2:23).	*Calvinist:* Jesus only died for the elect, not for all people. *Arminian:* Though Jesus died for all, not all will meet the conditions for salvation, so that it is no better than if He had not died for them.	To say Jesus died only for the elect is a partisan Calvinistic assumption, nowhere stated in Scripture. To say all men will not meet the conditions for salvation is to assume, without scriptural warrant, that the opportunity to do so is limited to this life only.

Argument for the View	Cross-Examination of Argument	Further Discussion of the Point
12. Jesus died for all, not merely some (John 1:29; 1 Tim. 2:6; Heb. 2:9; 1 John 2:2).	*Calvinist:* The words "all" and "the whole world" can be referring only to the inclusion of all races and all classes of people—not every individual.	The Bible abundantly affirms that God shows no partiality, as He would have to if He selected only a fraction of the human race to save by His grace.
13. If all are not saved, Jesus paid for something He did not receive. He is then cheated, and the enemy wins.	*Calvinist:* Jesus only died to save the elect, and they will all be saved. *Arminian:* Jesus paid for the whole world, knowing that only some would be saved. This is the price He was willing to pay for the few.	The Bible says that Jesus died for everybody (1 John 2:2), and that God is not willing that any should perish (2 Peter 3:9). If any ultimately are lost to Him, He will be disappointed. There is no reason for God to accept disappointment, when He could continue pursuing each one until He has saved all.
14. Jesus's impact on the race for salvation was superior (not inferior) to Adam's impact for condemnation.	All have been harmed by Adam's sin. Christ died to recover "many" (Mark 10:45; Rom. 5:15, 19). Christ does not recover as many as Adam harmed.	Paul says "the many" whom Christ saves are the same "the many" that Adam harmed (Rom. 5:15, 19). "The many" are identified as "all men" in verse 18. What Christ accomplished for the race was "much more" than Adam accomplished against it (Rom. 5:15, 17, 20)—not "much less."

Argument for the View	Cross-Examination of Argument	Further Discussion of the Point
15. God has purposed to reconcile all things to Himself in Christ through the cross (Eph. 2:10; Col. 1:20).	First, "all things" can be a hyperbole, as is often the case in Scripture. Second, the creation can also be "reconciled" to God by the fact that the rebellious element has been eliminated in hell.	What God desires to reconcile are "all things" that were created (comp. Col. 1:16 and 20). The reconciliation of all things is "through the blood of His cross" (meaning salvation), not by the loss and/or destruction of most things.
16. Every knee will someday bow, and every tongue confess that Jesus is Lord to the glory of God (Phil. 2:9–11).	First, the verse says *should* bow, not *will* bow. Second, many may bow and confess grudgingly and in resentment.	The verse is alluding to Isaiah 45:23, which is quoted also in Romans 14:11. In both, it says they "shall" or "will" bow and confess. The language and context of Isaiah 45 and Romans 14 (as well as Philippians 2) all require that this is true worship. Besides, it is "to the glory of God," which insincere worship would not be.
17. The gospel is "good tidings of great joy . . . to all people" (Luke 2:10). The good news is to all people—not good news to some and bad news to others.	It is good news to all people to know that God is willing to save them. It is not His fault if they reject this offer.	But it is not news "of great joy" to all people, if most ultimately reject it. There will be no "great joy" in hell.

Argument for the View	Cross-Examination of Argument	Further Discussion of the Point
18. Christians cannot be glad if their loved ones are lost (Rom. 9:2–3; Phil. 3:18).	God will wipe away all tears from our eyes. Perhaps He will blot out the memory of them from our minds. Or it may just be that we will be perfected to the point that we rejoice to see His justice carried out, even against our loved ones.	If God can't make us happy without concealing His actions, this does not speak well of the innate goodness of His actions! If we are perfected, will that not mean "made perfect in love" (1 John 4:17–18)? How can we have less compassion on the lost, when our love is more perfect? How can we rejoice in the judgment of sinners, when God Himself does not (Ezek. 33:11)?
19. Jesus is the Victor over sin, death, and the devil (Isa. 42:4; Matt. 12:28; 1 Cor. 15:25–26; Col. 2:15; 2 Tim. 1:10; Heb. 2:14; Rev. 5:5; 11:15; 21:4) — the devil and death cannot win in the end.	(The author has never encountered an answer to this in the literature.)	

SELECTIVE BIBLIOGRAPHY

ETERNAL TORMENT (TRADITIONAL VIEW)

Blamires, Harry. *Knowing the Truth about Heaven and Hell: Our Choices and Where They Lead Us*. Ann Arbor, MI: Servant Books, 1988.

Buis, Harry. *The Doctrine of Eternal Punishment*. Grand Rapids: Baker Book House, 1957.

Chan, Francis, and Preston Sprinkle. *Erasing Hell: What God Said about Eternity, and the Things We Made Up*. Colorado Springs: David C. Cook, 2011.

Crocket, William, ed. *Four Views on Hell*. Grand Rapids: Zondervan, 1992, 11–131.

Gerstner, John H. *Repent or Perish*. Morgan, PA: Soli Deo Gloria Publications, 1990.

McClymond, Michael J. *The Devil's Redemption: A New History and Interpretation of Christian Universalism*. Grand Rapids: Baker Academic, 2018.

Morey, Robert A. *Death and the Afterlife*. Minneapolis: Bethany House, 1984.

Morgan, Christopher W., and Robert A. Peterson, eds. *Hell Under Fire*. Grand Rapids: Zondervan, 2004.

Peterson, Robert A. *Hell on Trial*. Phillipsburg, NJ: Presbyterian and Reformed Publishing, 1995.

Strobel, Lee. *The Case for Faith: A Journalist Investigates the Toughest Objections to Christianity*. Grand Rapids: Zondervan, 2000, 169–194.

Walls, Jerry L. *Heaven, Hell, and Purgatory: Rethinking the Things That Matter Most*. Grand Rapids: Brazos, 2015.

CONDITIONAL IMMORTALITY

Boyd, Gregory A., and Paul R. Eddy. *Across the Spectrum*. Grand Rapids: Baker Publishing Group, 2002, 254–264.

Crockett, William, ed. *Four Views on Hell*. Grand Rapids: Zondervan, 1992, 135–178.

Evans, David L., and John Stott. *Evangelical Essentials: A Liberal-Evangelical Dialogue*. Downers Grove, IL: InterVarsity Press, 1988, 312–329.

Froom, LeRoy Edwin. *The Conditionalist Faith of Our Fathers*, 2 vols. Washington, D.C.: Review and Herald, 1965–66.

Fudge, Edward William. *The Fire That Consumes: A Biblical and Historical Study of the Doctrine of Final Punishment*. 3rd ed. Eugene, OR: Cascade, 2011.

Fudge, Edward William, and Robert A. Peterson. *Two Views of Hell: A Biblical and Theological Dialogue*. Downers Grove, IL: InterVarsity Press, 2000.

Green, Michael B. *Evangelism through the Local Church*. London: Hodder & Stoughton, 1990; repr., Nashville: Thomas Nelson, 1992, 71–74.

Hughes, Philip E. *The True Image: The Origin and Destiny of Man in Christ*. Grand Rapids: Wm. B. Eerdmans, 1989.

Jacoby, Douglas A. *What's the Truth about Heaven and Hell?* Eugene, OR: Harvest House, 2013.

Powys, David. *Hell: A Hard Look at a Hard Question*. Paternoster Biblical and Theological Monographs; Carlisle: Paternoster, 1998.

Spiegel, James S. *Hell and Divine Goodness: A Philosophical-Theological Inquiry*. Eugene, OR: Cascade, 2019.

Taylor, Robert Allen. *Rescue from Death: John 3:16 Salvation*. Denver: Outskirts Press, 2012.

Wenham, John. *The Enigma of Evil*. Grand Rapids: Zondervan, 1985.

Wenham, John. *Facing Hell: The Story of a Nobody*. Carlisle, Cumbria: Paternoster Press, 1998.

Website: "Afterlife." *The Conditional Immortality Association of New Zealand*. http://www.afterlife.co.nz.

Website: *Rethinking Hell*. http://www.rethinkinghell.com.

UNIVERSAL RECONCILIATION

Allin, Thomas, and Mark T. Chamberlain. *Every Knee Shall Bow: The Case for Christian Universalism*. USA: xulonpress.com, 2005.

Beauchemin, Gerry. *Hope Beyond Hell*. Olmito, TX: Malista Press, 2007.

Bell, Rob. *Love Wins: A Book about Heaven, Hell, and the Fate of Every Person Who Ever Lived*. New York: HarperCollins, 2011.

Bonda, Jan. *The One Purpose of God: An Answer to the Doctrine of Eternal Punishment*. Grand Rapids: Wm. B. Eerdmans, 1998.

Gulley, Philip, and James Mulholland. *If Grace Is True: Why God Will Save Every Person*. San Francisco: HarperCollins, 2004.

Hart, David Bentley. *That All Shall Be Saved: Heaven, Hell, and Universal Salvation*. New Haven and London: Yale University Press, 2019.

Klassen, Randy. *What Does the Bible Really Say about Hell? Wrestling with the Traditional View*. Telford, PA: Pandora Press, 2001.

Kronen, John, and Eric Reitan. *God's Final Victory: A Comparative Philosophical Case for Universalism*. London/New York: Continuum, 2011.

MacDonald, Gregory. *The Evangelical Universalist*. 2nd ed. Eugene, OR: Cascade, 2012.

Ramelli, Ilaria L. E., and Robin A. Parry. *A Larger Hope?* 2 vols. Eugene, OR: Cascade, 2019.

Talbott, Thomas. *The Inescapable Love of God*. 2nd ed. Eugene, OR: Cascade, 2014.

Website: *Hope Beyond Hell.* www.hopebeyondhell.net.
Website: *Tentmaker.* www.tentmaker.org.

COMPILATIONS PRESENTING MORE THAN ONE VIEW

Boyd, Gregory A., and Paul R. Eddy. *Across the Spectrum.* Grand Rapids: Baker Publishing Group, 2002.

Crockett, William, ed. *Four Views on Hell.* Grand Rapids: Zondervan, 1992.

de S. Cameron, Nigel M., ed. *Universalism and the Doctrine of Hell.* Edinburgh: Rutherford House, 1992.

Fudge, Edward William, and Robert A. Peterson. *Two Views of Hell: A Biblical and Theological Dialogue.* Downers Grove, IL: InterVarsity Press, 2000.

Miller, Kevin. *Hellbound?* Kevin Miller XI Productions Inc., 2013.

Parry, Robin A., and Christopher H. Partridge, eds. *Universal Salvation: The Current Debate.* Grand Rapids: Wm. B. Eerdmans, 2003.

Sprinkle, Preston, ed. *Four Views on Hell.* 2nd ed. Grand Rapids: Zondervan, 2016.